EQUIVOCAL
CHILD ABUSE

EQUIVOCAL CHILD ABUSE

Sandra B. McPherson
Farshid Afsarifard

CRC Press
Taylor & Francis Group
Boca Raton London New York

CRC Press is an imprint of the
Taylor & Francis Group, an **informa** business

Cover: Image design by Jeffrey Donnelly from an original photograph by Phil Campbell.

CRC Press
Taylor & Francis Group
6000 Broken Sound Parkway NW, Suite 300
Boca Raton, FL 33487-2742

First issued in paperback 2017

ISBN 13: 978-1-138-11431-9 (pbk)
ISBN 13: 978-1-4398-4776-3 (hbk)

Library of Congress Cataloging-in-Publication Data

McPherson, Sandra B.
Equivocal child abuse / author, Sandra B. McPherson, Farshid Afsarifard.
p. cm.
Includes bibliographical references and index.
ISBN 978-1-4398-4776-3 (hardcover : alk. paper)
1. Forensic psychology--United States. 2. Child psychology--United States. 3. Child psychologists--Legal status, laws, etc.--United States. 4. Custody of children--United States. 5. Child abuse--Law and legislation--United States. I. Afsarifard, Farshid. II. Title.

KF8965.M39 2012
346.7301'73--dc23
2011034193

Visit the Taylor & Francis Web site at
http://www.taylorandfrancis.com

and the CRC Press Web site at
http://www.crcpress.com

DEDICATION

We would like to dedicate this book to the children whom
we strive to serve and to the parents who love them
and want them to have happiness in their lives.

Table of Contents

Acknowledgments   xiii
About the Authors   xv

1   Equivocality in a Complex Legal Context   1

Context   1
Principles of Chaos Theory as They Relate to the Arena Under
Consideration   2
Summary Point   3
Principles of Therapeutic Jurisprudence as They Relate to the
Arena Under Consideration   4
    Basic Argument   7
Legal, Historical, and Psychosocial Background   7
    Legal Concepts   8
    Legal History   12
    Relevant Sociolegal Trends in Divorce   14
    Best Interests Standards and Shared Parenting Legislation   18
    Psychosocial Concepts and Research   26
Two Problematic Psychological Concepts   27
Conclusion   30

2   The Courts: Views Across and Within   31

The Course of a Case   31
    Case in Point   34
        Comment   36
The Rule of Law and the Law of Rules   37
    County Court Rules   38
    A Parenting Time Rule   39
        Comment   43
    State Rules   43
    Research Findings   45
The Play of the Participants   46
    The Litigants   46
    The Guardians   46
    The Lawyers   47
    The Experts   47

The Judges   48
  Judicial Perspectives   48
  In Camera Interviews   48
Pretrial Peregrinations   51
  Motions—Adversarial and Agreeable   51
  Depositions   52
  The Settlement Conference   53
Days in Court   53
Conclusion   54

3   Investigation   55

Current Theory and Research on Brain Function   56
The Particular Problem of Lying   60
  Linguistic Analyses of Transcripts   61
  Polygraph   62
  Voice Stress Analysis (VSA)   63
  Neuroscience Enters the Picture   63
  Nonverbal Interview Behavior   64
  Summary   64
Abel Testing to Identify Potential Perpetrators   64
Perspectives from Investigators   65
  Comment   68
Perspectives of Child Custody Evaluators   69
Legal Standard Issues   70
Some Case Investigations   72
  Case A   72
  Case B   73
  Case C   75
  Comment   76

4   The Expert in the Courtroom   77

Types of Witnesses in DR Court Cases   78
  Evaluators   79
  Guardians *ad Litem*   79
  Treating Professionals   81
Rules of Evidence   83
  U.S. Tradition   83
  Expert Evidence in Canada   85
  The Problem of Expert Opinions on Credibility   86
    The *Brown* Case   87
    Implications   88

      Scientific Evidence   89
      "Consistent With"   89
      Recommendations   90
    Hearsay   91
      Comment   92
      Ohio Case Law Illustrations Regarding Hearsay   93
    Implications of the *Daubert* Decision   94
    Specialized Forensic Instruments   99
    Presentation of Expert Evidence   99
    Preparing Evidence as an Expert   99
  Summary   101

5 Practitioner Hazards   103

  Legal Risks   106
    Licensure Board Complaints   106
    Civil Suit and Malpractice Actions   112
  Personal Safety and Physical Risks   116
    Personal Risks   116
    Risks to Others   117
    Risks of Danger for the Practitioner—Professional
    Perspectives   119
    Emergence of the Internet   123
  One Psychologist's Experience   125
  Practicing Defensively   127
    Ethical Perspectives   127
    Evaluation and Investigation   129
    Some Practice Recommendations   130
      Basics in Risk Management   130
      Informed Consent   131
      Documentation   131
      Consultation   132
      Financial Issues   132
    Some Recommended Procedures   134
    Checklist for Defensive Practice   138
  Conclusion   139

6 Intervention Options   141

  Initial Filing Phase   142
  Interim Pretrial Phase   144
  Hearing and Judgment Phase   144
  Post-Decree Phase   145

Intervention Options   145
    Supervised Visitation   146
    Paid Professional Supervision Services   147
    Relative Supervised Visitation   148
Therapy for Children   148
Child Therapy as a Means of Establishing Security   152
    Age of the Child   152
Reunification Therapy   154
Mediation   156
Parent Coordinator Process   159
Parental Alienation Syndrome   161
Summary   164

7   Mental Health Issues   165

Borderline Personality Disorder   165
Borderline Personality Disorder and Child Abuse   170
    Recommendations   175
    Case Management   175
        Comprehensive Psychological Evaluation   175
        Experienced Treating Clinicians   176
        Parenting Coordinators With BPD Knowledge   177
        Provision of Psychological Reports to Intervenors   177
Narcissistic and Related Personality Patterns   178
    Construct of Psychopathy   178
Affective Disorders   182
    Bipolar Disorder   182
    Major Depressive Disorder   185
Substance Abuse   187
    Current Patterns of Abuse   188
    Equivocal Allegations of Substance Abuse   190
    Investigative Options   191
    Psychological Testing   192
    Nicotine and Alcohol—Some Further Issues   193
    Some Intervention Options   195
Summary   195
Conclusions   196

8   Working Model for the Forensic Evaluator   197

First Step—Conducting the Evaluation   197
    Primary Contacts   197
    Ancillary Contacts   201
    Pretrial Attorney Contacts   202

Second Step—Reportage   202
   Referral Question and Procedure   204
   Results   204
   Discussion Section   204
Recommendations   205
Conclusion   207

9   Top Cat   **209**

Equivocal Communication   211
Change   213
Summary   216

Appendix A: Recommended Guidelines for Interviewing
Children in Cases of Alleged Sexual Abuse   **219**
JACK S. ANNON
General   219
The Interview   220
Evaluation of the Interview   224

Appendix B: Affidavit Example   **227**
SANDRA McPHERSON
General Background   227
Training and Experience Regarding the Investigation of
Allegations of Child Sexual Abuse   228
Accepted Protocols and Procedures for the Investigation of
Allegations of Child Sexual Abuse   229
Protocols for the Presentation of a Child's Testimony in Court 232
Relevant but Not Exhaustive Resources   233

Appendix C: Semistructured Interview Guides   **235**

Appendix D: Billing Policy: Forensic Evaluations and
Statement of Financial Responsibility   **237**

Appendix E: Instructions for Enhanced Security   **245**
Secrets   245
Roving Reporter   245
Possession Parent Tape   246

Appendix F: Consultation Example: Critique of a Child
Interview   **247**

References   **263**

Index   **279**

Acknowledgments

Writing a book such as this one presented rather specific challenges, as do all such efforts. In this case, there was the need to put together insights, experiences, and guidance from multiple sources toward the end of helping courts, evaluators, guardians, and lawyers both understand and deal with what are often seen as the "bad" custody cases. Some materials have been created in an effort to make case management more feasible but we know of no strategies that will cover every contingency that presents itself. To some degree, professionals have to attend to the basics of their work, exercise due diligence in how they follow their own rules and procedures, and rely at times on "instincts" born from experience to make decisions under fire. In that regard, they are not entirely unlike US Airways pilot Chesley B. Sullenberger, who landed a damaged plane in the Hudson River with all passengers rescued: there can be no specific preparation and rehearsal for such an exigency, but training and experience and exceptional capacity can combine with good results when the situation is unique. The people on whom we relied for insights were those with that kind of exceptional capacity in their fields.

Some systematic inquiries were conducted using semistructured interviews and in some cases a formal protocol for content analysis. All persons participating in such studies were provided confidentiality. No identifying information has been preserved and multiple geographic locations were involved. None of the studies was either large enough or would meet any systematic standards for representation; on the other hand, the general thematic uniformity of responses spoke to a commonality of experience in dealing with cases in this area.

All case histories presented in this book have been disguised as to identifying information, but the dynamic relationships presented and the behaviors illustrated have actually occurred either in the experience of the writers or as reported by the resources we contacted.

We thank the following Fielding Graduate University Research Assistants for the information gathered and their contributions to its presentation: Mary Dang, Whitney Keener, Tania Lodge, Susan Moraes, and Kimberly Watson. For the input and help we received we also thank veterans in this field, including sitting judges, lawyers, and guardians *ad litem*, especially from Ashtabula, Cuyahoga, and Lake counties in Ohio. We were particularly assisted by police officers and social service workers in a sample from the United States and Ontario, Canada, who agreed to provide their insights based on significant investigative experience in a difficult field. However, anything and everything that has been provided in this book represents our perspectives and for that we take full responsibility.

An undertaking of this kind is not possible without highly competent and incredibly supportive staff assistance. Our office manager, Kathy Lynn, transcribed multiple versions, kept some order in the proliferation of chapters that ensued, held out an expectation that the work would in fact be completed in the face of our periodic pessimism, and made the project into a formatted acceptable manuscript. Her husband, Ron Ilkanich, an engineer by background, created Excel tables and other detail work. Jeff Donnelly donated graphic arts talent. Dr. McPherson's husband, Donald McPherson, and Dr. Afsarifard's wife, Kathy Afsarifard, both professionals in their own right, had to read or listen to what we were doing throughout the year, give critical input, and claim with straight faces that they liked it all.

Sandra B. McPherson, PhD, ABPP
Farshid Afsarifard, PhD

About the Authors

Sandra B. McPherson, PhD, ABPP, has been involved in both clinical and forensic psychological work for more than 40 years in the Cleveland, Ohio, area. She holds the American Board of Professional Psychology specialty diploma in clinical and in forensic psychology. She has a particular interest in participating in international collegial contacts and has been a member of the European Association of Psychology and Law since its earliest years. She has published in professional journals, authored several book chapters, and coedited two editions of a text on forensic and clinical aspects of methamphetamine. Her forensic practice has focused on a combination of domestic relations cases and criminal court work, notably involving death penalty mitigation. Dr. McPherson recently retired from active teaching as part of the Fielding Graduate University clinical psychology program. She has long been a member of the advisory board for the guardian *ad litem* program for the Juvenile Court of Cuyahoga County and regularly provides input to the GAL continuing legal education programs of the local bar association. Dr. McPherson was secretary and president of the original licensure board for the State of Ohio and also has served as the president of the Ohio Psychological Association.

Farshid Afsarifard, PhD, was born in Tehran, Iran, and came to the United States in 1976. He obtained his PhD in clinical psychology in 1999 from the Fielding Institute, now known as the Fielding Graduate University. His clinical work has focused on the application of dialectical behavior therapy to different populations such as treatment of adolescents and of individuals with addiction, recovery, and mental health diagnoses. His forensic interests and activities are in criminal and civil competencies, child custody, termination of parental rights, civil commitment, and mitigation in sentencing.

Dr. Afsarifard also has had extensive administrative experience and was the president and chief executive officer of the largest free-standing psychiatric hospital with a full continuum of care in Ohio. During his work in this capacity, he was involved in the development and implementation of innovative programs that provided evidence-based treatment to a variety of clinical populations. At the present time, he has organized a multiservice practice that includes psychologists, psychiatrists, and social workers and provides ongoing training opportunities for mental health professionals.

Equivocality in a Complex Legal Context

1

When she walked into the office of the evaluator with videotapes of her questioning her child, the psychologist knew it was going to be a difficult case. With repeated and inappropriate leading, she managed to get the youngster to, if not endorse, not protest that the father was an abuser. When the tapes were later referenced in the report, her counsel was unhappy that she had not heeded his advice not to submit them. But it took time, the child was repeatedly exposed to misinformation through the processing of the case as well as by the mother, and the relationship of the child with the father required professional input. This case and others illustrate the problems where the presence of risk, the operation of belief systems, multiple sources of variance, unanticipated effects, legal process, and advocacy conditioned by an adversarial system of justice all combine in a very special and hazardous context. Handling problem cases of this sort in the domestic relations arena is what this volume addresses. It is our hope that some of the ideas obtained from various experienced mental health professionals, investigators, attorneys, magistrates, and judges, along with guidelines from our experience, will be of help in minimizing the unnecessary harm to children and their families.

Context

Over time, the study of dynamics in large systems has come to include concepts that have been variously referred to as chaos or complexity theory. Although having a substantial and sophisticated mathematical aspect, the approach of those who look at the world through the lens of complexity theory involves the notion that behavior occurs in consequence of multiple factors with dynamic interactions, such that depending upon the level of observation, the appearance of randomness exists. A number of concepts were originally developed in the context of molecular systems with applications to biological as well as physical science; however, they have been applied to both social and individual psychological functioning. A number of intriguing concepts characterize the complexity theory approach, including the notion that small events in a highly diversified and interrelated set of factors can ultimately produce substantial results, although perhaps not predictably depending upon the level of observation (Bütz, 1997; Waldrop, 1992; Williams & Arrigo, 2002).

Principles of Chaos Theory as They Relate
to the Arena Under Consideration

As indicated in Williams and Arrigo's (2002) application of chaos theory to the
legal system, the primary characteristics or features of complexity theory are
iteration, sensitive dependence on initial conditions, bifurcations, and period-
doubling points, attractors, and fractals. Iteration indicates repetition of some
pattern. Iteration is essentially a mathematical concept. It involves a process
whereby a phenomenon is present that acts in such a way that it reannounces
itself; however, although this iterative pattern involves similarities over time,
there is also a progression so that new organization eventually occurs.

The notion of sensitive dependence on initial conditions has to do with
the fact that at the beginning of this iterative process there are certain factors, some of which may or may not be known at the time, that will play a
very significant part in the changes that occur. However, there is little way
to anticipate which of these factors are going to be the powerful ones, if any.
One of the implications of this concept for social science involves its significance for the rather common practices of eliminating unusual outliers in
databases or of rounding off numbers in certain calculations, both of which
are done under the assumption that little if any impact is being sacrificed. In
fact, the study of large and complex systems shows that these outliers may,
but not necessarily will, be definers of the patterns of the future, and remov-
ing them or not considering them may well be acts of profound importance
leading to significant error.

Bifurcation is a concept that is familiar in law and usually references a
court proceeding that is sectioned off so that each stage has its own process,
although one stage may be dependent on the outcome of another (capital
trials are bifurcated for the guilt phase and the sentencing phase). In complexity theory, bifurcation refers to points at which some kind of critical
mass is reached and a destabilization occurs with a new pattern emerging.
When bifurcations occur, systems that appear to be out of control may then
revert to a more controlled iterative process until the next point of destabilization is reached. Interestingly, in looking at the bifurcation process in
nature, it is found that each time there is such an event, the time needed for
the system to become stable is twice what it was from the last bifurcation.
Thus, bifurcation involves a multiplicative pattern. The "system oscillates
between two separate modes of behavior. If the level of disorder continues
to grow, the system will approach another bifurcation...at this point the system branches again to produce four possible behavioral outcomes around
which it oscillates. At the next critical value, the system again bifurcates and
has eight possible outcomes" (p. 63). Williams and Arrigo go on to note that
there is a point at which there is, in effect, a branching into infinity, which is

considered "chaos," and the idea is that identifiable patterns cease to appear at this point, although within what is apparent disorder, there is some type of emerging pattern.

Attractors are factors that describe more or less stable patterns within a system. These patterns seem to have the power to actually pull the system into conformity, at least for a while. However, there are "strange attractors." These patterns resemble each other but are never exactly the same (snowflakes, for example) so that they can always be identified but never entirely predicted. Finally, fractals are structures that grow out of an "iterative, self-referential process" (Goerner, 1994, p. 40). Fractals are very special patterns (again of which snowflakes would be one) in that they have a pattern and that pattern is repeated on a smaller scale the more magnified the view of the original is. These concepts allow description of the way in which self-organization takes place in a large system so that there is a general patterning; depending upon the vantage point, the pattern can be perceived and there is some predictability but there is always a dynamic presence such that a simple linear approach that might secure certainty in decision making is never present.

Summary Point

When self-organizing complex systems, themselves not entirely predictable in the linear sense by their very nature, become interactive with each other, further layers of operations ensue and can only be viewed from a different distance than might be ideal for understanding any one of the systems. Thus, one can review what is taking place in the legal system by learning procedure and seeing how it is being implemented in the courtroom. At a different level, one can look at whether the decisions that are being made in the processing of cases reflect allowable case features or some nonlegitimate characteristics of people, such as race. What one cannot do from *that* vantage point, however, is to understand entirely what is taking place. This uncertainty operates particularly with respect to domestic relations cases. Judges seeking assistance have obtained a different level of observation when they authorize custody evaluations. The mental health professionals called upon look at individual psychology and functioning and family dynamics, and try to consider the unique self-organizing systems of each individual in the patterns of interaction relevant for the decision making which is about to take place.* Less well appreciated, though hinted at in some writing, are the

---

* The forensic assessment process, which *itself* is a complex and varied set of operations influenced by multiple individual variables, is quite limited for any capacity to effectively linearize the legal system's functioning. If anything, it is a source of further complex system dynamics.

particularities of the self-organizing systems of the attorneys and the judges (see, for example, Stolle, Wexler, & Winick, 2000) and the often unique properties in the way in which each court system operates and reflects its own history. All of these in interaction become the system that ultimately must deal with cases. In the particular case of equivocal abuse allegations in family situations, desirable objective facts are not known and may not be knowable. Nonetheless, these unknown actualities are of substantive importance for being potentially disruptive and dangerous to children and their parents, particularly when courts administer life-affecting decisions and orders.

Principles of Therapeutic Jurisprudence as They Relate to the Arena Under Consideration

Another area of theoretical importance for this volume involves therapeutic jurisprudence (TJ). Although a recent entrant in the arena of theories of law and legal procedure, TJ has achieved some acceptance and actual implementation in various Western legal systems, including those of the United States, the United Kingdom, Australia, and Canada. The essence of TJ looks at ways in which legal procedure may not only allow the resolution of disputes within a framework of a legal system, but also how it may affect the people involved such that there is a more positive impact on their emotional and social health. In effect, it goes beyond the importance of fairness, which is an intrinsic value to the legal procedures that essentially began with the Magna Carta and have continued to date in the legal systems influenced by that tradition, to also look for ways in which an individual may feel a sense of satisfaction and respect regardless of the actual outcome of the dispute (Stolle et al., 2000). Stolle and colleagues provided a fairly complete discussion of how law can act as a helping profession, merging concerns of mental health and legal adequacy. Much of the work in this approach has focused on the civil arena and specifically that concerned with mental health law and actions. However, there have been some applications to the criminal courts and to family law. In effect, in a complex system of competing interests and complicated processes, TJ looks for ways in which the involvement of the various persons can be experienced as empowering regardless of the shape of the ultimate outcome. In a way, TJ argues for making even more complex—less predictable— a system that already operates according to nonlinear dynamics.

In looking at a traditional legal system, there is a definite procedure and the deceptively simple notion that by applying that procedure in a uniform and fair fashion across both sides of a given dispute, the weight of the evidence will result in an outcome that reflects the truth of the situation. The concept of blind justice is intrinsic to this notion. Should the system so operate, then it would be possible, certainly by the end of a trial, to predict exactly what the results would be because in most cases the weight of the evidence would be obvious. If there is sufficient "tippage" (referencing standard of proof), then the aim sought by one side or the other will be reached. In fact, however, the prediction of case outcomes is fraught with hazard as any practicing attorney well knows. The justice system, whether civil or criminal, is riddled with the input of factors that are theoretically noncontributory to decision making. Thus, studies notably by Baldus and others have clearly demonstrated the input of racial factors into death penalty decision making (see, for example, Baldus & Woodworth, 1998; Baldus, Woodworth, & Pulaski, 1990; and Weiner & Haney, 2004). A more present illustration that nonlegitimate factors are known to operate powerfully is seen in the current planned study in Cuyahoga County, Ohio, of the criminal justice system from charging to outcome in order to identify and reduce the operation of nonlegitimate bias (Gomez, May 14, 2010; *The Plain Dealer* Editorial, Dec. 9, 2009).

Our argument, however, goes beyond a concern with nonlegitimate bias. It is our contention that human decision making rests on the complex system of cognition wherein interactions of people multiply the interplay of intrinsically complex but nonetheless lawful systems. In effect, although linear logic systems may constrain in beneficial directions, it is only by appreciating the true nonlinearity that is the essence of complex human institutions that a more accurate understanding of the legal system emerges that can inform more adequate solutions through the courts.

In the family court arena, it is argued that an even higher potential exists for nontraditional evidentiary variables to play a part in the outcomes than is found in criminal courts. First of all, there is no jury involved (all decision making is undertaken by a judge or magistrate). The evidence that is presented, although there are procedural safeguards, may exceed what is theoretically allowed. For example, there is significant potential for hearsay to wander into the court through various doors, not the least of which is the psychological report. In addition, in a custody dispute, triers of fact not only absorb the independent evidence but also may be more immediately affected by the behavior of the individuals. Courts sometimes ask for input from the children at issue through *in camera* interviews, designed to protect children from the exposure of open court and testimony in front of their parents. These interviews also have no exact procedural rules of inquiry as are present in direct and cross-examination of the adults and vary in terms of the judge's expertise in communication with children who present at various levels of development and capacity. Furthermore, by the time a case reaches the point that motions for *in camera* interviews are made, the children usually are more than exposed to the points of view of their respective parents and to the attitudes and reactions of extended families; in addition, they frequently have arrived at a perception of their own interests, which may or may not have the advantage of much wisdom and foresightedness. Nonetheless, what they say will become one of the sources of information that will be a part of the judicial decision making. For all these reasons, it is argued that the standard and traditional processing of matters pertaining to family systems in family, domestic relations, or juvenile courts is a cauldron of unexpected, sometimes unknown, and often unappreciated inputs, each of which has its own rhythm and set of variables that are themselves dynamic in their function and in their impact.

Anderer and Glass (2000) provided a TJ-based approach to family law in which they created a schematic where these kinds of factors were clearly present. They considered what they were doing a "developmental model" and they stated, "We began our analysis by asking: 'Where do family law disputes start and where do these disputes fit into people's lives?'" (p. 209). That focus question makes it clear that what needs to be understood to apply this model is history with its multiple factors of individual, family, and societal origin, and the present with its multiple motives and conditions. They proceeded further to analyze where and how lawyering takes place in the course of a case and they also looked at the interrelationship between legal processing and the efforts of mental health practitioners to deal with questions of child custody. In their examples, they noted that the behavior of attorneys can itself affect the perceptions of the parties. Where those perceptions are essentially negative, even if the outcome is in the general direction of a party's desire, the seeds are laid for future disintegration. It has to be remembered that in a child custody case, settlements are created, orders are made, decisions are handed down, but post decree, people continue to interact either in negative or positive or combined directions, leading to more or less disputation. Not only what but how things are handled can be a critical set of variables. For example, a judge's decision to attempt a resolution of a case by having the lawyers work it out in chambers may create the groundwork for one or both of the parties to feel a sense of never having had any chance to present issues and always to have some trust concerns about whether there was proper representation.

The goals of TJ are benevolent and informed by a strong body of mental health and psychological literature. However, the potentials of a TJ-based set of procedures may not be sufficient to overcome the negative dynamics of the worst domestic relations cases, which perhaps could be described as representing apparent chaotic behavior among multiple variables in patterns that ultimately create what, in another arena, has been called the perfect storm.

Basic Argument

It is the goal of TJ to find ways to implement the law so that the outcome is mentally healthy as opposed to destructive. Toward that end, taking into account psychological aspects of the process, including perception and the sense of personal power and efficacy, becomes an important component regardless of legal context. It is further asserted that a complexity theory–based view of any social system's activity is particularly applicable to the processing of human affairs in courts of law where the notion of a linear logic process is more fiction than fact. Under those presumptions, it seems reasonable that an analysis of how to handle particularly difficult custody and visitation situations in the courts can be enhanced with a model that responds to nonrational but nonetheless psychologically sensitive aspects of importance to the futures of children who are central to such cases.

Legal, Historical, and Psychosocial Background

Coming from the above perspectives, we can consider the history, legal parameters, and psychological factors that interact in the domestic relations court and are of substantial importance in understanding and dealing with cases that involve high conflict and high uncertainty. The stakes, of course, are indeed high as well and not just for the nuclear families involved. The future of children significantly depends upon the experiences they have as they grow and develop in the family setting. The impact on children of experiences of violence, conflict, and particularly the impact of being drawn into becoming players in dysfunctional family situations is well known to be pervasively negative (Fonagy & Target, 1997; Fonagy, Target, Gergely, Allen, & Bateman, 2003; Ghasemi, 2005; Graham-Bermann & Seng, 2005; Kashani & Allan, 1998; Lanier, Jonson-Reid, Stahlschmidt, Drake, & Constantino, 2009; Roisman, Padron, Sroufe, & Egeland, 2002a,b; Weinfield, Sroufe, & Egeland, 2000). Some children grow up and do well even when they have highly unhappy childhoods and inadequate protection from negative input. However, for every child who rises above such insults and inadequacies, a great number do not, which, of course, is why the studies using aggregated data regularly show the negative results that they do (Brayden, Altemeier, Tucker, Dietrich, & Vietz, 1992; Budd, Holdsworth, & HoganBruen, 2006).

Reducing the number of children for whom the childhood period has involved significant damage will benefit not only the individuals themselves, but also society as a whole. It is a general and well-documented principle that human beings repeat what they experience and that the parenting they experience is often seen in style and substance in the parenting they provide. Good domestic relations decision making, which effectively establishes as much of a positive base for growth and happiness as is feasible in individual situations, can make a very significant contribution to a more adequate society.

Legal Concepts

This book depends largely upon concepts and materials that come from both the legal and mental health literatures. Certain legal concepts are of particular importance in understanding the area under consideration. First of all, the overall area of law that is under discussion is referenced by terms such as domestic relations law and court, family court, matrimonial law, and custody law. All of these phrases refer to either the venue or the body of legal literature that controls or affects the decision making in this area. Different jurisdictions have a family court approach versus a domestic relations court.

Family courts involve a model wherein all or most legal matters pertaining to children and families are handled under one judicial roof. Such courts typically cover what is usually processed in juvenile court as well as the matrimonial matters typically reserved to domestic relations courts. However, various locales have differences in how their models work. Examples follow:

1. New York City Family Court has the authority to consider abuse, neglect, adoption, custody, visitation, domestic violence, foster care, guardianship, juvenile delinquency, paternity, "persons in need of supervision," and child/spousal support. (http://www.nycourts.gov/courts/nyc/family/index.shtml. Retrieved Nov. 14, 2009.)

2. The Family Court Division of the Philadelphia Court is one of three divisions of Common Pleas and itself involves two branches, juvenile and domestic relations. However, it operates under one umbrella with an overall presiding judge. (http://courts.phila.gov/commonpleas/family. Retrieved Nov. 14, 2009.)

3. Rhode Island Family Court. This court is an integrated court that looks at all issues relating to families and children. On its Web site is stated, "Goals are to assist, to protect, and, if possible, to restore families whose unity or well-being has been or is threatened." The Rhode Island model includes all the functions that are usually found in both domestic relations and juvenile court settings. (http://www.courts.ri.gov/family/defaultfamily.htm. Retrieved Nov. 14, 2009.)

4. Family Court of Clark County in Nevada. The Web site for this court noted that the court is a division of the 8th Judicial District Court and began as of January 1993. It is an integrated venue. Interestingly, on its

Web site is stated, "A large portion of the cases in the family courts are initiated and finalized by parties who do not have the benefit of working with advice of counsel (pro se)." There is a special center for self-help that is linked to the site that facilitates access to the court by those who are not represented. Other links included a mediation center and the Family Violence Intervention Center. (http://www.clarkcountycourts. us/ejdc/courts-and-judges/family.html Retrieved Nov. 14, 2009.)

5. Superior Court of DC—Family Court Operations. An integrated family court model is involved. The Web site notes that the design allows cases that come from juvenile or domestic relations to be heard by the same judge to "minimize court appearances, reduce the risk of conflicting court orders, and insure quality decisions based on the full knowledge of the issues affecting the family." Its Annual Report to Congress 2008 detailed activities in all spheres of a family court. There is a significant emphasis on alternative dispute resolution. (http://www.dccourts.gov/dccourts/superior/family/index.jsp. Retrieved Nov. 14, 2009.)

6. Superior Court of California, County of Nevada. This venue, again, is an integrated site where cases are handled that reflect not only all aspects of divorce, but also juvenile court process and domestic violence. As with other such courts, the emphasis was on finding ways to negotiate settlements in most cases. (http://court.co.nevada.ca.us/ services/general_info/index.htm. Retrieved Nov. 14, 2009.)

Family court as a concept has its supporters but there are also potential negatives. On the positive side as indicated in the above and reflected in the messages on the various sites, it is seen as a means of judicial efficiency and continuity. Given the generally stated goal, inherent in best interests statutes (see below), of preserving as best possible that which is positive in troubled families, the idea is that a presiding judge will have the advantage of ongoing knowledge as to the particularities of a case and therefore will be enhanced in decision making consistency when cases reappear over time. However, it could be argued that where bias might exist for whatever reason, the potential for a child or family to benefit from a fresh look is less in such a model.

Efficiency of operation is another potential benefit of the family court system. Given that some cases languish literally for years during which time young children are growing up with ongoing uncertainty, the lack of definitive action may victimize families as much as their internally disrupted operations. That uncertainty may also fuel ongoing disputation as each side feels either justification for, or continued optimism about, achieving victory.

The emphasis seen on facilitating access to the legal system which is found in domestic relations or family court also is considered a two-edged sword. In general, as shown, liberalization of matrimonial law has opened doors to the court. By making it easier to litigate,* filings increase and people rather than seeking harder ways to deal with problems through personal change and compromise move more quickly to the legal warfare of contested custody. It is hypothesized that couples already prone to interact competitively and negatively are in a sense more comfortable staying with that approach than in choosing some cooperative means of handling their issues. Recognizing the need to encourage nonadversarial means, the approach of alternative dispute resolution has arisen across many court systems and venues; both family and domestic relations courts have established mediation programs and often require divorcing couples to attend workshops aimed at reducing ongoing disputation.

Other important concepts about which to be aware include the types of custody that exist. Sole custody refers to a model in which one parent has unilateral decision making capacity and the other parent, in most cases, has certain privileges that can be exercised as well, such as a regular visitation schedule and access to medical, psychological, and educational records. However, under a sole custody order, health, education, and other decision making capacity devolves to the holder of the custody. In spite of that unilateral parental authority, a request for services for a child can create some issues for mental health professionals. Most guidelines for psychologists and other therapists include that even where sole custody exists, it is appropriate to inform the other parent as to the proposed treatment program and preferable to obtain the agreement of that parent, even where the parent does not have the decision making option. Otherwise, clear danger exists of putting the child in a relationship situation (therapy) that is opposed by a parent and the child then once again contends with being caught in the middle of conflict between important adults. To pursue such a course may offend against ethical considerations, notably the prohibition against doing harm (American Medical Association, 2008–2009; American Psychological Association, 2003; Canadian Psychological Association, 2000).

Types of custody are denoted by a number of terms, which themselves are somewhat variously defined depending upon the source. However, in general, joint custody is a model that may be joint legal or physical or both. Joint legal custody establishes that both parents are denoted the legal custodians of the child or children and both are involved in major decision making. Wherever a joint legal custodianship exists, any nonemergency treatment must have the

---

* Some years ago, McPherson was told by an attorney with experience in San Francisco that the amount of litigation activity in that city's matrimonial court increased immediately upon the acquisition of a fax machine, which led to easy ways to quickly file motions.

approval and agreement of both parties. Joint physical custody, which may or may not be part of a joint legal custody arrangement, involves a companionship time schedule that is relatively close to evenly distributed between the parents. Other terms often referring to joint arrangements are coparenting and shared parenting, although the term coparenting is sometimes used more loosely to designate the process by which parents should collaborate in the raising of their children post decree. The term in more frequent use at this point is shared parenting and may involve not only the joint legal custody, but also any number of arrangements for companionship time, varying from school year with one parent and summer with the other (sometimes the approach to geographic separation occurring between the two parents) to a traditional every other weekend to the nonresidential parent, or to some kind of mathematically equivalent arrangement such as a week by week or even half-week by half-week approach. Schedules can be complex or simple, and some inquiry has been done as to how to adjust schedule design to the developmental needs of children (see Kelly, 2010a; see also Mart, 2009, for a critique of scientific adequacy; further consideration of this area is found in Chapter 2).

Another area of significant legal definition involves the notion of legal standards. In law, it is common to establish standards that define the basis for making decisions. As the standards are articulated in statutory law and further defined in case law decisions, there is developed a body of literature that guides fact finders in specific applications. In the area of specific focus for this book, particular interest is in the standard that guides custody decisions. At this point, the best interests doctrine is the guide for most of the United States and also the standard found in Canadian federal and provincial laws. Under best interests, it is necessary to look at multiple factors and make custody decisions on the basis of what will optimally serve in the case at hand. This standard requires that judges look at cases in extremely complex fashion and be particularly aware of the myriad psychological and social factors that can have an impact in individual cases. It is the best interests doctrine that has led to increasing input of mental health expertise into the family law courts as an assist to the judicial process. Thus, the National Council of Juvenile and Family Court Judges, on its Web site in the domestic relations section, notes that the organization "provides training and technical assistance about family law issues, with an emphasis on the latest psychological, scientific, legal, and technological information affecting children, including custody, visitation, paternity, and child support for divorcing and never married parents, as well as safe and appropriate alternative dispute resolution techniques and options for unrepresented litigants." (http://www.ncjfcj.org/content/blogcategory/183/386. Retrieved Nov. 14, 2009.)

Legal History

It has been generally supported that it is not possible to legislate morality; in fact, however, law does affect behavior and results in changes in any number of both minor and major lifestyle processes. Furthermore, it is well demonstrated that behavioral changes do in fact lead to changes in thinking and attitudes (see, for example, Reinecke, Dattilio, & Freeman, 2003). In fact, the basic premise of cognitive behavior therapy is that by making conscious behavioral changes, accommodated by exercises that require practicing different ways of thinking, the result is substantial improvement in multiple domains, including those involving how the individual thinks about him- or herself and him- or herself in relationship to others.

Law in the United States and Canada is significantly based in English Common Law. In looking at legal history, it is appropriate to consider that original legal foundation because of its pervasive influence. D. C. Wright (2002) provided an extended discussion of a history of English matrimonial law and the cases and events that influenced its development. Both England and subsequently the United States initially operated according to the presumption of the father as the custodian. An interesting legal concept was developed called coverture, which was what Wright defined as "the legal fiction of the unity of husband and wife." The notion was that because legally husband and wife were one, it was not possible for one to sue the other, thereby foreclosing from two spouses any ability to sue each other for divorce. However, coverture was used primarily as part of the barriers established to keep women from rights of access to the courts.

As of the 1700s, significant change began to occur that continued until approximately midway through the 1800s. Initially, the place of women before the law was extraordinarily minimal as to rights and options. Thus, in Great Britain, women initially could obtain an ecclesiastical divorce if they could prove the cruelty of their husbands, but the ruling was that regardless, the father had the right to the custody of any children. Furthermore, women had to prove that they were entirely innocent of any fault. If women remarried, especially if they had an ecclesiastical divorce, they were viewed as adulterous, which became another "proof" they were not appropriate as decision makers for their children (D. C. Wright, 2002). It must be said that women themselves failed to raise significant protests in many cases because they agreed with the naturally superior male ideal. Even after petitions were successful in changing the law to follow a tender years doctrine, which recognized the preference of placing very young children in custody of their mothers, a strong presumption of the rights of the father existed.

Up through 1856 in England, only men could get a divorce and in fact usually only rich men, the ecclesiastical separation with no right of remarriage excepted. In 1857, a law was passed that allowed women to get a legal divorce if they could show that the husband was unfaithful, brutal, or drunken. (Interestingly, Scottish law was not the same as that of its southern neighbors and much earlier incorporated notions of male and female equality before the law when it came to the burden and standards involved.) However, in England and Wales, it was not until 1937 that grounds for divorce came to include desertion, cruelty, drunkenness, or insanity as stand-alone causes with no difference applied to the male or the female. The 1937 change reflected the growing success of the development of the women's movement (D. C. Wright, 2002).

With respect to the custody issue specifically, between 1700 and 1839, there was some legislation that allowed women to petition for children, even though their likelihood for success was very limited.[*] Between 1839 and 1857, there was initiated a procedural adjustment that allowed the court the power to make both interim and final custody orders. Given the often extended time that the legal process takes, the ability to make interim orders with respect to custody at least allowed for some potential stability for children involved (D. C. Wright, 2002). That capacity remains with the courts to date and is seen in initial temporary custody or other interim orders, the purpose of which is to stabilize the situation until further evidence is brought forward.[†] Between 1851 and 1880, more potential for women to have custody developed, along with their capacity to own and operate property and make certain decisions for themselves. (The right to vote in national elections, of course, would not be conveyed until the 20th century.) Over time, cases arose involving a nonparent petitioning for custody of children, which had some impact in eroding the sanctity of fathers' rights as the primary standard.

In the United States and Canada, the same kind of patterning pertained. Initially, fathers' rights were paramount in decision making. In the 1920s, the tender years doctrine was articulated and led to the next 40–50 years of decision making favoring women. In effect, the burden was on men to prove either unfitness of the mother or very special circumstances in order for them to assume custody of a child, particularly one very young. In effect, in the 1800s the law and decisions made pursuant to the law clearly underlined and supported the inequitable status of males over females. As of the

---

[*] The saga of Caroline Norton is detailed at www.absoluteastronomy.com/topics/ Caroline_Elizabeth_Sarah_Norton. She was an author and socialite who obtained a divorce from an abusive husband but who lost her children in consequence. She was able to obtain from the British Parliament legislation that opened doors to maternal rights. Her case history is one that mirrors many heard in courts today.

[†] However, another vehicle to access court action prior to a final hearing is the *ex parte* motion in which one party asserts an emergency and asks for immediate relief. *Ex parte* motions subvert the process of each side being heard, are generally viewed with disfavor, but nonetheless continue to be granted by courts under the pressure of alleged imminent danger.

1920s and forward, the law did a paradigm shift, at least in this area, and ostensibly placed women in the upper position. (It could be argued of course that a complex consideration of this state of affairs would note that women were often designated as having *only* the natural capacity for bearing and raising children rather than for being out in the world and making decisions in boardrooms or holding other positions of significance. The decision making that shifted the child custody preference to the female did not necessarily raise her status in other arenas of equal rights and opportunities.)

Relevant Sociolegal Trends in Divorce

In any discussion of divorce rates, some caveats are in order. Although it is common to see referenced figures at or around 50% reflecting the rate of divorce, in fact the figures on which such statistics are based have significant flaws and therefore their use in further analyses is questionable. Hurley (2005) provided some discussion of the problem of the use of the commonly reported figures wherein there is a comparison of the annual divorce rate with the annual marriage rate. Because the divorcing population is not the same as the marrying population in a given year, comparison of the two figures is problematic. Somewhat more accurate reflectors of divorcing behavior can be found when the comparison is to number of marriages that end in divorce or by looking at specific population cohorts. Even so, all such indicators have to be viewed as tentative (Americans for Divorce Reform, 2010).

It is reasonably considered that divorce rates will reflect multiple social factors, among which is the economy. The general notion is that as economic indicators show recession potentials, divorce rates will reduce. Another factor, however, on behavior generally, and divorcing is no exception, is the legal structure. When that structure changes to either facilitate or inhibit target behaviors, effects on the behavior are often found. However, the effects of legislation are often not as direct as those who enact laws might presuppose. Thus, there was the effect of the well-known experiment of prohibition, which clearly did not stop people from using alcohol, although arguably it did result in the solidification of criminal organizations and an assault on constitutional protections (Gray, 2000; McPherson, Yudko, Murray-Bridges, Rodriguez, & Lindo-Moulds, 2009).

In the case of divorce law, provisions that would enhance the ease of obtaining a divorce, especially including changes to no-fault statutes, are of significance in their impact on the population. Unemployment rates are considered a fairly good reflector of general economic health in the country. Vanneman's (1999) calculations provide a basis for some contrasts (see Figures 1.1 and 1.2).

The unemployment rates nicely reflect some of the periodic recession and recovery periods and may be used as a rough indicator of economic health.

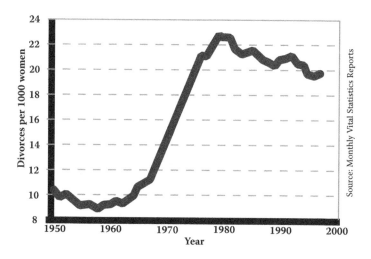

Figure 1.1 Divorce rates. (Used by permission of Reeve Vanneman, University of Maryland.)

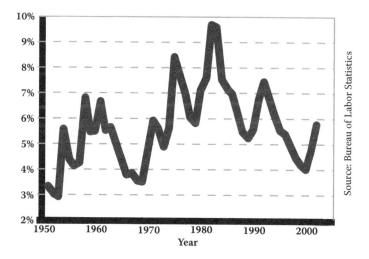

Figure 1.2 Unemployment rates. (Used by permission of Reeve Vanneman, University of Maryland.)

Between 1950 and 1970, a case could be made for rising unemployment rates to be associated with low rates of divorce (although not necessarily implying causality). However, after the 1970 drop in unemployment, the same rates rose to previously unachieved levels (nearly 10%) in the early 1980s, only to drop back to the more acceptable level of 4% by 2000. At this point, of course, they have returned to 9.7% (U.S. Department of Labor, 2010a). In spite of the return to high levels of unemployment, however, the divorce rate, which spiked in the mid-1970s, has been holding at a 40–50% level since. Furthermore, it can be noted that although 50% of first marriages end up in divorce, 67% of second marriages and 47% of third marriages follow suit. Some of the analyses of divorce statistics have also suggested that the presence of children is associated with slightly less than the 50% figure (U.S. Department of Labor, 2010b).

In Canada, the picture is not particularly different with current reported rates at approximately 48%. There has been a fairly steady rise since 1968 forward that may have reflected the passage of the Divorce Act of 1968, which for the first time allowed a general statute for divorce. Prior to this time in Canada, one obtained a divorce through a special process of petition, which was undoubtedly both cumbersome and expensive. The 1968 federal law pertained until the Divorce Act of 1985, which liberalized the standards and also preceded the further rate increases that brought their divorce rate to the 50% level (Marriage and Conjugal Life in Canada, 2010).

It is perhaps interesting and illustrative of the complexity that exists in this area that in the United States approximately 37% of children have no visitation with their fathers, but in Canada it is reported that 50% of the children never see their fathers post decree (Marriage and Conjugal Life in Canada, 2010). The factors that may account for such a difference are not at this point articulated. However, to the extent that children result in binding parents who may have extreme negative agendas with respect to each other, the potential for the kinds of cases about which we are concerned is raised. In the perhaps quite regrettable—depending upon case specifics—instance of children who never see their fathers again, there would also be no ongoing disputation and confrontation, nor would it be likely that any allegations, ultimately true or false, of abuse would be raised for evaluation.

As the law evolved, the idea of no-fault divorce arose. In 1969, California became the first state to pass no-fault legislation as the only grounds for divorce. Prior to this development, all divorce statutes required that one party prove fault of the other as a basis for divorcing. That statutory requirement led to scenarios involving use of private investigators to obtain incriminating photographs and the use of other less than savory techniques, the results of which were paraded before the courts in order to get a divorce where one party may not have wished to agree to it. Additionally, even divorces where each party wished for an end to the marriage had to involve petitions that specified a basis in fault that usually was covered under the phrase "mental cruelty."* With no-fault divorce, petitions were possible on the basis of the

---

* Technically, it was unacceptable for the two parties to collude in the development of these motions; in doing so, the rules of the court were being breached, which arguably could reduce respect for the process.

agreement of the parties that marriage was no longer viable. By 1974, 45 states had passed similar legislation and all 50 had done so by 1996 (Milbank, 1996).

In the case of the liberalizing of divorce legislation, there has been some research on the impact of no-fault divorce and divorce rates. However, the studies that were done primarily up through the mid-1990s were based on varying dates of no-fault legislation. The problem of retaining reliable dates that would reflect the actual date from which no-fault legislation would be in force in the various jurisdictions is that the laws are written differently, there is a time lag between passing a law and its actual implementation, and some no-fault legislation was achieved by amendment to existing divorce acts whereas elsewhere there were new statutes. Some no-fault legislation was achieved by specifying or reducing the separation period that would allow an immediate no-fault divorce rather than by passing specific no-fault statutes (Vlosky & Monroe, 2002).

Vlosky and Monroe (2002) addressed the problem and applied a set of decision rules that allow somewhat more comfort in that the resulting dates for no-fault legislation could be considered comparable across the 50 states. Their decision rules do not eradicate all of the potential variance but clearly are an improvement over the simple use of effective dates that are specified in the various laws and also allow comparisons to states where an amendment process was the vehicle for change. Those dates were used in our analysis of potential relationships. When Vlosky and Monroe's dates are considered in relationship to calculations of divorce rates during the same period of time, it can be seen that following the period of highest passage of these laws, the divorce rate had moved to its current level and has been maintained since with some possible slight reduction recently (see Figures 1.3 and 1.4).

In completing the above calculations, divorce rates used were both Vanneman's (1999) and those from the Bureau of Vital Statistics representing aggregated monthly figures, both of which may be slightly more accurate ways of tracking divorce levels. As can be seen, the curves are essentially identical. What is particularly striking is the similarity between the cumulative graph of the number of no-fault states by year and the curve for divorce rates. These analyses provide support for a potential link between changes in divorce law and rates of divorce. Furthermore, the pattern of economic factors as reflected by the unemployment graph for the same period does not mirror the divorce rate.

What cannot be parsed from this type of data is the exact identity of and degree to which relevant and important variables are responsible for the changes seen. For example, passage of liberalized divorce laws may well reflect more pervasive changes in the society that are part of attitudes toward sexuality, the impact of scientific findings on worldviews, and secularization trends replacing what had been a more traditional religious foundation.

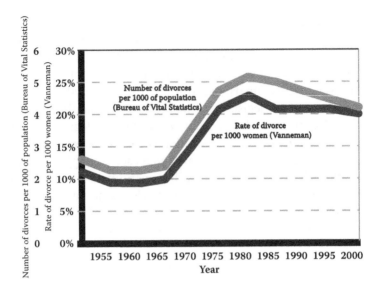

Figure 1.3 U.S. divorce rates by 5-year periods.

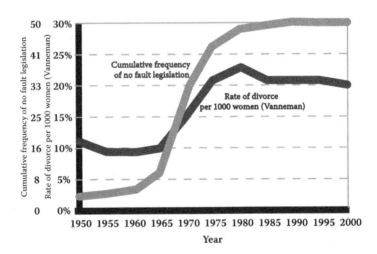

Figure 1.4 U.S. divorce rates and cumulative no-fault legislation by 5-year periods.

Best Interests Standards and Shared Parenting Legislation

We have already indicated that it is our thesis that legislation may influence social behavior with an impact on attitudes and values that form a basis for moral decision making. We would argue further that in particular in this area, significant effects on society have occurred as a function of changes in the legal structure and function. One of the more dramatic correlations that illustrates that position is the increase in the divorce rate that has accompanied the reduction of difficulty and criteria needed to get a divorce. At the level of social values, the increased divorce rate has been accompanied by a change from the moral disapproval of divorce that was standard up through the first half of the 1900s to the contemporary acceptance of some for the idea that marriage may be entered as a temporary state and terminated when it is not seen as happy. As the second half of the 20th century was completed and the 21st began, a kind of complex set of attitudes emerged. Marriage was valued, but alternative lifestyles were also endorsed. Marriage came to be seen as an ideal but not as a necessity. These changes reflected many factors, but among them were the changes in the domestic relations legal structure (Amato, 1988; National Healthy Marriage Resource Center, 2010; Pew Research Center, July 1, 2010, Nov. 18, 2010; Whitehead & Popenoe, 2000).

A major change has involved the evolution of the best interests standard, a notion that focused on case-specific and multiple characteristics aimed at defining for children a post-decree model that would gain them the best combination of their now split family system. However, there have been detractors of the replacement of tender years with best interests. That change has been criticized as having the result of eroding the position of women rather than leading to equality. The notions expressed by these critics have included that the opportunities for women to relocate, to make parenting decisions, and to have independent control of their lives post decree are reduced inasmuch as fathers (in most cases) will have coparenting responsibilities and rights (Chesler, 1987; Fineman, 1991, 1995; Polikoff, 1983).

Although the concept preceded the Michigan legislation, that state's law has been viewed as a model for defining best interests. At this point, in the United States as well as Canada, most matrimonial laws contain provisions reflective of that original material. Specifically, the Michigan statute specifies the following 12 factors (Michigan Compiled Laws, Section 722.23):

1. The love, affection, and other emotional ties existing between the parents involved and the child
2. The capacity and disposition of the parties involved to give the child love, affection, and guidance and to continue the education and raising of the child in his or her religion or creed if any
3. The capacity and disposition of the parties involved to provide the child with food, clothing, and medical care or other remedial care recognized under the laws of this state in place of medical care, and other material needs
4. The length of time the child has lived in a stable, satisfactory environment, and the desirability of maintaining continuity

5. The permanence as a family unit, of the existing or proposed custodial home or homes
6. The moral fitness of the parties involved
7. The mental and physical health of the parties involved
8. The home, school, and community record of the child
9. The reasonable preferences of the child, if the court considers the child to be of sufficient age to express preferences
10. The willingness of each of the parties to facilitate and encourage a close and continuing parent–child relationship between the child and the other parent or the child and the parents
11. Domestic violence, regardless of whether the violence was directed against or witnessed by the child
12. Any other factors considered by the court to be relevant to a particular child custody dispute

Using a somewhat adjusted list to enhance mutual exclusivity, an extended review of the best interests statutes across the country was conducted to determine the degree of similarity and differences in the legal definitions of the states. Table 1.1 provides that analysis of the legislation.

Forty-six statutes and the law for Washington, DC, were retrieved and analyzed against the 12 Michigan categories (as reconfigured). Table 1.1 illustrates not only the influence of the Michigan law but also the variability that is characteristic of independent state lawmaking. The most "popular" defining characteristics were 1 (bonding), 9 (preferences of child), and 11 (domestic violence). (The 12th category, Other, was the most popular but represents content that itself is extremely variable.) Nine states showed consonance with Michigan for nine or more of the categories (Alaska, Illinois, Louisiana, Minnesota, New Hampshire, Nevada, New York, North Dakota, Virginia). Six states had very limited commonality with three or fewer categories checked (California, Kentucky, South Dakota, Vermont, Wisconsin, Wyoming). The rest varied from four to eight common categories; two states had no "Other" category. Of interest from the perspectives of this book, Arizona has a specification that proven false allegations or coercion or duress as part of obtaining an agreement should be considered in the awarding of custody. The presence of the popular "Other" option includes a wide variety of different considerations and not infrequently includes the option for the judge to consider and articulate unspecified factors as a basis for the decision. The essential ambiguities created have been criticized from a legal scholarship standpoint (Chambers, 1984; Goldstein, Freud, & Solnit, 1979; Mnookin, 1975); however, proposals for more definite and limited categories are, in the opinion of these writers, likely to create significant problems simply due to the complexity of the cases and the considerations that they present to judges. For example, the American Law Institute in 2002 proposed

Table 1.1 Content Analysis of Best Interests Statutes

		AK	AL	AZ	CA	CO	CT	DC	DE	FL	GA	HI	IA	ID	
Bonding	1	1	1	1	·	1	1	1	·	1	1	1	·	1	10
Capacity for Love	2	1	1	·	·	·	·	·	·	1	1	1	·	·	5
Capacity to Provide Physical Support	3	1	1	·	·	·	·	·	·	·	1	1	·	·	4
Capacity for Emotional/Educational Support	4	1	1	1	·	·	·	·	·	1	1	1	·	·	6
Continuity	5	1	1	·	1	·	1	1	·	1	1	·	·	1	8
Moral Fitness	6	·	·	·	·	·	·	·	·	1	·	·	·	·	1
Mental/Phys Health	7	·	·	1	1	1	·	1	1	·	1	·	·	1	7
"Home, School, Community"	8	·	·	1	·	1	1	·	1	·	1	·	·	1	6
Preferences of Child	9	1	·	1	1	1	·	1	1	·	1	1	1	1	10
"Support Relationships, Child with Other Parent"	10	1	·	1	·	1	·	·	·	·	1	·	1	·	5
Domestic Violence	11	1	·	1	1	1	·	·	1	·	1	·	1	1	8
Other	12	1	1	1	1	1	1	1	1	1	1	1	1	1	13
		9	6	8	5	7	4	5	5	6	11	6	4	7	

Continued

Table 1.1 (Continued) Content Analysis of Best Interests Statutes

		IL	IN	KS	KY	LA	MD	ME	MN	MO	MS	MT	NC	ND	
Bonding	1	.	1	1	.	1	1	1	1	1	1	1	.	1	10
Capacity for Love	2	.	.	.	.	1	.	1	1	.	.	.	1	1	5
Capacity to Provide Physical Support	3	1	.	.	.	.	.	.	1	.	.	.	1	.	3
Capacity for Emotional/Educational Support	4	.	.	.	.	1	.	.	.	.	.	.	1	.	2
Continuity	5	1	.	1	.	1	1	1	1	.	1	1	.	1	9
Moral Fitness	6	1	.	.	.	1	.	1	.	.	.	.	.	1	4
Mental/Phys Health	7	1	1	1	.	1	.	.	1	1	1	1	.	1	9
"Home, School, Community"	8	1	1	1	1	1	.	.	1	1	1	1	.	1	10
Preferences of Child	9	1	.	1	.	1	.	1	1	1	1	1	.	1	9
"Support Relationships, Child with Other Parent"	10	1	1	.	.	1	.	1	1	1	.	.	.	1	7
Domestic Violence	11	1	1	1	1	.	1	1	1	1	1	1	.	1	11
Other	12	1	1	1	1	1	1	1	1	1	1	1	1	1	13
		9	6	7	3	10	4	8	10	7	7	7	4	10	

Table 1.1 (Continued) Content Analysis of Best Interests Statutes

		NE	NH	NJ	NM	NV	NY	OH	OR	PA	RI	SC	SD	TN	
Bonding	1	1	1	1	1	1	·	1	1	·	·	·	·	1	8
Capacity for Love	2	·	1	·	·	1	1	·	·	·	·	·	·	·	3
Capacity to Provide Physical Support	3	·	1	1	·	1	1	·	·	1	·	1	·	·	6
Capacity for Emotional/Educational Support	4	1	1	·	·	1	·	·	·	1	1	1	·	·	5
Continuity	5	·	·	·	·	·	1	·	·	1	1	·	·	·	3
Moral Fitness	6	·	·	·	·	·	1	·	·	·	·	·	·	·	1
Mental/Physical Health	7	·	·	·	1	1	1	1	·	·	·	1	·	1	6
Home, School, Community	8	·	1	·	1	·	·	1	·	·	·	·	·	·	3
Preferences of Child	9	1	1	1	1	1	1	1	1	1	1	1	1	·	12
Support Relationships, Child with Other Parent	10	·	1	1	·	1	1	1	1	·	·	·	·	·	6
Domestic Violence	11	1	1	1	·	1	1	1	1	·	1	1	1	1	9
Other	12	N/A	1	1	1	1	1	1	1	1	·	1	1	1	11
		4	9	6	5	9	9	7	5	5	2	6	2	4	

Continued

Table 1.1 (Continued)   Content Analysis of Best Interests Statutes

		TX	UT	VA	VT	WA	WI	WV	WY	
1	Bonding	.	1	1	1	1	1	1	1	7
2	Capacity for Love	.	.	1	1	1	.	.	.	3
3	Capacity to Provide Physical Support	.	.	1	.	.	.	.	.	1
4	Capacity for Emotional/Educational Support	1	.	1	.	.	.	1	1	4
5	Continuity	.	.	.	.	.	.	.	.	0
6	Moral Fitness	.	1	1	.	.	.	.	.	2
7	Mental/Physical Health	1	.	1	.	.	.	.	1	3
8	Home, School, Community	.	.	1	1	1	.	.	.	3
9	Preferences of Child	.	.	1	.	1	1	.	.	3
10	Support Relationships, Child with Other Parent	1	1	1	.	.	.	.	1	4
11	Domestic Violence	1	.	1	.	.	.	.	1	3
12	Other	1	1	1	.	1	1	1	1	7
		5	4	11	3	5	3	3	6	

that best interests could be defined by reference to the party who had the most primary caretaking involvement with the children prior to the filing of divorce. However, in many dysfunctional family situations, such a criterion would perpetuate factors harmful to the children and would rule out a careful evaluation of alternatives that might exist.

Furthermore, inasmuch as the degree of operational definition is not high, as is not infrequently the case in law, the result is that judicial interpretation may reflect unanticipated sources. Words are used that may communicate within the shared experience of the culture, but which nonetheless leave room for idiosyncratic input. Studies of judicial decision making patterns have documented such external to the statute sources, and a study of judges' perspectives on their own decision making has documented the operation of gender-based influences (female judges were more likely to be egalitarian than male judges with respect to mother versus father preferences for custody), age-related attitudes (older judges favored the no longer statutory tender years doctrine more than younger judges), and political differences reflecting traditional family concepts versus more liberal definitions of same (Artis, 2004).*

Referencing the definitional problem, Jameson, Ehrenberg, and Hunter (1997) reviewed the best interests concept and recognized that there was a need to articulate at more specific levels in order to guide the courts and those serving them toward the goal of meeting best interests standards. Of some importance for the matters under current consideration, their survey noted that the top two areas of importance to decision making in the view of judges were sexual or physical abuse of a child by a parent. In our view, the fact that abuse issues are of paramount importance to judges, and rightfully so, further underlines the importance of developing rational and psychologically informed ways of dealing with those situations where determining whether abuse has occurred cannot be secure nor satisfactorily resolved for each of the parties.

It is also argued that another legal event has occurred which facilitates divorce: the increasing adoption of shared parenting as a preferred outcome. As already indicated, a certain confusion or overlap of terms characterizes the literature about newer forms of custody. Specifically, the notion of shared parenting is a term that sometimes refers to an order that specifies 50% companionship time scheduling along with the responsibilities of joint legal custody. However, for purposes of this volume, shared parenting is used interchangeably with joint custody and implies the joint responsibilities for

---

* Interestingly, some judges in the Artis (2004) study indicated they were not entirely familiar with the statutory language, which would mean they were actually applying their own experiential base for defining the best interests concept and applying it to cases at hand.

major decision making but does not specify the dimensions of companionship scheduling. Over time, shared parenting has come to be in effect, if not *de jure,* the default or presumptive arrangement, with courts less and less ordering sole custody and only doing so when clear indications of potential detriment to the child or children pertain or when the parents have themselves proposed the sole model. However, although a joint form has come to be the preferred mode, the statistics on the actual living situations of children have not changed a great deal: in the 1970s, 85% of children lived with their mothers; currently, 80% are with the mothers; fathers have gained from 10% to 15% in being primary caretakers; the remainder are in varying arrangements, presumably reflecting closer to 50/50 (Kelly, 2010b).

At this point, the presumption of the shared parenting approach is being reflected in legislative reform. Bills are being introduced in both Canada and the United States that require shared parenting unless proven otherwise (Allison, 2010; MacLean Family Law Group, 2010 Members Bill C-422; Wolf, 2007). In both countries, however, cautions are being raised both on the basis of whether the model truly benefits all children and families, based on psychological studies, and on the basis that within certain family contexts, especially involving domestic violence and other pathology, the presumption poorly serves the needs of protection and welfare. Additionally, critics point out that research supports the importance of children accessing both parents, but no research has supported a particular scheduling of that contact (Shaffer, 2010).

Psychosocial Concepts and Research

Although the standard of best interests has been present in the legal system only since 1970, there has been some ongoing research to investigate effects and factors of relevance that may guide decision makers. Contrary to the expectations, or perhaps the hopes of those who developed and supported the legislation that has come to define the field, shared parenting has proven to be a mixed blessing. In situations where people are able to use another relatively recent process, that of dissolution, and design together an approach to dealing with their children post decree, it is frequently the case that the children do very well. However, in the case of shared parentings that occur in the context of contested and conflict-ridden divorces, the picture is not quite so promising. Kline, Tschann, Johnston, and Wallerstein (1989) did not show a significant advantage of joint physical custody over other models. However, it was noted that boys were more vulnerable to problems than girls, that parental depression and anxiety could play a part, and that interparental hostility and aggression were of substantial importance. In looking into models where parental conflict is associated with frequent access, the difficulties were clear, leading to a reasonable conclusion that shared parenting may not be an appropriate model if the parties are incapable of effectively working together to design the way things will be handled (Johnston, Kline, & Tschann, 1989).

Many judges and professionals have taken the position, generally speaking, that shared parenting cannot work where there is inadequate communication. Certainly, where parents cannot speak to each other, or speak to each other only to articulate further levels of conflict, many take the position that a shared parenting order should not be attempted. It is interesting to note that the law has evolved in this respect as well. As indicated above, over time, some statutes that originally indicated shared parenting could be ordered only with the agreement of both parties came to include that judges could order it over the disagreement of both parties, but the wisdom of doing so has been consistently challenged.

Two Problematic Psychological Concepts

In the field of forensic psychology or psychiatry, it has often been noted that the marriage of mental health and law is known to produce some problem children. That metaphor may be particularly apt in this context. Two of the more questionable contributions to family law venues have been parental alienation syndrome (PAS) and the child sexual abuse accommodation syndrome (CSAAS). Both of these concepts arose out of family and juvenile law concerns. Both have been presented in courtrooms as if they were scientifically validated, and both have been and continue to be seriously misused in both clinic and court. Nonetheless, both are of some relevance to the issues of focus in this book.

PAS, the creation of Gardner (1987, 1991), specifies that alienation develops out of one parent teaching the child to view the other parent as a negative force often involving reportage of sexual or physical abuse. At conscious and unconscious levels, the input by the usually primary care parent is such that the child comes to believe the allegation and ally with the alienating parent against the other. The concept of parental alienation is a valuable one and can be of assistance in judicial decision making. Where it describes a conscious or unconscious attempt by one party to significantly affect the thinking and behavior of a child or children to reject and dislike the other parent, it is of significant legal as well as psychological importance. Such manipulations clearly imperil the child's growth and development, the self-concept of the child, and the behavior of the child *vis à vis* the other parent. Such a campaign ultimately, if carried out successfully, will cost the child a parent. Additionally, causing a child to dislike a parent offends against one of the legal criteria found in many statutes to guide identification of custodial adequacy, the capacity and willingness to support the relationship of the child with the other parent.

However, a significant error occurred in the development and presentation of the parental alienation concept to the court system. PAS has utility as a syndrome in the strictest sense of that word, namely, a set of behaviors that under some circumstances exhibit a heightened likelihood of co-occurrence. PAS may describe how a child acts when he is alienated—in a negative orientation—toward a parent in a divorce or separation situation. A syndrome, however, is only a description of co-occurring behaviors. It is not an indication of the causes of those behaviors. Syndromes, when identified, need to be further investigated in order to assign causes or interventions that will be effective. The fallacy of how PAS came to be applied in the divorce situation can be laid in part to Gardner and his development of a "test" that had no psychometric integrity and the acceptance by the court system of testimony that implied or asserted that the behavior of a child or children was a reliable indicator of actions and behaviors on the part of the primary caretaking parent. Furthermore, Gardner's "findings" were reported in his self-published materials and lacked scientific peer review and confirmation, which meant the concept was vulnerable to effective challenge even when the data were applicable to a given case. Furthermore, he overstated the incidence of false allegations well beyond what careful research has supported. In fact, children can become alienated from a parent not only when the other parent is transmitting negative information about the former spouse and providing some kind of obvious or not so obvious rewards for alienated behavior, but also when that target parent is acting in an abusive or pathological fashion.* Children may exhibit the alienation syndrome when they have, in effect, a very good reason to do so. The problem for the case investigator in such situations is to determine the causes of these kinds of behaviors using reliable investigative methods. The further problem, which is our focus, is that some cases, even where properly and rigorously investigated, do not allow for firm conclusions. In such cases, very special approaches are needed as recommendations for the courts. (Although developed for cases where alienation is a function of a parent's hostility toward the other parent, Lowenstein's [2008] suggestions can be helpful in fashioning solutions; see Chapter 6.)

In a similar fashion, the CSAAS developed by Summit (1983) was an observation of behaviors that have co-occurred in a subset of children *known*

---

* Subsequent publication of implications of PAS have addressed this issue by specifying that PAS only appears in those cases where there is action by one parent against the other. Cases of parental misbehavior that lead to child rejection of the parent are excluded (see Gardner, Sauber, & Lorandos, 2006).

to have been abused. CSAAS included that some sexually abused children, who had disclosed that abuse, subsequently recanted. A number of reasons were offered as to why that recantation might occur, including direct pressures from the perpetrator, experience of family disruption and a desire to restore what was apparent normalcy, or fearfulness induced by contact with the legal system. This observed patterning, unfortunately—and Summit himself recognized the problem in a 1992 paper—was distorted by scientifically inadequate experts who were allowed to testify that the presence of a recantation was proof of the accuracy of the original disclosure.[*] Any serious logical inquiry into this state of affairs quickly reveals that when the truth of a statement is proven by its retraction, the capacity for there to be an alternative is eliminated. In effect, this behavior of recantation was nonlegitimately treated as an index of truthfulness, where, in fact, it is a demonstration that on at least one occasion (the first disclosure or the recantation itself) the child was not telling the truth.[†]

When the demands of science and logical inquiry are ignored, and when the court system allows experts to provide scientifically indefensible evidence on the basis of which decisions then come to be made, the most regrettable progeny of the marriage of law and psychology are created. Fortunately, the courts have mandates to be careful of the quality of scientific evidence, particularly since *Daubert* (1993), which required that triers of fact evaluate when necessary the presentation of scientific evidence for the degree to which it meets scientific criteria (see Chapter 4 for more extended consideration of this decision and its implications for these cases).

---

[*] Summit, however, brought some significant scientific flaws to his initial involvement in the evaluation of abuse allegations. He was active in the early 1980s supporting the notions promulgated by the worst of the daycare panics, lectured about how wives' vocational ambitions were related to husbands' incestuous wishes, and readily accepted bizarre and unfounded allegations involving eating feces and drinking blood in the context of sexual rituals of abuse against children. He proceeded from unproven theoretical positions to conclusions of acceptance of reports that were based on flawed investigations (Frankfurter, 2006).

[†] More recently, Bernet (2008) proposed that parental alienation disorder (PAD, as distinguished from PAS) be considered for inclusion under the *DSM–V*, the current revision underway for the *Diagnostic and Statistical Manual of Mental Disorders*. In his conceptualization, PAD is a relational disorder and would be defined as the child having false ideas as to the nature of one parent, would be alienated from that parent by virtue of those ideas, and would have come to those ideas either by virtue of the actions of the other parent or by aligning himself with one side of an ongoing and difficult struggle. Not included would be a child alienated by virtue of the actual abusive behavior of the other parent. However, the determination that the child is proceeding on the basis of a false idea cannot be made on the basis of the child's behavior, which was the case of Gardner's application of PAS, and is the essential fallacy that can occur in many of these kinds of situations.

Conclusion

In an arena where behavior is complex and variably determined, which describes most of the settings in which human interaction occurs, and where there is motivation to distort relevant sources of information about significant factors involved, it can easily become impossible to conclude definitively regarding those factors. In the specific area of child abuse allegations occurring in the context of a high-conflict domestic relations dispute, equivocality not infrequently is present and the risks of error in assignment of cause can be high. Such error, regardless of what its nature might be, whether a false positive or a false negative, precipitates a child to lifelong negative consequences. Nonetheless, handling of these cases unfortunately is one of the duties of the court system, as well as becoming, at different points, a focus for mental health practitioners. This chapter has explored foundations on the basis of which contested custody cases including the subset of equivocal abuse cases have been handled. We have emphasized the complexity of the subject matter and of the underlying processes involved in legal decision making as well as the influence of social forces and changes in the law. Ensuing chapters look at sources of ongoing authority in the field, at models that may be applied to reduce the risk levels, and at such empirical sources of data as may be brought to bear on creating a more reliable set of guides than currently exist in the statutes alone. The goal is to lead to more positive outcomes for children and their families when the wisdom of the courts must be substituted due to the lack of combined will of the parents.

The Courts
Views Across and Within

2

As has already been indicated in the preceding chapter, courts differ across the country existing in the legal contexts of the 50 states, all of which have their own codes and regulations. In addition, even within a state, different courts make local rules with the result that procedures vary from one jurisdiction to the next. When cases are ambiguous, as by definition equivocal abuse cases are, the development of any models for investigation and processing have to be flexible enough to be adaptive to these varying court systems and focused enough to actually generate potential solutions.

The Course of a Case

In a relationship that begins in all optimism, there can come a time when one or both of the parties realize that they no longer want to be together. There are varied causes, and although there are general categories of determinative factors leading to divorce, each situation is a unique conflict between two people who have their own idiosyncrasies. One or both parties seek advice from attorneys and at some point one side formally files for divorce. In the vast majority of the cases, the parties reach an agreement as to the division of property and allocation of parental rights and responsibilities, develop a parenting time schedule, and, at this point, usually a shared parenting agreement that enables them to manage the postdivorce family affairs in an uneventful manner. There will still be arguments and angry exchanges from time to time, but such interactions are not constant and occur outside the legal arena. The main job of the domestic relations court in such cases is to ratify the agreement that has been drafted by the parents or their attorneys.

Domestic relations courts spend the majority of their time and effort on a minority of cases that are contested and require adjudication. Financial matters are very important to divorcing couples, as resources are going to be divided and the same income and financial means that used to support one household are going to be allocated to two homes. However, most financial issues such as division of property, alimony, and child support are determined by formulas that utilize the income of the parties or their imputed income, and the length of time they have been married, to calculate what is due each spouse. The complex issues are related to parenting time schedules and the control over decision making for the children regarding healthcare, education, and extracurricular activities. It is in this context that most of the conflicts in a divorce arise and posturing and gamesmanship by parents and their counsels occur.

In most contested custody cases, there is a parenting schedule that the parties follow in the interim when a formal agreement is not yet in place. In some high-conflict cases one parent tries to prevent the other from visitation and having time with the children. It is in this type of situation that allegations of abuse are made. The party that attempts to block visitation is usually asserting the visitation is going to be detrimental to the child or that the child would be in immediate risk of being harmed if she or he is with the other parent. The complicating factor in the early part of the process is that usually there are no court orders in place that define the situation, freeing the parties to engage in these types of behaviors without being in violation of any mandate.

When allegations of abuse are brought against a party, the appropriate social service agencies are notified either directly by a parent who reports the abuse or through other individuals such as pediatricians, school teachers, and daycare workers. An investigation follows and a report is generated that contains an opinion regarding the allegations. If the allegations are determined to be indicated or substantiated, the party expressing concern about the abuse may file a motion (often *ex parte*) to restrict the child's contact with the alleged offender. In many situations, arrangements are made for supervised visitation and the parent has some time with the child. In some instances when one party files a motion with the court for no contact and the social service agencies do not provide a great deal of direction, contact may be terminated temporarily and a psychological evaluation is requested by one of the parties and commonly granted by the court. Along with this process, a guardian *ad litem* (GAL) can also be appointed to ensure that the partisanship between the parents does not interfere with someone advocating for the best interest of the child.

The evaluation process can take a great deal of time, which can be detrimental to the parent–child relationship. In some instances there are countermotions filed by the accused parent to have some type of visitation and depending upon the recommendations of the GAL and the nature of the report from the human services agency, some allowance is made for visitation. The court may order unsupervised but time-limited visitation with no restriction, or it could require different levels of supervision provided by either professionals or trusted family members of the accused. Grandparents are often chosen to provide this type of supervision at their homes because it is a familiar and somewhat natural environment for the children.

There are other situations when professionals are involved to facilitate the visitation and supervise it appropriately. For example, in Ashtabula County, Ohio, the Children Services Board owns and operates a house called Rooms to Grow, where scheduled supervised visits take place. Social workers and case managers are assigned to provide a range of supervision that includes being in the room or observing parent–child interaction from behind a two-way mirror. In the majority of cases, the Ashtabula Court appoints a clinician to conduct a psychological evaluation of the parties and the minor child or the children involved in the case (a detailed description of how such evaluations are usually conducted is outlined elsewhere in this volume). If one of the parties objects to the evaluator that the court appoints or the other party recommends, the court instructs the objecting party to choose one from a group of qualified experts who are known to the court. The court then orders the parties to participate in both evaluations and cooperate fully with the experts.

When there are two experts, eventually two reports are presented to the court, the parties' attorneys, and the GAL. Evaluators obtain permission from the parties to release the information. The authors have a form that they utilize in these types of cases that require the authorization of the parties to send the report to the court and the attorneys. At times, when the evaluator is specifically chosen by one side, the report will only be released to the counsel for the party that has retained the expert. (Parenthetically, in all court-related evaluations, but particularly in the highly charged and conflicted ones of the domestic relations court, it is important to carefully read the content of the court order to make sure what the questions are and who gets the report. In one such case the expert who was retained by the one side sent the report that he had generated to the attorneys from both sides and the GAL, claiming that because the court had agreed that he could conduct the evaluation, he was considered the court's expert and therefore he acted in that fashion. The attorney who had retained him objected and asked that his report be suppressed. It was initially not allowed as evidence although later it was permitted based on the petition from the other attorney.)

After the attorneys get the report they usually review it with their clients and consider the recommendations. There are some informal discussions between the parties as to which recommendations are acceptable, which ones are in need of modification, and which ones are unacceptable. A hearing is scheduled to review the material and attempts are made to settle the case prior to going to trial. In cases where the parties are close to an agreement, experts are asked informal questions regarding some of the recommendations and on some occasions they are invited into the conference room to participate in the settlement discussions with the hope that an agreement can be reached between the parties.

If the settlement conference/hearing does not result in an agreement, a pretrial date is scheduled to ensure that all the pieces are in place for the trial to proceed. Further attempts are made to settle the case during this meeting and at times the magistrate or the judge presiding over the case may provide some directions as to how he or she expects to conduct the trial. (Judges vary stylistically as to their degree of activism, with some vulnerability to criticism whether they choose a more distant or immediate hands-on stance.)

In highly contested cases and in situations where there are allegations of abuse the case usually goes to trial. The parties prepare and call witnesses to testify. In regard to the allocations of parental rights and responsibility, the expert(s) who have conducted the evaluation will be called to testify as to their findings and their recommendations. They will be subjected to direct and cross-examination and sometimes redirect and recross to have the expert explain the opinions and recommendations that are made in regard to the case.

It is not uncommon that even during the trial, depending upon how the case is going, that attempts are made to reach a settlement. Viewed from a more objective or neutral stance, in a significant number of these situations, the parties do not seem to be that far off from each other, and with minor adjustments they each could achieve their objectives of having a good relationship with their child(ren) and being involved in their lives. However, the anger over the divorce, the hurt of the rejection, the need for revenge, the input of extended families, and even at times the encouragement from the litigating attorneys can contaminate the situation and prevent the parties from reaching an amicable solution regarding parenting issues for their children. In equivocal cases of abuse, these fires could be on one side fueled by the belief that the other parent is abusing the child and on the other by a party feeling outraged for being falsely accused of harming the youngster.

Case in Point

This case involved an attractive woman with a compelling kind of dependency that seemed to have particular impact on men in her environment. She had a mildly exotic presentation that enhanced her sensuality and attractions. In the ongoing conflict over custody of the child between herself and the child's father, allegations were raised, re-raised, and re-re-raised. She obtained support from a retired professional man who accompanied her to many of the sessions and meetings, and even the court hearings, and who manifested a rather fatherly interest in how he related to her that probably included an appreciation of her female attributes as well but in no way reflected any kind of ongoing romantic relationship. Up until the case was finally resolved by the court, he supported her version of what was going on and suggested there could be dangers for the child.

In the course of the original custody evaluation, the father alleged infidelity on the part of mother. He also claimed she was overly prone to have doctors and therapies for the child. For his part, he minimized the presence of any medical or developmental needs in the face of clear indications to the contrary. The mother alleged domestic violence. She made multiple assertions of the father's inadequate parenting. Her own use of speech, her word choices, and the way in which she conceptualized things were suggestive that she herself may have had some kinds of verbal developmental issues. The child had excellent verbal capacity albeit some atypical expression modes and social behaviors. (His good vocabulary and the ability to communicate were extremely helpful because it allowed him to respond to investigative interviews.) Not only did the youngster have to cope with ongoing conflicts and problems between his parents, but there was an extended history of very unusual and highly dysfunctional involvements by family members, some of which directly affected him at different points.

The evaluation included reviewing fairly extensive medical and mental health records reflecting the treatment of the child. Recommendations reflected input from both sides of this parental conflict. Included were suggestions for therapeutic input to the child but only with involvement of both parents rather than only one or the other. Joint parental input for decision making in a number of areas was specified and control over contacts with problematic family members was specified. Therapy was recommended for each of the parents.

Following the release of the report, yet another sexual abuse allegation was raised and an investigation was completed by both the social services and police. A request was made by the attorney for the mother that the evaluator once again see the boy from the standpoint of the new allegations. The procedure for that second evaluative phase included a review of the social services interview, which had been preserved on tape. That interview was relatively brief but well handled. The child was able to respond to questioning, and the interviewer spent some time emphasizing the importance that she only wanted to talk about that which was real versus anything that might be in any way made up. She saw the child alone. One of the ongoing allegations that had been periodically raised and was re-raised at this time was that the father would arrange it so that the child would sexually stimulate him. At this point, the child had elaborated that story and created many details that were not logical or for that matter possible. In the follow-up interview of the child, he began referring to the father by the latter's first name and indicated that was his custom at this point. Although the child was very bright and had excellent verbal skills, a lot of the sentences that he provided simply did not make sense. Thus, the interviewer said, "And you call him by his name?" The child answered, "Yes. And then daddy makes it look without me seeing what that happens." Another question prompt, and then the child said, "Well, he didn't let me see him walking the dog and he locks the door." The boy when asked said it was a closet door, but inquiry determined there were no locks on the doors inside the father's house. The boy continued to build on the story, introducing new characters and improbable activities. It became clear that he had interwoven real experiences, things he had been told to tell, and fantasies or stories that he had picked up along the way. It was also clear that he had learned to support his mother against his father.

In the meantime, it was indicated by the guardian that the mother's counsel had her take a private polygraph and reported that she had passed. In dealing with that finding, the evaluator pointed out that there are some reliability questions about the polygraph, but even presuming that the poly was well handled, the implication was that the mother believed that which she was saying as opposed to knowingly lying, in some ways making the situation even more complicated but also allowing a position of support insofar as her character was concerned. In the course of this case, a deposition of the mother was held and was made available to the evaluator by the father's counsel. That deposition documented a lot of confusion and a lack of good organization in her presentation. It also illustrated that she was either very naïve about male behavior or very prone to misconstrue the meaning of what was happening in her world at times.

This case was not as troublesome as it might have been because of the careful activity of the professionals involved. Independent gathering of information using good investigative techniques was characteristic of the social services and police investigations. The information obtained allowed some confidence by professionals that the child was not in danger from the father but did not affect the mother's beliefs that the father might be dangerous to the boy. However, the validation of some of her quite legitimate concerns along with some security procedures (and also the reduction of threat to her primary residential status) allowed her to go forward without continued sabotaging of the child's relationship with the father.

Comment

A positive outcome, as is seen above, can be achieved in these types of situations. When both sides feel and believe that they have been able to get some concessions and also have learned to give some, when they walk away with a sense that they never want to repeat this process, and when they feel sufficient security to adhere closely to the recommendations that are provided to them and at times mandated by the court, a new and more productive set of patterns is instituted. From a complexity theory perspective, one might characterize the process as illustrative of change occurring on what appears to be the edge of total disorder with the emergence of new patterns not typical of those seen earlier during the period of highest dysfunctionality. Children in these situations often are provided with a safety plan that includes access to a competent mental health professional who has experience and training in the area of domestic relations high-conflict cases and is able to work with them to develop healthy coping skills and to find their new "normal" in the aftermath of their parents' divorce. The parents also are taught adaptive ways of protecting their children and also to communicate effectively with their ex-spouses about their children's lives.

Good intentions and good actions can create positive outcomes. However, given the nature of conflict between the parties and their historic difficulties in communication and collaborative problem solving, it is unfortunately true that for a subsection of cases, the drama will continue and the problems perpetuate. The best measure of success is whether these cases do or do not end up back in court and whether the children are able to work through the stress and to develop positive and healthy relationships with both of their parents.

The Rule of Law and the Law of Rules

Every court has its own jurisdiction, within which its rules pertain. However, there are constraints and limitations. In the case of Ohio, there are Rules of Superintendence issued by the State Supreme Court and there are decisions and statutes that limit the kinds of rules that may be articulated and enforced. A rule of course, as with any other legal constraint, can be challenged and upheld, or found in some way defective. Generally speaking, the rules operate to allow the court to have a consistent procedure and approach to the area of the court's concern. In the case of domestic relations, these rules have tended, particularly in recent years, to be relatively extensive and to reflect a court that is clearly concerned with more than the basic administration of matrimonial law. Perhaps as a function of the increased divorce rate, the focus of the domestic relations courts has been more and more on the plight of children and the need to educate parents in order to reduce the degree of negative impact. Judges are interested in research that has focused upon the impact of divorce on child and family functioning and often ask experts appointed by the court to validate or comment upon the state of knowledge that exists in the area.

From a therapeutic jurisprudence (TJ) perspective, the concept of the "Peacemaker Test" has been developed (Mumford, 2007, 2010). Its analysis of legal rules focuses on five questions, each of which is answered in regard to the rule being considered. Is participation limited to the interested parties? Is respect for the parties encouraged? Does the rule incorporate respect for the courts and their officers? Does it promote finality of decision making? Does it lead to reconciliation? In an informal discussion of possible application to the rule making in Domestic Relations (DR) courts, it was noted that finality is often difficult to achieve in the context of ongoing family dynamics and that reconciliation can be even more elusive between parties who have severed the marital bond. Nonetheless, the conceptual approach to evaluation of rules, given the desire of courts and lawmakers to create potentials for resolution that decrease conflict and increase collaboration on behalf of children, is one that may be appropriately applied. We would argue that the rules studied below do encourage respect for parties and the courts and attempt to move in the direction of finality (with courts endorsing that nonreturn of the parties and stability of the parenting orders is the desired outcome). Although reconciliation may be at issue, an outcome of mutual respect and capacity for coparenting, which is in place for the vast majority of divorces, is at least potentially achievable and may indeed be enhanced by facilitative rules of the type currently seen. Research into this area may further shed some light on these matters and give some direction to those who fashion the regulations that establish the court processing of cases.

County Court Rules

In a review of rules from the 88 counties in the State of Ohio, certain commonalities and some differences were observed. In general, when it comes to parenting time, rules will specify that the desirable mode is for the parents to agree upon a schedule that suits their particular life situation and the needs of the children. Absent such agreement, the rules will then state that the court's own schedule becomes the default. For the most part, such schedules, from both rural and more populated and urban counties, have reflected some variation of the traditional standard schedule of every other weekend Friday to Sunday, a midweek time, and some vacation time to the nonresidential parent. The rules may specify 6:00 p.m. Friday to 6:00 p.m. Sunday, 7:00 p.m. Friday to 7:00 p.m. Sunday, or some other variation. Some rules have incorporated developmental knowledge, specifying smaller amounts of time and more frequent contact when children are in their first two years, and then moving to the more standard approach. Some rules also explicitly recognize that teenagers must be treated differently from preteens and need to have somewhat more control over where they will be in order to pursue their own positive agendas. Parents are encouraged to work with their teenagers rather than expect them to conform to some definite and unyielding set of parameters.

What is also clear in the reading of the various rule documents is that an immense amount of thought has gone into wording the rules, whether in regard to visitation schedules or other areas of concern—with trying to so describe and delimit the arena—such that there will be less basis for a return to court for some type of adjustment. In fact, many of the things in the rules can be seen as driven by a need to stabilize and create at least semipermanent systems that will work for the families being served. Thus, it is general for rules to include requirements for attendance at educational seminars that teach about the needs of children in the divorcing process and to further specify programs such as conciliation, mediation, and parent coordination, with an eye to moving families beyond the legal system and into some ongoing living patterns. The Summit County Court contains a list of links to social service agencies as well as to the internal court services that exist.

Another area that is found embedded in the rules are instructions for those who would approach this arena from a *pro se* point of view. Carefully worded directions are in place that facilitate obtaining the proper forms, filing of motions and petitions, and handling other specifics. To some degree, this area also reflects the court's interest in facilitating dissolution wherein the two parties file together to achieve the end of the marital union and the conditions under which they will work post decree. Remember that in Chapter 1, the issue was raised as to the degree to which that kind of facilitation encourages the lack of marital stability as opposed to simply responding to it. Certainly, that question could be raised. Perhaps it is instructive in that regard to note that a recent Pew (11/18/10) study has documented that marriage remains a popular arrangement for the college-educated and economically adequate population but has been opted for much less by those who are of lower socioeconomic status. The results of the inquiry documented a desire on the part of the lower socioeconomic sample to want marriage but to condition actually moving to that status on obtaining some kind of higher-level economic security, which for many would be a goal impossible to meet. The Pew Study looked at marital status from 1960 to 2008 and essentially showed that although 72% of couples were married in 1960, only 52% were married as of 2008. The widowed cohort stayed about the same, 9% versus 7%. The divorced group moved from 5% to 14%. Interestingly, the survey also documented a changing and expanding concept of what constitutes a family. The marriage rate would not be the only factor in these changes, however, inasmuch as there is much more acceptance at this point of alternative lifestyles including the unions of gays and lesbians and more acceptance of single persons having and raising children, including adopting them (Pew Research Center, Nov. 18, 2010).

A Parenting Time Rule

The following section from the parenting time in the default schedule from Ohio's Lorain County Domestic Relations court (2011) is fairly consistent with what is found throughout the state:

Guidelines for Parenting Time

These guidelines are designed to provide assistance to parents in the resolution of issues relating to parenting time and to provide assistance to the Court in formulating parenting time orders when the parents are unable to reach an agreement. The underlying purpose of any such agreement or order is to provide for the best interest of each child after giving full consideration to the facts and issues that are relevant to each family.

These guidelines are based on the premise that:

A. Both parents are suitable;
B. Both parents desire to have an ongoing relationship with each child;
C. Both parents are able to carry out the childcare plan;
D. Any negotiated solution between parents is preferred to a court imposed solution;
E. It is usually in the children's best interest for each parent to have frequent, meaningful and continuing access to the children;
F. Children need reliability, predictability and consistency on the part of each parent.

A number of commonsense guidelines should be followed in every case. Except as otherwise ordered by the court:

A. Both parents are entitled to access to records and information on the medical care of the children directly from the healthcare provider as well as from the other parent. Each parent should notify the other promptly of any significant medical treatment;
B. Both parents are entitled to access all school records of the children directly from the school as well as from the other parent. School reports should be photocopied promptly after receipt and supplied to the other parent. Both parents should be notified promptly of all child-related activities which encourage or allow parental participation;
C. Both parents are reminded that parenting time and child support, while they may be emotionally connected, are separate legal issues. Parental access may not be denied due to failure to pay child support and child support may not be withheld due to failure of a parent to allow access to the children;
D. Parents should share with each other their residence and work addresses and phone numbers;
E. Each parent should encourage the children to initiate telephone, e-mail, and/or mail contact with the other parent on a regular basis, and allow the other parent reasonable contact with the children while in their care;
F. Parents should not discuss their problems with the other parent with the children, nor should they speak ill of the other parent in the presence of the children;
G. Parents should not attempt to buy the favor of the children with presents, special treatment or privileges, or promises;
H. Parents should not make their children choose between the two parents;
I. Parents should not question their children regarding the activities of the other parent;
J. Parents should be prompt with appointments with their children. Children should not be kept waiting, nor should they suffer the disappointment of a parent failing to show up. When unforeseen circumstances prevent arrival within approximately 30 minutes of the scheduled time of exchange, immediate notification should be given, if possible, and appropriate alternative arrangements should be made;

K. Parents should coordinate plans regarding bedtime, discipline, homework schedule and other household rules;

L. Any clothing accompanying the child should be returned in the same
condition as it was sent;

M. The parent exercising parenting time is responsible for transporting
their children to and from the other parent's residence. If the parent
is unavailable for the pick-up or return of their children, an alternate
driver may be used, provided that driver has a valid driver's license and
is known to the children. Any person transporting children must adhere
to all child restraint laws. Both parents are expected to have their own
child restraint devices. No person transporting children may be under
the influence of drugs or alcohol;

N. When either parent's plans include travel out of the area, a travel schedule including destination and emergency phone numbers (if available)
should be forwarded to the other parent prior to departure, with one week
notification being preferred.

Suggested Parenting Time Plan

A. Alternating weekends from Friday at 6:00 p.m. to Sunday at 6:00 p.m.,
commencing the first weekend after the date of filing the journal entry.

B. One midweek day from 5:00 p.m. to 8:00 p.m. If the parties cannot agree
upon a day for the midweek parenting time it shall be Wednesday.

C. For the purpose of parenting time, there are ten (10) holidays as follows:
   1. New Year's Day
   2. Martin Luther King Day
   3. President's Day
   4. Easter
   5. Memorial Day
   6. Independence Day (noon 7/4 until noon 7/5)
   7. Labor Day
   8. Thanksgiving
   9. Christmas Eve
   10. Christmas

   In the odd-numbered years, the mother/father shall have the children
   on odd-numbered holidays; and the father/mother shall have the children on the even-numbered holidays. In the even-numbered years, the
   father/mother shall have the odd-numbered holidays; and the mother/
   father shall have the even-numbered holidays. Holiday parenting
   time shall supersede regularly scheduled parenting time and is from
   9:00 a.m. to 8:00 p.m., unless otherwise noted above.

D. The alternating weekend parenting time sequence shall not be inter-
rupted as a consequence of the holiday schedule. If the weekend immediately preceding a Monday holiday and the holiday parenting time
are both scheduled with the same parent, holiday parenting time shall
commence Friday at 6:00 p.m. and end Monday at 8:00 p.m. Should the

parent having the Thanksgiving holiday also have the weekend immediately following the holiday, holiday parenting time shall commence
Thursday at 9:00 a.m. and end Sunday at 6:00 p.m.

E. On Mother's Day and Father's Day, no matter whose weekend for parenting time, children will be with the appropriate parent.

F. For children of school age, the parents shall split the winter vacation
from school in the following manner: The parent designated to have the
Christmas Eve holiday shall have the children for the first half of the winter vacation, beginning 9:00 a.m. the day immediately following the last
day of school until December 24th at 8:00 p.m. The parent designated to
have the Christmas Day holiday shall have the second half of the winter
vacation, beginning 8:00 p.m. December 24 until 8:00 p.m. December 31st.

G. For children of school age, the parents shall alternate the spring vacation from school in the following manner: The parent designated to have
the Easter holiday shall have the children from 9:00 a.m. the day immediately following the last day of school until 8:00 p.m. the day prior to
reconvening of school. Spring vacation parenting time will supersede
any regular weekend visitation.

H. Four (4) weeks of parenting time each summer. Notice shall be given
to the other parent of the dates of intended parenting time thirty (30)
days in advance of such parenting time. The parent exercising extended
summer parenting time has priority in scheduling over the other parent's choice provided the thirty (30) days notice is given, unless the other
parent's vacation choice is an annual mandatory shutdown of their place
of employment. If either parent chooses to exercise extended summer
parenting time for three or more consecutive weeks, the other parent
is entitled to exercise their alternating weekend parenting time schedule during that time period, unless the extended summer parenting time
involves travel out of the local area.

1. Children are to be in the residential home for school purposes one
week before commencement of the school year. No extended summer parenting time is to be scheduled by either parent for the week
prior to commencement of school.

2. Children not of school age may go for extended parenting time
throughout the year, provided the parents comply with the thirty
(30) day notice requirement.

I. Children shall celebrate their birthday in the home of the residential
parent for school purposes, unless it falls on a day when the other parent is exercising parenting time. The other parent may make up for the
birthday with a separate birthday party if desired.

J. Such additional times as may be agreed between the parties.

K. Absent reasonable notice and good cause for delay, children and/or
the other parent have no duty to wait for the other parent for more than
thirty (30) minutes of a scheduled parenting time. A parent who is later
than thirty (30) minutes without reasonable notice and good cause for
delay shall forfeit that scheduled parenting time.

L. If either parent intends to move from their current residence, that parent shall file a notice of intent to relocate with the court pursuant to Ohio Revised Code Section 3109.051(G)(1).

Comment

A reading of the above shows the kind of scope that is not atypical in writing these rules. Embedded are hoped-for lessons about how to proceed without needlessly distressing children and actually implementing their interests. Also clearly present in this rule is some recognition of the special circumstances that have to occur in the course of ongoing living. What also can be said is that in spite of the active attempts to educate by program and by rule, there are those who cannot hear or whose concerns lead them to reject any system other than the one that they propose for the protection of their children as they perceive it.

State Rules

States in various ways have mechanisms for ensuring some degree of consistency in how the laws are administered by various local courts throughout the state. The Ohio State Constitution has given to the State Supreme Court "General powers of superintendence over the courts of Ohio." The Supreme Court of Ohio established a special commission to assist in rule making. That commission is made up of 20 members from among nominees primarily made by the Chief Justice and other judges. Appointees must include an attorney in practice, a clerk of court, and a court administrator; the others may be judges. The commission meets on a regular basis and considers the needs across the state for various kinds of rules. In common with all state rule making, mechanisms exist for proposed changes to be publicized and for input to be obtained from interested parties and citizens. In the areas relevant to domestic relations practice, the Ohio Rules for Superintendence, among other things, spell out procedures and forms to be used in the case of domestic violence, provide requirements for the qualifications of mediators, and provide detailed expectations for the functioning of GALs. The GAL rules go to the qualifications, the duties, and the requirements for ongoing education. Once a Rule of Superintendence is adopted, local rules are adjusted to be consistent with or to elaborate what that rule has mandated.

Similarly, Massachusetts has "Domestic Rules of Relations Procedure" that are statewide and "govern the procedure in the probate and family court department in all proceedings for divorce, separate support, and custody of minor children..." (Massachusetts Trial Court Law Libraries, Massachusetts Rules of Domestic Relations Procedure, 2010). The rules then proceed to detail the filing procedures, modes of service, property issues, how time is calculated insofar as legal deadlines are concerned, and

pretrial procedure (which includes that the court may suggest "simplifica-
tion of the issues," limitations on what shall be filed and what numbers of
expert witnesses may be presented, and may call for consideration of possibility of settlement). There are procedures regarding discovery and there is
interesting provision for the appointment of a Special Master on motion of
the parties or the court's own motion who has the decision making authority to resolve discovery disputes and levy penalties (with parties disputing
those decisions having access to a court hearing). The rules are extensive
and detailed, but there is a specific rule (83) that permits each court to govern by its own rules as long as there is consistency with the state rules or the
local rules cover areas on which the state rules are silent.

The proliferation of rules within states and across states, with their commonalities but detailed specificities and differences, has created in the eyes of
some attorneys an unnecessarily complicated situation. Attorneys licensed
to practice in a given state have to conform their approaches to myriad
detailed expectations, which change depending upon the jurisdiction in
which they may find themselves trying cases. Given the mobility of people
and the scope of most practices, attorneys and others serving the domestic relations courts have to stay abreast of these various approaches. Some
have thought it would be better to have at least state level uniformity with
rules promulgated that define such basic areas as parenting time, as well as
some of the more commonly held procedures across the state. Certainly, the
Ohio Rules of Superintendence and equivalent state level regulations found
elsewhere across the country do have that impact to some degree. It can be
argued, however, that if all of the courts did not have the capacity to develop
their own rules within the scope of such state regulations that currently exist,
the system would be less likely to respond to new developments, changes
in the family structures and systems, and changes in the population. In Ohio,
although the general default in parenting time is every other weekend and
a midweek, along with the usual days of special meaning and—with some
variation—a number of weeks of summer vacation, there are some "outlier"
courts that approach from a slightly different philosophy than is embedded
in the traditional schedule.

The traditional schedule implicitly endorses a potential conventional
family system in which there is a primary homemaker and child caretaker
and a primary breadwinner. That model, of course, has long since ceased to
be a viable description for contemporary family systems. Most families, if
they are surviving at all economically well, involve two breadwinners and
there is no longer a presumption that the male will be the primary income
producer. As indicated above in the Pew research, the actual construction
of the family is changing and there is a reduction in the number of people
who are in fact marrying (which means that where there are disputes, the
same kinds of problems that exist for the domestic relations courts are going

to be handled in increasing numbers in the juvenile divisions except where there is a unified family court model). Many but not all of the rules reviewed in the State of Ohio did not include detailed approaches to developmental differences. Some of those with age specifications acknowledged the needs of very young children; somewhat fewer explicitly recognized the particular situation of the older child who is approaching his or her own majority. In the case of Cuyahoga County, the default schedule markedly differs from the old standard in that it has a four-week cycle: first and third weekends are Friday at 7:00 p.m. to Sunday at 7:00 p.m.; the second weekend is Friday from 5:00 p.m. to 9:00 p.m. There is no visitation on the fourth weekend. The midweek includes 5:00 p.m. to 7:30 or 8:00 or 9:00 p.m., depending upon the age of the child. There is a six-week vacation period for the nonresidential parent. Another innovation is found in the Erie County schedule where the specification is from alternating Thursday 6:00 p.m. to Sunday at 6:00 p.m. with the midweek occurring from Thursday to Friday at 6:00 p.m. on the weeks that the long weekend does not occur. The way this rule was written, it maximizes the degree to which the schedule would be experienced as similar to week-by-week.

Research Findings

What is clear when looking at the psychological research, however, is that there is no strong empirical base for supporting either the popular traditional default schedule, the innovative schedules, or any other schedules that parents may themselves agree to, with the explicit blessing of the court of their doing so. Research that has been done has indicated the importance of considering a variety of aspects of children's behavior and development and the importance of consistency. Interestingly, the most systematic inquiry into this area found that overnights were not crucial in and of themselves but that girls were more likely to benefit from them than were boys (Pruett, Ebling, & Insabella, 2004). There is, as has already been discussed, substantial evidence that the presence of conflict and the lack of parental ability to communicate victimizes children (see Chapter 1). Therefore, to the extent that the rules of the courts would be so contrived that they actually affected to lower the degree of conflict and discord in the divorcing family systems, there would be a result consistent with the goals of both law and mental health. However, there is as yet no basis for saying that one or the other of the court defined and mandated schedules, which are imposed in the absence of agreement and accord, will be better or worse. In fact, there are no good studies to support any models, originating either in court rules or in recommendations of experts or in the agreements of parents (with the caveat that it is generally observed that agreements made by the parties have a more solid foundation of support by both).

The Play of the Participants

The Litigants

Persons entering the courts with a petition to end their marriage may do so by dissolution or by divorce. Those creating the agreed document that, usually with legal consultation, specifies the terms of their postmarital life represent the lowest conflict portion of this population. They will have created the basis for property, support, other conditions, and parenting in that document. The process is relatively quick and, by contrast to contested situations, relatively painless (if the revision of an anticipated permanent life circumstance can ever be said to be easy to handle). Many persons, however, still choose the option of divorce, in which there is created an adversarial initiation; however, most of these petitions wind up being handled through formal or informal negotiations and do not rise to the level of severe conflict. In the cases where equivocal allegations become central, high conflict pertains and the emotional costs are significant for the parties and children and often others in the immediate families. In these cases, the litigants are in a highly adversarial stance. Their views of each other not infrequently could be characterized in enemy terms, and they will be prone to the same kind of cognitive distortions and beliefs that are found in the literature about how enemies come to see each other. They will devalue and denigrate, often dehumanize or demonize, expect only the worst from the other, and generally attribute negative qualities for the other and those allied with the other. The negative events and traits will be remembered; positives will be minimized (Keen, 1986; McPherson & Donnelly, 2005; Silverstein, 1989).

The Guardians

In high-conflict settings, the cases are more likely to have appointed GALs who must represent the best interests of their wards (the children). Rules determine much of their functioning, as already indicated. Their duty is to maintain objectivity, to investigate thoroughly, and ultimately to make recommendations to the court. Those recommendations are often of substantial importance in the shape of the orders that eventuate. They are compensated, although usually at a much lower rate than is charged by attorneys; they are more frequently than not attorneys and need that background. If they do their job well, they have access to the kind of information that allows a balanced view across the ground created by the two parties. They not infrequently collaborate relatively closely with evaluators, both providing and obtaining information (McPherson, 1990).

The Lawyers

Lawyers are first and foremost advocates. They are pledged to support the interests and positions of their clients. They do have the opportunity to exercise some influence when client behavior is actually self-defeating. However, in the end, and unless what the client wants is not legally allowable, they must move ahead with the case as the client wishes. The concept of client control is often raised in the context of whether the lawyers are able to persuade the parties they represent of the wisdom of some particular direction and whether significantly negative behavior can be reduced if not eliminated. Many of them welcome the opportunity to work in a conflict resolution mode and may meet with guardians and sometimes evaluators in pretrial settlement efforts. Some few of them will engage in practices that unnecessarily prolong the struggle (increasing the fees) and ultimately contributing to what may be very negative outcomes.

The Experts

Although it is generally the preferred model according to most authorities, the court appointed evaluator is not the only or necessarily most common choice across the country. In California, that model has a statutory basis and a detailed set of implementation rules (see Rule 5.220, California Rules of Court). Furthermore, the court must appoint a qualified evaluator (as specified in the rules) where there is "…a serious allegation of child sexual abuse" (California Family Code, Section 3118). In Ohio and some other states there is no statutory requirement. However, the more common occurrence is for a single evaluator by way of an agreed judgment entry, in which the counsels for both parties agree to an evaluator. Nonetheless, many cases involve appointed experts for each side, very much as one finds in traditional civil (tort) cases. Within that model of experts appointed to each side, there are situations in which the order specifies the experts are to consult with one another and share test results, often involving only one administration of the instruments and data provided to both, or the experts may be involved in a coordinated fashion, sharing all the data and sometimes even jointly presiding over a negotiated solution. However, in some cases, perhaps even most of those where experts are obtained by each side, neither expert releases the report or any information to the other side, but only to the retaining attorney, again referencing the model from traditional civil case work. The attorney retaining the expert determines whether to put the expert on the witness list.

The Judges

Judicial Perspectives

Two magistrates and a sitting judge provided some response to a semistruc-tured inquiry into aspects of their work related to ambiguous cases. All were highly experienced in their work in family law. All three indicated experi-ence in dealing with cases where allegations were raised but no clear evidence developed to allow a finding one way or the other. In some cases, agreement between the parties was reached, but when negotiations are unsuccessful, decisions must be rendered in the face of the uncertainties presenting. None of the respondents felt there were any specific socioeconomic or related fac-tors held in common by the cases. These factfinders all had made use of GALs and psychology evaluators to assist in cases with these characteristics. All indicated the addition of these appointees was helpful to managing the case. As one indicated, where cases are clear cut, there is no need for a trial. When these cases go to trial, however, there is always the need for more informa-tion than is usually available. Adding the data and perspectives of the GAL or evaluator is therefore specifically desirable. These respondents also indicated experience with the mechanism of the *in camera* interview. They referenced training and reading they had done in order to assist children and increase the potential for good information to be the product of the session. In their discussions of the process of conducting such interviews, they articulated concern for the child, for the needed rapport, and for understanding both the obvious and more covert aspects of communication. They also recog-nized that in many cases, the interviews did not help the children, sometimes giving them a false hope that they could control the outcomes and always maintaining them in the undesirable middle in which they were living. Respondents indicated they spent time trying to help children understand the legal parameters of the situation and the limitations that pertained. One respondent noted as particularly helpful an American Bar Association publi-cation by Walker (1999) that is based on a linguistic perspective.

In Camera *Interviews*

Interviewing children by judges in contested custody cases arose as a func-tion of the best interests legislation and its specifications, variable to be sure across jurisdictions, that children's wishes were to be considered as part of the process. In some statutes, children's wishes become somewhat control-ling of the outcome, depending upon their age. In Ohio, following best inter-ests legislation, the statute, up until 1993, allowed children the right to have motions filed to make an election as to their custodial arrangements, man-dating that children over the age of 12 would have the right to be heard in such matters and would likely control the outcome with the burden on the parent who opposed the election to present evidence contrary to the child's position.* Furthermore, children at 11½ might be given that option as well. That option ended with amendments to the legislation occurring at that time. Since then and up to the present, the right of election no longer exists in the state, although the statute indicates that the age and maturity of the child provide a basis for the court to assign some weight to expressed preferences. In practice, it is generally agreed that as children proceed through their teen years, their preferences are considered more and more compelling.

Whenever the statute allows the court to consider a factor, including one of the child's preferences, procedures necessarily follow that have to do with how that factor is to be evaluated in cases. The development of those procedures is what led to the *in camera* interview. As indicated by L. Wright (2002), the purpose of the interview is to provide a protected place for the child wherein he or she can express desires as to custody and visitation. In Michigan in 2001, an appeals court reviewed and came to the following conclusion as to the *in camera,* stating that it was "limited to a reasonable inquiry to determine the child's parental preference and...any records of the interview must be made available to the parties if the interview affects an additional child custody factor and that information makes a difference in the outcome of the case" (*Molloy v. Molloy,* 2001; cited in L. Wright, 2002, p. 298). As that appeals case indicated, the purpose of the *in camera* involved providing a forum so that children's preferences could be presented.

One of the reasons the Ohio statute was changed was in recognition that when children are brought into the court in what becomes an adversary position to one of their parents, the psychological impact is negative, the potential for further disruption in an already problematic family situation is raised, and the risk for a serious loss of relationship with a parent clearly presents. It is interesting, however, that the *in camera* interview was viewed as a place that would be safe and comfortable for the child as opposed to open court, even while it was made clear and explicitly required that these interviews were to be recorded, were part of the record, and the parties may have access to them (in many instances and depending upon the jurisdiction, such access is mandated).

In L. Wright's (2002) presentation of appropriate interview procedures for these interviews, the following protocol was presented. Ideally, the interview would take place in a "safe environment" and would not be held in the formality of a judge's chambers. Judges are instructed not to wear their robes and not to sit behind a desk. If there are two children, it may be best to interview them together first and then separately, thus observing the dynamics of the siblingship, as well as giving each child a chance to present information without the influence of the other. The format involves asking the child

---

* In our observation it was the usual case that the child's plea was with substantial adult and one-sided input.

what he or she understands about why the interview takes place. If the child has an idea, he or she should be asked who instructed him or her. The child should be told that there is ongoing recording, but the mechanism doing so should be less than prominent if possible. The child needs to be told that he or she may refuse to engage in the interview. Depending upon the jurisdiction and also in the guidelines of the model Marriage and Divorce Act, the court may permit counsel for each parent to be present. It is not uncommon that the GAL is present during the interview, and in some jurisdictions it is mandated.

Wright's interview format goes on with the usual instructions that are found in almost all child investigative interview guides (see, for example, Aldridge & Wood, 1999; Kuehnle & Connell, 2009; Milne & Bull, 1999), which involve staying at the child's level, using open-ended questions, and using the child's own words to further explore a response the child has given. Several concerns can be raised about the whole procedure at this point. Wright's carefully crafted approach to interviewing notwithstanding, and for that matter the existing guides that are consistent with same also considered, the fact is that this is an intrinsically unsafe procedure, and to believe otherwise is to engage in self-deceit. To suggest to the child that the procedure is safe is to engage in inappropriate misleading of the youngster. In most cases, by virtue of the way in which the legal system works, when decisions are made, the foundation for those decisions must be articulated. When that foundation includes information and impressions obtained from an *in camera* interview, the evidence from that interview needs to be part of the record. That principle has clearly been incorporated into the procedures. However, that very safeguard of the principles of due process means that the child will, in effect if removed by a brief period of time and space, make known his or her wishes to the parents, each of whom has a stake in the outcome. Thus, in the *in camera* interview, no matter how skillfully it is conducted and how sensitive the judge may be to the pressures on the child brought into a situation like this, the impact is more likely than not to be negative. An exception to that outcome might be found in those cases where what is said is irrelevant and therefore the record does not become part of the case (in jurisdictions where such exclusion is permitted).

It is interesting to note that in Wright's discussion on how to proceed, he talks about relatively benign factors that may influence a child in ways which could distort actual underlying preferences, such as being brought by a parent who had just provided an exceedingly delightful weekend experience or being brought by a parent the morning after there was a serious disagreement around matters of homework or other house rules. Nowhere in Wright's article does he cover the situation that pertains where there is advertent or inadvertent programming of a child's situation with one parent actively working to get the child to reject the other parent.

The *in camera* interview is thus a device that arose in order to address one aspect of how the court process itself, outside and beyond the ongoing disputation in the family, actually acts to harm the child or children and the potential for family unification, only to wind up being confronted with another level where the solution merely creates a different place for the same effect.

Another problem that touches upon the difficulties of the *in camera* interview goes to the capacity of children to handle these kinds of legal situations. Woolard, Reppucci, and Redding (1996) addressed the distinction between capacity and performance. They defined performance to include "...the processing activities required to demonstrate knowledge, as well as the interpersonal and contextual factors affecting performance" (p. 220). Performance is defined further to be that which is in evidence under "ideal circumstances." Capacity, however, is defined in terms of specific legal context. The authors indicated there is not sufficient research to look at the degree to which performance is affected by the legal context, and, furthermore, there is not a clear understanding that very often capacity references the ability to engage in decision making that is found in the adult world. Crosby-Currie (1996) investigated the area by looking at judges, lawyers, and mental health professionals as to how they evaluated competency for children to be involved in articulating wishes regarding the custody situation. They found some interesting differences between the groups, with mental health professionals more likely to follow due process protections (recording of the interview, allowing parents to see the results, and even allowing parents to be present). Judges were more likely to make the record available for attorneys or allow them to be present. The actual interview approaches were not substantially different. Finally, all groups tended to give substantial weight to the age of the child in making a determination as to whether competency or capacity was likely to be present.

Pretrial Peregrinations

Motions—Adversarial and Agreeable

In high-conflict cases, multiple motions filed by each side are the rule. Some of the filings are usual and customary and the necessary operations to get matters before the court that have to be decided in order to move the case from its initiation to a final order stage. When allegations occur, motions are filed to reflect the stance of the parties in regard to the issues being raised; not infrequently, there are *ex parte* motions presented on an emergency basis, the purpose of which is to at least ostensibly secure the safety of the children from the perceived danger and responsive motions that assert a contrary position and may ask for visitation or even placement of the children in temporary sole custody with the respondent. Although the granting of emergency motions without a formal hearing is not something most courts wish to do, if such is done, a formal hearing is scheduled as quickly as feasible. However, hearings scheduled within the times required by rule may in some cases be subsequently deferred for some reason deemed necessary by the court. Most motions reflect the ongoing "warfare" in the situation; however, some motions may be jointly filed and represent agreement of the parties with respect to some particular issues or to obtain the expert evaluator.

Depositions

Deposition is a time-honored discovery procedure that can incline toward settlement in any civil venue. By deposing witnesses, especially experts, each side gets to know what will be presented in the court and what are the potential strengths and weaknesses of the testimony. An educated understanding comes to exist across both sides as to what is likely to be the outcome and what limits may exist for reasonable goals. Deposition of experts is not entirely unusual in domestic relations cases; in equivocal abuse cases, the potential for such procedures increases. The use of deposition is much more common in high-profile and highly funded cases. It is, of course, an expensive procedure involving multiple attorney fees, court recorder charges, and transcription costs. Depositions may be scheduled for each of the parties by the opposing side and for a variety of witnesses on the lists of each party. Each side's evaluator is likely to be deposed by the other side, or in the case of an independent evaluator, there may be a deposition by either or both sides to determine what can or will be said prior to giving evidence in court. If there is a GAL, these depositions are attended by that individual.

These authors are aware of an instance in which an attempt was made to schedule a deposition for the guardian. In Ohio, until the passage of Rule 48, which was adopted Jan. 22, 2009, the general approach has been to protect the position of the GAL as an extension of the court and to hold the guardian as unavailable to the same kinds of discovery procedures that apply to parties. Many of the courts and most of the training of GALs emphasized that reports would not be presented until the end of the trial if at all, at which time the GAL would make known his or her recommendations. However, changes in the state rules have specified that GAL reports must be tendered a week prior to the trial, unless the court rules otherwise. In the case referenced above, that ruling had been made and it was specified that the report would be presented after all other evidence was heard; the report was to reflect the totality of the information including trial presentations. The late filed motion for deposition was not approved; a motion to protect the GAL based on the prior ruling was upheld.

This sequence points out the way in which procedural rules define in certain ways the functional role of the domestic relations court, in this case moving toward more formal litigation and away from a somewhat less defined and best interests founded but almost paternalistic function. It is our observation that in extended litigation emanating from equivocal abuse cases, there is more potential for elaborate procedural strategies and what might be considered technical legal maneuvers than is common for much civil litigation but not necessarily characteristic of family court operation.

The Settlement Conference

In Ohio and most of the jurisdictions we reviewed, courts have some procedure for a final pretrial with the purpose being to see whether the case can be settled without going into a full evidentiary hearing. This procedure, incorporated by rule, reflects the ongoing interest in resolving the conflict through alternative means rather than by adversary processing. This conference may involve significant negotiations in chambers, with parties waiting, and attorneys delivering to them proposals for their agreement or amendment. When those conferences result in an outcome that is satisfactory, they also serve to limit how costly the divorcing process becomes. When either of the parties feels that the process has not allowed a fair outcome or that important information has been neglected, the post-decree result can lay the foundation for the case to re-present, sometimes with accompanying allegations and other markers of high conflict. In some courts, the pretrials, including the final one, are more formal and are documented by court reporters with transcripts subsequently available. In those cases, it could be argued that there is less chance to negotiate successfully, but it also ensures that a clear record exists with the imposition of some of the protections of due process. In the kinds of cases considered in this volume, the advantages or disadvantages of formal versus informal proceedings are probably not importantly relevant, inasmuch as the cases are driven by factors outside the courtroom that are not likely to respond to either mode.

Days in Court

A young lawyer from Brazil, visiting the United States for an extended period, attended a trial in progress featuring two quite intransigent parties and two attorneys known for their opposite courtroom styles and shared potentials for prolonged litigation. He watched some not atypical courtroom antics (the one attorney was bombastic and melodramatic, often running around the courtroom gesticulating as he questioned the expert; the other attorney was pedantic and focused his questioning with excruciating thoroughness on every detail that might conceivably have some relevance and quite a few that had none). After about seven hours of the respective performances, the expert (McPherson) was dismissed, and the trial continued for the rest of the week with multiple fact witnesses and testimony by parties. The Brazilian turned to the expert outside the courthouse and said (with apologies for being critical), "In my country, we schedule two hours for divorces with custody issues, and I think we make quite good decisions."

One of the more important functions of the court is its ability to issue a "final appealable order." In other words, the court's authority and mandate is to end the conflict by imposing conditions that will meet statutory requirements for the ongoing care of children. That capacity alone can be argued to have therapeutic potentials inasmuch as the most difficulty for children occurs when conflict is most active, and conflict is heightened when the warring parties each perceive the potential to "win." Such orders are denoted "appealable" because in any action of a lower court where there is dispute as to whether the law and legal procedure have been faithfully followed, an aggrieved party can initiate access to the appeals review process. In many ways, this system is an elegant one whereby bias and error should they be present can be addressed and justice served. The system, however, is not so elegant in the extended time that any appeal requires, the money involved in mounting such an appeal (effectively foreclosing the option to those with limited funds), and the prolongation of case conflict to the detriment of the children who grow up within that context.

Conclusion

In looking at court functioning and the codes that underlie their procedures, complexities clearly abound. When one considers additionally the interplay of experts, court options, court rules and state rules, and the overriding structures of law and precedent, the enormous difficulty of attempting to provide rational and effective frameworks for couples separated by chasms of mutual paranoia should be evident. The expert role is further and appropriately constrained by scientific and objective findings. The expert functions best by acknowledging the significant limitations of his or her contribution. Ultimately, the finder of fact will determine issues of what is credible and what is not and will further decide what is at risk and how to minimize that uncertainty.

Investigation

3

Investigations start with people: those who are the targets and those who seek to enlarge an understanding of a situation. What happens because of the investigative process is driven by numerous factors, including the characteristics and training of investigators, the types of procedures that have been characteristically employed including the adequacies and inadequacies involved, and the special problems that present in the situation being evaluated. An underlying philosophy that is part of the overall approach in this volume is the need for investigation to follow cases rather than for cases to be constrained by investigative protocols (or even worse, by premature theories). The desirability of having some standardized procedures is not disputed. Primarily, however, guidelines such as those promulgated by the American Psychological Association (2009) and the Association of Family and Conciliation Courts (2006) secure that investigations will not omit certain kinds of critical activities. However, if a custody evaluation is defined to be adequate because these guidelines procedures are followed, in the most problematic of cases the investigation will not be complete and the potential for error will be drastically increased. As is well known by persons doing more conventional kinds of investigations, as data are developed in a situation, there should be decision making about whether to pursue one line or another of additional information. No investigation can afford to provide all lines of possible evidence, nor would such an uneconomical procedure yield much in the way of regular value. However, we would take the position that investigation can involve a series of decisions as to how to proceed and those decisions can be informed by certain kinds of procedures. Furthermore, we would argue that through awareness of the likely particular problems with these kinds of cases, the necessary decision making for evaluative strategies is further enhanced.

However, in all domestic relations cases, the goal, whether from the standpoint of a custody evaluator, a guardian *ad litem* (GAL), or the court, and even sometimes counsel for the parties, is to have an understanding of the realities of the situation rather than resting upon the perspectives or distortions of those realities as they may be presented by the parties. Distortions come about not only from conscious desires to achieve certain ends, but perhaps more largely through the unconscious operations that are characteristic of human functioning. People generally see the world in ways compatible with their pre-existing assumptions, their goals and history, and their expectations.

Current Theory and Research on Brain Function

In order to understand the difficulties that exist at the level of society and its courts and the search for accuracy and truth, it is necessary to consider the complexities that underlie human mechanisms for thinking and reasoning. In many respects, the potential of investigation, no matter how well carried out, to develop what is needed by the courts is limited by the nature of the human brain, which directs the functioning of the objects or targets of investigation and the functions of the investigators themselves. It is well beyond the scope of this volume to provide detailed analyses of the multiple systems and functional properties that underlie human behavior, but some appreciation of this area will allow an understanding of limitations that exist for those working in the field.

Starting at the level of the organization of the brain, the thinking prior to the recent explosion of data from cognitive neuroscience essentially approached understanding the brain either by looking at it from a stimulus–response point of view or by looking at functioning of individuals with known brain injury and mapping what they could or could not do with reference to the areas of damage. Thus, either the brain was a black box where its nature was not important and the only information went to the description of the affecting variable and the dimensions of the subsequent activity, which would characterize a strict behaviorist position (see Gardner, 1985, for a discussion of the contrast between original behaviorists and the early development of cognitive science), or the brain was more centrally included but identified functionally in discrete area terms. Thus, Broca in 1863 identified the area associated with language production, and Wernicke in 1874 amplified the Broca findings by demonstrating that the area of language comprehension was entirely different from the Broca area for production. Luria, on the other hand, coming from the more modern perspective that reflected the advances of Russian research, developed a theory which essentially identified that there are functional aspects that go into a variety of more global activities and require communication within the brain and multiple area responding. That approach was detailed by Kosslyn and Koenig (1992), whose concept of wet mind represented a revolution in the approach to conceptualizing about the brain. They defined reasoning as involving the selection of a goal and then creating a way of meeting that goal. Elaborating further, they detailed that there had to be a perceptual encoding system, some imagery processing to allow the individual to do vicarious trial and error involving the operation of memory subsystems, auditory subsystems to process verbal instructions, and ultimately a decisional system that "…orchestrates the others so that a specific goal is achieved…" (p. 403).*

Consistently, the basic overall theory of brain organization involved the notion of parallel distributed processing. That model envisions levels of functioning, cortical and subcortical, interwired and operating on feedback mechanisms, associational bonding, with complex and dynamic interrelationships that are changing and developing throughout the lifetime of the organism (Rumelhart, Hinton, & McClelland, 1986).

Considering some of the relevant areas of cognition even further, the research from perception, memory, emotion, and consciousness allows further elaboration of Kosslyn and Koenig's basic posture. In order to be able to react to something going on in the world, the individual has to perceive or see it through some set of sensory systems. The study of that perceptual processing initially involved the development of a number of different theories which addressed questions such as whether the individual was genetically wired to understand the world globally or came through experience to develop the immediate perceptual recognition processing. However, not unlike the case in physics with wave versus quantum theories, both of those approaches turned out to have supportive evidence. In a recent article, Dilworth (2005) developed a theory called reflexive theory. From his point of view, an adequate theory has to accommodate findings from both the behavioral studies of global responding as well as the more learning-theory-based materials, and the functional neuroscience developments. The following quotations give a sense of his theory.

> The current view will more specifically be a *dispositional* version of functionalism.…Such a view is theoretically flexible in that (as with any dispositional view) the perceptual acquisition of such dispositions need not immediately—or ever—involve an actual behavioral output, in that the right external conditions for the disposition to be manifested may not be present, just as the fact that salt has the dispositional property of being soluble in water does not imply that a given sample ever will be in contact with water. (p. 20)

and:

> Nevertheless, the view can be flexible enough to recognize that some cognitive activities constructed upon this dispositional perceptual base, such as speculative thoughts of various kinds, may not themselves involve any direct behavioral dispositions. (pp. 20–21)

---

* Although Kosslyn and Koenig articulated a more complex and likely more adequate explanatory basis for brain function, what they did not do was get beyond describing what might be characteristic rather than really reaching explanatory levels, in part because of the impossibility of obtaining the kinds of observations at the level of neuron interaction that would be needed.

Thus, at the level of theorizing about perception, it is obvious that we are dealing with selection, with personal history, and with the potential for an individual to literally see the world differently than another individual, and therefore truthfully relate the nature of that world and act upon it based on a perception that varies from his or her neighbor.

When we look at memory, it has been empirically demonstrated since 1932 (Bartlett) that a constructive process exists. The implications of constructive memory and the potential for the human being to remember as real that which never occurred has become fundamental as a problem for investigations into allegations of abuse (Kuehnle & Connell, 2009; London, Bruck, Ceci, & Shuman, 2005; London, Bruck, Wright, & Ceci, 2008). At a more molecular level, which may add to an understanding of why these investigative difficulties are the case, the current research into memory systems has secured the facts of complexity, construction, and variable impacts of environmental inputs. There are different brain systems involved in the acceptance and coding of stimuli and further different systems involved in categorizing those stimuli and then storing them in memory. Not everything that is seen or understood at the moment is actually encoded. Not everything that is initially encoded is stored. Thus, one individual may be in a situation and differ in what he or she takes out of that situation and has available for later reflection and reportage than is true for another equally exposed person. The brain then operates to process that which in fact was categorized and stored and has even different systems that get involved in recall and reporting. Moreover, the process of retrieval of a memory changes it every time the retrieval is performed. A kind of Heisenberg (1927) indeterminacy principle exists: the measurement—in this case subjective review of content or outward reportage—changes the content for the next round. There are different brain pathways of explicit, implicit, and emotional memories. Explicit memories involve essentially factual or personal data. Implicit memories involve those things that come to be known but are not necessarily conscious, such as driving a car, riding a bike, and aspects of playing a musical instrument. Emotional memories are those memories that are stored and have a significant emotional component as part of the stored information. Traumatic events of an individual involve significant and usually negative emotional components. All of these aspects vary in complex and interactive ways, depending upon the nature of the experience, stimulus, history of the individual, and internal brain properties (Kolb & Wishaw, 2009).

As if that were not enough to consider, the function of emotion is of specific concern in this area. One recent finding at a behavioral rather than neurophysiological level is that the presence of emotional arousal can increase the amount of detail in later reports of the event but reduce the potential for accuracy (Kensinger, 2010; Phelps & Sharot, 2008; Richardson, Strange, & Dolan, 2004). Such a finding has obvious implications for the arena about which we are concerned. The original notion in the study of emotion was that there was a specific system for encoding, namely the regional limbic system, but in common with all other aspects of contemporary brain research, that type of localization is not supported. The studies also indicate that the operation of the amygdala is significant for encoding, but the specifics of that function are not yet known for retrieval. An additional caution is warranted: a lot of the current neuroscientifically based studies are limited as to generalizability due to the small samples and characteristics of participants involved (Richardson, Strange, & Dolan, 2004; Ward, 2006).

Finally, in this extremely brief and not comprehensive consideration of some relevant knowledge as to human functioning, the area of consciousness has also received current attention. For many years, consciousness was the stepchild of all behavioral research and there were certainly some who treated it essentially as an epiphenomenon, a function that didn't have any relevance for understanding why people acted as they did and simply existed to reflect what was going on automatically. However, the general finding from evolution studies and other areas of scientific exploration is that nature abhors an unnecessary process, and at this point it would be generally agreed that consciousness is an important component and one that must be better understood. Generally speaking, consciousness is considered to be an awareness of internal and external sources of information including memories, emotional and other feeling states, and things that are occurring. It has been demonstrated that multiple brain areas are active when conscious alertness is demonstrated and become inactive in sleep and pathological states that represent unconsciousness (coma, significant general anesthesia, persistent vegetative states) (Soslo, Maclin, & Maclin, 2008; Tsuchiya & Adolphs, 2007). From the standpoint of the usefulness of the unconscious, Vandenbos (2007), in defining unconscious processing, noted its importance in multitasking and certain kinds of learning and decision making.

In the experiences reported by many people, and specifically those in situations that may be considered emergencies that require extremely fast decisional operations, there are indications that individuals are able to come to conclusions that are correct without having the conscious experience of going through an articulate process. That rapid decision making constitutes one aspect of what is thought of as the unconscious level of consciousness. In addition, there is a venerable literature from the psychodynamic viewpoint that speaks to the purposive activity that unconscious functioning can represent with individuals protecting themselves from unwanted knowledge and operating to not have access to some at least previously known life events due to traumatic inputs. However, although the current research is not definitive on the presence or absence of some variations of what has been referred to as repression and associated operations, it has been clearly demonstrated that the claims of those who posit a combination of motivated forgetting of severe and extensive traumas as well as notions that the "repressed" material remains impervious to any postevent alterations have little if any foundation. It is probable that some type of complex functioning can take place involving psychological protectionism, which may be readily available to conscious report or not, and is a necessary part for understanding why people say the things they do, some of which may turn out to be factually false statements (Piper, Lillevik, & Kritzer, 2008).

In this brief discussion of brain functioning, it has been hoped to illustrate that any work that involves complex processing of information by individuals is an area where a simple dichotomous outcome and one often desired by the legal system flies in the face of the nature of what is available. Because of this characteristic complexity of human functioning, investigation of human activity is not easy, a fact that is well known from the world of criminal justice (see, for example, the work of Gudjonsson, 2003, and Shuy, 1998). The well-known triad in criminal investigation is that of motivation, opportunity, and means. Although perhaps not directly applicable in all cases, thinking in those kinds of terms is not an inappropriate perspective to bring to bear in these kinds of cases. As shown below, investigating police officers approach questions of child sexual and physical abuse from just such a perspective and in some ways have less tolerance for letting a case stay at the equivocal level than do social workers and perhaps psychologists.

The Particular Problem of Lying

Another variable in conducting investigations is the difficulty of separating truthful statements from those that represent lies. The truth/lie distinction is one that is and has been a subject of much research, inquiry, and procedural development. However, the essence of the criminal justice system has acknowledged that although there may be higher than appreciated levels of incidence of a crime, the system itself is tilted in the direction of not punishing the innocent over allowing the release of the guilty. That position was actually overtly challenged by some, notably in the 1980s, who took the position that child sexual abuse was the one area that should be treated separate from the presumption of innocence and requirement for conviction at beyond reasonable doubt. Such thinking not only offends against the integrity of the Western judicial system and the rights that it protects (and its own over 1,000-year history at this point), but it also in a subtle way supported some in taking the position that the evidence obtained in these kinds of investigations should not be subjected to the same kind of scrutiny as would be true in other contexts, and to some degree asserting that the evidence should not even be available to such scrutiny. In fact, there are still those who take the position that there should not be videotaped interviews of alleged victims because the tapes may allow cross-examination that discredits the report.* This total lack of appreciation of both the science of memory and the principles of a justice system presents a serious problem in these cases.

The problem of evaluating the credibility of a verbal report is one that is well known in investigation; the difficulty of discriminating truth-tellers from liars is in some ways the essence of most investigative activity. Research into the identification of truth-telling has yielded fairly clear results. There are no methods that reliably discriminate those who are lying, those who are telling the truth, those who are telling the truth as they know it but are operating on the basis of false beliefs, and those who present an honest and accurate account of a target event (Gudjonsson, 2003; Raskin, 1989; Wojcikiewicz, 2009; Wrightsman & Kassin, 1993). Policework and the legal system properly rely upon confirmations and independently obtained evidence, on the basis of which a reasonable discrimination can be made. Certain legal protections exist in the form of the burden of proof, which in the criminal justice system is on the prosecution, and the standard of proof, which, again in the criminal system, is beyond reasonable doubt. Although McPherson was present at a training session held during the mid-1980s where a speaker took the position that sexual abuse allegation cases should be exempt from both of those constraints and that persons should be convicted in spite of the lack of proof at that level in order to better protect children, the legal system has not been so "reformed." Of course, the conundrum remains. How can these cases be managed, given the potential damages that present on both sides?

In attempting to reduce these uncertainties, the misuse of an inadequate science is not unknown. A particular issue that may become part of the equivocal abuse case is the notion that a complaining witness, the party raising the allegation, can be shown to be telling the truth, and the alleged perpetrator can be identified as lying, by the use of the linguistic analysis of verbal products, polygraph, or even more problematically, the Voice Stress Analysis (VSA) technology or nonverbal behaviors.

Linguistic Analyses of Transcripts

In the pursuit of behavioral indicators of truth versus lying, the notion has been put forth that certain kinds of linguistic analysis of interview content or

---

* Faller (2007) provided a detailed discussion of the controversies that have been raised, noting that it was in the latter half of the 1980s and beyond that a variety of agencies and law enforcement units opposed taping, fearing it would set a precedent for other kinds of forensic inquiries, make investigators vulnerable to attack on the witness stand, and provide a basis for impeaching victims. She noted, however, that currently the use of veridical means of interview preservation is generally supported, citing the fact that guidelines have been developed for the process by the American Academy of Child and Adolescent Psychiatry (1997).

written statements can be evaluated for truthfulness. The first such attempt that was focused on the area of abuse interviews was that of Criteria Based Content Analysis (Undeutsch, 1982). That foundation was elaborated, supposedly to reflect research by linguists and psycholinguists and then sold as Statement Validity Assessment (SVA); Vrij (2010) has provided a *Daubert*-based analysis of the adequacy of those techniques that included a focus on the original Undeutsch (1982) based Criteria Based Content Analysis as well as the current SVA noting extremely high error rates and concluding usefulness as investigative tools but not presenting as eligible to be admitted as expert evidence. Another more recent linguistic approach is that of Schafer (2007, 2010), but it has no substantive independent research base. Science proceeds with baby steps and its findings are tested, examined, and ultimately applied under whatever limited conditions that have been demonstrated to be secure or most secure. Scientists look for levels of confidence at 95% or better before they feel justified in supporting a conclusion. Such a high bar can be frustrating to those who work in the field and want answers to serious questions. The conventions of science may be considered irrelevant by those who would prematurely sell—and profit from—a new technology. To those with a primary profit motive, the niceties of high standards have little importance. However, when decisions are made in the court, the observance of true scientific standards is a necessity for the protection of the interests of all.

Polygraph

The warhorse in investigating truthfulness has been the polygraph. That technique has a long-standing record as an investigative tool but is generally rejected as evidence of credibility under both *Frye* (1923) and *Daubert* (1993; Wojcikiewicz, 2009). The appeal that led to its exclusion (*Frye*, 1923) set the standard for the admission of scientific evidence in the courtroom. The reasoning underlying *Frye* was that scientific evidence had to meet a requirement of general acceptability in the scientific community. The polygraph presented with a problem of statistical adequacy that was sufficient to exclude such acceptability. The findings were that the polygraph could be useful as an investigative tool. It allowed a focus on an individual's report and could generate hypotheses on the likelihood of lying (either raised or reduced) as a function of failing or passing the instrument. What the instrument could not and cannot do, however, is to compensate adequately for the number of false positive and false negatives that occur, leading to well below any kind of scientific acceptability for discriminatory power.

Voice Stress Analysis (VSA)

VSA is one of the somewhat newer tools. Its theoretical base involves the notion that when persons are extremely tense and anxious, qualities of vocal production change. VSA appeared on the scene in the late 1970s and a fair amount of research has been done since. In spite of the assertions of those who are proprietors of this technology (and despite their withholding some of the data that represent studies of same), the instrument has an even less impressive accuracy of identifying truth-tellers from liars than the polygraph. There has been good evidence developed for its capacity to reflect stress, and a number of studies are consistent with same, including those done in both laboratory or simulated stress conditions and those using actual recordings of persons responding under stress. What has not been demonstrated, however, is that the presence of voice stress is associated with lying such that a positive finding rules out truth-telling with any kind of adequate probability. In fact, the studies have allowed the conclusion that the flipping of a coin would be as good a predictor (Virginia Department of Professional and Occupational Regulation, 2003). Under such conditions, one would do better to either take the position that children ought to be protected and therefore all allegations by persons about the perpetration of abuse should be accepted as true, or all allegations should be accepted as false and the rights of persons about whom allegations are made are best protected theoretically to the detriment of children. Neither of these solutions is particularly attractive to any investigator. The fact that those are the only kinds of approaches that can be recommended on a statistically acceptable basis clearly supports that VSA technology has only minimal utility for investigators (whose personal intuitions arguably may be better, depending upon their years of experience and the accuracy of their investigative conclusions) and no place as evidence in the court for credibility.

Neuroscience Enters the Picture

Current findings in contemporary neuroscience are looking at functional magnetic resonance images under conditions of truth-telling and lying and have developed some intriguing patterns that may be associated with truth-telling. However, findings have been variable, and as yet none of these has arrived at the level of reliability and validity that they have been admitted to courtrooms as evidence against (or for that matter, for) anyone. One exception involved an Illinois case where the brain scan was admitted as evidence of an individual's mental illness although not of his veracity; one lawyer in a

New York civil case has offered the results as a basis for witness truthfulness or the lack thereof (Hsu, 2010a).[*]

Nonverbal Interview Behavior

Any number of schemes for identifying nonverbal indicators of lying have been proposed or studied. Some have held up somewhat better than others, but the most effective ones may be best identified from within the range of behaviors of an individual necessitating an analysis of individual actions while truth-telling versus lying (see, for example, Memon, Vrij, & Bull, 2003). Other methods, notably the Reid technique, contain "indicators" that are simply misleading (Gudjonsson, 2003; Inbau, Reid, Buckley, & Jayne, 2001). Some of the tools of the Secret Service have shown reliability in the field, but no independent studies of their adequacy are available. Schafer (2007, 2010) has done some research and provides ongoing consultation to federal law enforcement relative to such behavioral indicators as investigative tools. To our knowledge, there are no systematic studies that would allow translation of even the best of these methods to the behavior of young children in the interview room.

Summary

The primary finding from a review of all of the attempts to use the analysis of verbal, written, or nonverbal behavior as a way to ferret out those who tell the truth from those who do not is that science has not arrived at a point where it can enter the courtroom on the witness credibility issue. In the meantime, there will continue to be cases where the evidence that derives from good investigation cannot result in resolution. Those cases need to be handled as equivocal and as therefore needing some kind of approach that can maximize safety issues across the disturbed family systems from which they emerge.

Abel Testing to Identify Potential Perpetrators

Abel (2011), after conducting research on a technique he designed, formed a company in 1995 to sell the use of the approach to law enforcement and others needing a basis for identifying sexual interests of a deviant sort. The technique, known as Abel Assessment for Sexual Interest (AASI), is based on the theory that latency of looking at different pictures in a series will reveal underlying sexual interests. For any number of reasons, that theory is flawed;

[*] Two days later, the judge ruled the evidence inadmissible (Hsu, 2010b).

the length of time one looks at any visual stimulus is variably determined and may reflect associations of a personal sort, remembered historical events, or other reasons including the patterns and colors that could be important to someone of artistic capacity. If a picture depicts some sexual aspect, it is not unlikely to cause most adults to view it with some interest but not necessarily to reflect a personal proclivity; otherwise, the sensationalism that sells newspapers and feeds much of mass entertainment would be an indicator of extraordinarily broad cohorts of sexually deviant individuals. A case can be made for some involuntary and unconsciously mediated responding as determining such latencies; however, the other part of the test involves rankings of the pictures as to their "disgust" level, with the notion being that the findings allow insight into the mind of a perpetrator who presumably will rank his or her sexual deviancies as less disgusting than will those who lack such potentials.

Abel, however, has refused to allow his data, on the basis of which the test is reputed to allow identification of child abusers and pedophiles, to be examined by independent researchers. It may be that this instrument has some value for providing information from admitting abusers about the scope of their predilections which would then allow focus of treatment programming. In that regard, the technique may be considered a potential tool. However, when it comes to the use of the AASI as a way to ferret out those who are denying they abuse children from those who are telling the truth, there is little or no scientific basis. Ewing (2006) provided a clear psycholegal discussion, referencing the scientific weakness, the proprietary issue, and the findings from *Daubert* analyses on the basis of which the AASI has been properly excluded from the courts.[*] Therefore, attorneys who do not allow their clients in these cases to "take the Abel" are engaging in good practice; the refusal to undergo this test cannot be viewed as having any meaning other than the avoidance of personal hazard and victimization by pseudoscience.

Perspectives from Investigators

Using a semistructured interview format (see Appendix C), both police and social services respondents were obtained from Canada and the United States in a small sample of opportunity. The responses showed consistency across a

---

[*] Ewing quoted the judge, who excluded the assessment as worthless for identifying molesters from nonmolesters, as stating, "For all we know, they and their components could be mathematically based, founded upon indisputable empirical research, or simply the magic of young Harry Potter's mixing potions at the Hogwarts School of Witchcraft and Wizardry" (*Ready v. Commonwealth*, 2005).

Table 3.1   Investigator Sample (Police and Social Workers)

Group	Education				Experience		
	H.S.	Some College	BA	MA/MSW	General	Special	No. Cases
Police	1	5	2	0	14+	7+	ca. 231
Social work	0	0	4	2	11	10	ca. 500

number of dimensions and as such may well have some representative value. Table 3.1 provides a sample description.

In this sample of 14 respondents, educational level was quite adequate (only one respondent had no college-level training). The sample included eight police officers and six social services workers. Range of general experience included 3 to 27 years with means of 14 and 11 for police and social services workers, respectively. Special experience with sexual abuse investigations ranged from 2 to 15 years, with means of 7 and 10 years. The mean number of cases referenced was 231 for police officers and 500 for social services workers. The group as a whole was clearly coming from significant work in the field.

In terms of procedure, the Canadian model was relatively clear. (Most of the officer respondents were Canadian; American procedures do not adhere to the same standards.) All investigative interviews with children are videotaped and all follow what is variously referred to as an open-ended or cognitive interview or "pure version technique interview." Officers interpreted that approach to start with as open-ended questions as are possible given the age and stage of the child and then to inquire further after the youngster has conveyed what his or her report might be. Police officers emphasized that they would interview the child alone, but only after obtaining consent from parents. Some noted that depending upon the child, separation could be difficult, but for the most part they seemed to feel that they were able to proceed in that fashion. Officers indicated that there were times when they would need more than one interview in order to achieve clarity and to follow up on information that might develop subsequently, but for the most part they would rely upon the initial interview contact as such.

Again, consistent with the usual procedures of police work, ancillary interviews would be scheduled. There would be an interview of anyone to whom the child had disclosed abuse, and there might be other investigative activities that led to sources of information and further interviews. In Canada, all videos are kept, at least as long as any case that would be filed against someone would be active, including up through the end of the appeals process.

By contrast, social services personnel relied entirely upon note taking and did not use video- or audiotaping as part of their usual procedure, except under unusual circumstances. That finding is consistent with our experience and with the departmental policies of which we are aware.

Officers in general did not usually have ancillary or alleged perpetrator interviews with an attorney present. Social services personnel indicated they would have such interviews, but in that case their own agency attorney also had to be present. On the other hand, officers recognized that there were *Miranda* rights in the United States and comparable cautions in Canada, and those cautions were followed. Some officers noted somewhat wryly that doing an interview with an attorney present often made it a less than very effective investigative tool, inasmuch as attorneys would routinely advise against answering questions that might have the potential to bear investigative fruit.

The role of the therapist was generally seen as that of a person who should support the victim and assist the victim with the ongoing process, as well as with any problems that might be present as a function of traumatic experience. Officers indicated they did not expect therapists to become arms of investigation. One noted that in most of his cases, a therapist usually became involved with the child after prosecution rather than before. However, there were a couple of respondents who suggested that the therapist might develop more information that might be important for the investigation and were at least tacitly viewing a therapist as a potential partner in the investigative process. (The implications—and complications—for such a dual role are discussed in Chapter 5.)

In discussing the kinds of cases that could fit within the focus of equivocal status, police officers generally took the position that they would continue investigating until they could (at least within their own perspectives) arrive at a point where the situation was not particularly equivocal: either they could rule out abuse or they felt there was something ongoing and so open status remained in place. At the same time, all of them recognized that the biggest problems when it came to identifying whether a case could be closed as ruled out or maintained open as likely to involve abuse were in the context of the divorce cases. All responding police officers recognized the potential for people to make false reports in this context and, at the same time, knew that there would be the potential for an actual case to exist. Most took refuge in the idea that there needed to be more education and more impact at the level of the court when suspect allegations came forward to assist parents in understanding how their use of children in this kind of dispute and in this kind of way was a destructive set of activities.

Police investigators, in dealing with these kinds of cases, to some degree relied upon their experience and intuitive sensibilities, and most felt that reliance was well placed. In other words, they were of the opinion that often they could accurately discriminate between the false and the true allegations, and that they had some sense of when people were making it up.

Among this group there was probably an underappreciation of the factor of belief wherein people make honest allegations from the standpoint of their belief systems, but those allegations in fact are incorrect.

Comment

Perhaps the most interesting "finding" from this very limited sample is the general comfort expressed by investigating police officers in using the videotaped format that contrasted with the continuing reliance by social workers on note taking only and some kind of aversion, at least on the part of some, to videotaping. In many respects, police officers seem to have a better understanding of the importance of hard data from the standpoint of evidence and seemed not to be worried about the impact of having to defend their interview approach. Specific guides for proper interviewing have been available for some time (Aldridge & Wood, 1998; Milne & Bull, 1999; Perry & Wrightsman, 1991; Sattler, 1998; Young, O'Brien, Gutterman, & Cohen, 1987). All of these approaches, as well as that embodied in the current American Academy of Child and Adolescent Psychiatry, Practice Parameters (1997), recommend audiotape or videotape interview preservation. The literature in general supports that false statements can occur, and that in this area the divorcing process is a context within which that danger presents most significantly.

It is also generally agreed that the interview format needs to emphasize open-ended inquiry to the extent possible, developmentally appropriate questioning, and minimization of any kind of leading questions. Thus, Annon (1994) provided a list of 39 guidelines for interviewing and a further set of seven considerations to bring to bear when assessing the content of the information obtained (see Appendix A), all of which are solidly based in the ongoing development of literature about the suggestibility of children, as well as their capacity to report and reflect on their experience. Also helpful are recommendations reported by the American Prosecutors Research Institute (APRI, 2003), which provide some clear instructions as to how to not only proceed, but how to defend in court what was done. The APRI has as its primary focus how to pursue and successfully obtain conviction in criminal cases. There is a tendency in implementing that perspective to presume likely guilt. However, the approach incorporates the importance of objectivity and court-worthy evidence collection, and it also acknowledges the obligation to find the truth in situations. These guidelines reflect an understanding of the potential for suggestibility under conditions of poorly conducted investigatory contacts. Nonetheless, persons coming from a prosecutorial orientation are likely to be more skeptical about alleged perpetrator denials than they are skeptical of child witness statements. Because of that, there is also a tendency to accept as likely to be valid the techniques used by police departments in their investigations without appreciating the potential problems of some police enthusiasm for inadequate technology (see above).

Appendix B is a sample of a portion from a typical affidavit provided by McPherson that was presented as part of obtaining admissibility for testimony about procedure in a case. Appendix F provides an example of a consultation in which the principles of forensic interviewing were the basis for a critique designed to assist defense counsel in trial preparation.

Perspectives of Child Custody Evaluators

Child custody evaluators generally recognize these cases as having particular difficulties procedurally and in other ways as well. However, those with experience in these kinds of cases speak to the need for creating options that acknowledge the insecurity of parties, children, and the situation itself. Several experienced forensic practitioners responded to semistructured but largely open-ended inquiries (see Appendix C for the Interview Guide). Their perspectives were essentially similar. Mandatory reporting was expected and followed. In some cases, the report could facilitate managing the situation, but in some instances it enhanced the complications that then ensued. The importance of documentation was noted and the need to use videotaping for child interviews, if not also for adults, was acknowledged. The potential for these cases to have negative consequences for practitioners was noted (see Chapter 5).

An interview of one such experienced evaluator is illustrative: Dr. X has over 30 years of experience in dealing with cases that have included various levels of abuse and of equivocality as to the allegations. Over those years, she has designed an ongoing set of policies that reflect the need for objectivity, professional security, observance of legal rights, and protection for children. Her overall protocol begins with the first phone contact where there is immediate and careful determination as to whether the individual is seeking therapy or a forensic input of some kind. If there is any confusion in the caller's mind, and there is litigation in the background that has led to the call, she requests a copy of the order. In her handout at the initial interview, the role clarification is restated as well as the specifics of the financial policy; clients sign a signifying agreement. Forensic evaluations involving custody issues follow the requirements of the APA guidelines. Treatment cases that have legal aspects (children referred as part of the court's final orders would be an example) are carefully handled to maintain confidentiality and sustain that the therapist is not to become an expert in further litigation. Court-ordered therapy needs careful specification in order to establish the boundaries and potentials for any reportage. In cases being evaluated for custody purposes, she operates according to certain presumptions: if the child at issue in an equivocal situation is very young, she makes the supposition that actual truth may never be known at satisfactory levels. In many of these cases, it has been her experience that the common parameters are allegations from the mother that are not clearly founded in demonstrable facts and poor boundary behaviors on the part of the father. These behaviors in and of themselves may not be injurious, but they sustain the suspicion and the fears of the mother and are part of the dynamics that victimize the child.

To change that dynamic, she has designed a safety plan which she "sells" on the basis that the mother (in the typical case) needs to feel the child will not be hurt and the father needs to protect himself from misperception that can move to serious levels of threat to him and his reputation. That plan (which is implemented in a treatment setting) then involves the "Coparenting Team" consisting of the two parents and the therapist. In that context, certain teaching occurs, including how to handle "dangerous" areas (bathing, toileting, bedtime) and what to do if the child says something worrisome but not entirely distinct, other than an immediate call to authorities (options may vary depending on the case). Each parent, the child, and the therapist meet for an "inoculation" session in which the emphasis is on not having secrets, understanding body parts and boundaries, and each parent endorses this process with the child and the therapist. In cases where there has been some separation and the child may be confused or reluctant to begin parenting time, the plan specifies a gradual approach that starts in the therapy room, moves to the visitation setting, and ultimately reaches the level specified in the court order.

Legal Standard Issues

To complicate matters somewhat further, in the domestic relations courtroom the standard of proof is either "more likely than not" or "clear and convincing," both of which are well below the standard required for a criminal conviction. The notion in the civil justice system is that such a lowered standard, in effect, protects the interests of both sides; perhaps in some ways this lower standard implicitly acknowledges the likelihood that some truth is to be found on both sides of a civil dispute, including in the domestic relations courtroom. Every divorce has at least some diverging perspectives of the parties, and some divorces represent diametrically opposing views on many matters and historical details. Most of those differences can be reasonably treated as likely partial truths created out of varying perspectives. A solution that incorporates aspects of both is a probable wise outcome. However, when the perspectives include ambiguous allegations of what might be either criminal or hazardous behavior, or might be false facts, the potential for a court decision to cause serious damage is well above what the usual divorce represents. Children spend their lives primarily with one or another parent. If that placement turns out to be a wrongful placement, the child's whole life is encumbered to some extent.* Impacts on children for whom these decisions are not well considered or well founded include the development of personal psychopathology, the development of eating disorders, major depression, or disruption of adult relationship potentials. It could be reasonably argued that the domestic relations court when acting as the protector of a child, by making a decision that radically severs a child's relationship with a parent, should meet a higher rather than lower standard of proof. Too much of the time, the only available evidence before the domestic relations court is the opinions of investigators such as psychologist evaluators, guardians *ad litem*, the respective testimonies of the warring parents, or an *in camera* interview of the child or children involved. Those *in camera* interviews themselves have legal, factual, or psychological problematic aspects, and the judges who conduct them have acknowledged the difficulties (see Chapter 4 for further elaboration).

To address the problems that present in these kinds of cases, a model for custody evaluations tailored to meet the various hazards of these cases is presented in Chapter 8. By following good investigative principles as well as known custody evaluation parameters, an evaluator can provide a foundation for the presentation for more secure evidence in the courtroom and for the development of conclusions and recommendations that have a higher chance of actually reflecting the best interests of the child or children and minimizing the potential for unnecessary harm to the parents involved. On the other hand, although any below-standard professional work is unethical and may precipitate harm to the client, in these cases the reverberations created by unethical and below-standard functioning are particularly egregious in their impacts. One factor that can feed into and support such negative outcomes involves over-identification between an evaluator and one or a few attorneys, often with significant monetary incentives involved. In effect, such collaboration becomes collusion. It would seem obvious that the below signs or behaviors should be viewed with alarm, but it remains the case that they are found in what we would

---

* We are aware of a case where judicial ire and clever manipulation by one parent combined with poor courtroom behavior and decision making by the other resulted in an order that has precipitated a child to a disastrous and ongoing negative life experience. The child, who was of promising intellect and was happily prosocial is now socially isolated, depressed, producing poorly in school, and has developed several symptoms of an anxiety disorder. It can be reasonably predicted that the future of this individual will be seriously problematic.

argue are sophisticated court settings and represent the worst type of negative evaluator contributions:

1. Willingness to provide opinions in a case based on evidence from one side only (there can be license actions; however, there are those who operate cleverly to stay just this side of outright ethical violations). One tactic that has been seen is to acknowledge that the writer cannot make a custody recommendation, referencing the APA guidelines, and then discussing the child's psychological needs and making treatment recommendations that would require one rather than another outcome from the court.

2. A long association with only one or two attorneys such that a significant portion of the evaluator's work depends upon a very few reference sources, making the evaluator dependent on the source. In one such case, we are aware that the evaluator routinely submits reports to the referral source, who then track edits them, and the evaluator then clicks "Accept" and signs the result.

Some Case Investigations

The cases below are presented in the form of sequential activity and ensuing developments that illustrate the principles of following the case while maintaining an overall structure of the evaluative process. We have heard some practitioners suggest that psychological evaluation is different from investigation, but we take a contrary position to the effect that the necessary level of inquiry in child custody work, particularly where serious allegations have emerged, must combine good investigative principles with the development of more traditional psychological perspectives and expertise if the interests of children are to be served. In that stance, current authorities are generally supportive (see, for example, Melton, Petrila, Poythress, & Slobogin, 1997).

Case A

One of the more important investigative techniques is the creation of a time line that integrates the history of the case with its legal "events." In this case, both parents had significant mental health diagnoses and were in ongoing psychiatric treatment for same. When the mother was hospitalized, following the deterioration of the marital relationship, the father filed first for a protection order and then for divorce. The mother, once out of the hospital, filed responsively to freeze and restrict contact to certain very significant assets. Visitation with the son commenced and was immediately followed by the first allegation by the father of sexual abuse. Mediation of the custody dispute was cancelled. Mandatory reports resulted in both social services and police interviews of the mother. At her attorney's request, she took and passed a polygraph examination. A filing in juvenile court resulted in an adjudication of abuse and a reunification plan that included certain educational and therapy activities. In the Domestic Relations (DR) court, the civil protection order was dismissed after an evidentiary hearing and questions began to be raised about the legitimacy of the separation of the mother and the child. Of some import, the child was an extremely bright and verbally capable preteen. The father then filed a motion to relocate to a very distant state. The mother filed to prohibit. The mother, at advice of counsel, took and "passed" the Abel screening. In the course of the juvenile court involvement, the child was seen by two different forensic evaluators, only one of whom videotaped the interviews. At this point, the mother filed for approval of an expert to do an evaluation of the investigatory procedures that had been employed and an evaluation of the child's status. The procedure included a review of all available mental health records for parents and child, a review of the investigative tape and other investigative notes and reports, and psychological testing of the mother and of the child, in this case including some cognitive assessment. Two important aspects were covered in the review of prior evaluations: the degree to which procedures were consistent with existing guidelines and the degree to which the content of results raised any clear questions of the presence of unlikely events. The results of the procedures (which were interspersed with attempts to restrict access to needed materials that were overruled by the court) supported that generally the forensic interviewing followed appropriate patterns (except for the lack of the tape in the one case), that the mother had not maintained consistent good parenting practices, and that the specific sexual abuse scenarios recounted by the child literally could not have occurred as indicated (one involved the attribution of a penis to the mother, another created an event at a site that did not exist). Other allegations were physically unlikely, bizarre, or replete with highly deviant sex acts. The direct evaluation of the boy focused on the current status of the youngster, his belief systems and their malleability, and the potential to benefit from environmental inputs. There was no attempt made to engage at the level of "proving" the allegations one way or the other. The end result was a court order providing for ongoing assistance by the therapist in a graduated contact program with the mother.

Case B

In this case, allegations ranged from the sexual to physical to parenting judgment deficits. The procedure was relatively standard in that each parent was seen, and the child was seen with the mother (but not with the father initially because legal barriers had been erected in the form of protection orders that did not allow the father to be in the same setting as the mother, and the contact with the child had been suspended pending the resolution of the allegations.) The history included impulsive actions on the part of the father that nicely fed the mother's fears and became a basis for the ongoing lack of contact. The child, however, indicated no problems with seeing the father. The extended family of the mother was actively involved in the allegations, claiming the child's statements had confirmed same, and supporting an end to the father's parental rights. The mother's fourth husband was actively involved as well and she indicated a desire for the child to be free for adoption by that individual. The father's history included alcoholism and periodic drug abuse with a relapse to which he admitted almost a year prior (after which his visitation rights were suspended). The allegations arose when it appeared likely that supervised and ultimately normalized visitation might be ordered (again illustrating the importance of chronology). Complicating matters—and a factor not uncommon in these cases—the mother indicated a history of sexual abuse at the hands of her stepfather. In her presentation of what she believed the father was doing to the child, the details and her behavior both spoke to the active memory of her abuse experience (she rather graphically demonstrated one of the things done to her). When the father was given the chance to visit under supervision, he brought with him a present that he denoted was a children's storybook but which actually was an adult satire with comic book pictures, the content of which was of very questionable taste and clearly inappropriate for the 6-year-old. All of that said, when there was a contact visit/observation conducted as part of the evaluation, the child was delighted to see the father (even though she had a day earlier expressed concern while in the presence of her mother). She immediately initiated physical contact with the father. His play at times was overly rambunctious and stimulating for the small space but at no time suggested eroticization.

Following testimony, there was a court order for visitation with the involvement of a therapist. However, in the course of the ensuing two years, during which there were few times that visits actually occurred, the father and mother had some ongoing e-mail and U.S. mail contact, notably involving his extended and detailed and often accusatory statements to her. He seemed unable to comprehend that continuing the negative dialogue would not convince her of the rightness of his position. Ultimately, a new allegation surfaced, to the effect that the father was harassing and threatening the mother in his contacts. His written communications were turned over to a newly "trained" police officer for application of a type of content analysis known as Scientific Content Analysis (SCAN), a proprietary method that is advertised to show whether a person is telling the truth and if not what the hidden information might be, all obtainable by scrutinizing the subject's written statement about a given situation (see Laboratory for Scientific Interrogation, Inc., retrieved Jan. 20, 2011 from http://www.lsiscan.com). That officer opined that the analysis revealed that not only would the father likely harm the mother, but moreover that he had in fact assaulted the daughter. Expert testimony regarding the lack of adequate scientific foundation for this technique was provided by way of a trial deposition; following cross-examination, the criminal charges were dismissed on the basis of the record in place from the DR case and the unreliability and likely inadmissibility of the "evidence" from the SCAN application. However, contact of father and daughter remained ruptured and the father's insight into the contributions he made to the deterioration of the situation was at best superficial.

Case C

As any investigator will confirm, it is sometimes possible to come to conclusions because of fortuitous collection of data. A case that illustrates that phenomenon involved a child who was ordered into visitation with his father over the objections of his mother, who maintained that the father was potentially a danger to him. The father had remarried and relocated to an area several hours away. Upon the child's return from his first visit over the weekend, there was a social services report filed by the mother alleging that the youngster had been terrorized in the course of the weekend and further that he was sexually molested in his bed by his father with both his father and stepmother standing by with no clothes on. He repeated that story to the investigating social worker and then was seen for a taped interview as part of the ongoing custody evaluation, secondary to the mother's motion to modify custody and essentially end all parental rights. In the course of interviewing the mother, she was asked whether from her experience of the father during the period of their marriage there had been any unusual sexual behaviors or inclinations that she had observed. She did not have any specific examples, but she maintained that his interest in her had been very limited and volunteered that in her current relationship, which was now fairly long-standing, there was much happier intimate contact. For no consciously thought-through reason on the part of the evaluator, the mother was asked whether there were any things in the current relationship that would be considered unusual. She replied to the contrary except maybe some would find it strange that her lover preferred that she shave completely her pubic area. In her original report about the allegation, there was included that the boy had not been exposed to any adult material and the only woman he had ever seen unclothed was his mother. Armed with that information, the inquiry to the boy included a request to describe in detail the body of the stepmother as she stood there in his bedroom. He complied, faithfully indicating and confirming on follow-up focused but nonleading questioning that the woman had no pubic hair.

The clear lack of validity of this report was thus demonstrated (the wife of the father indicated she would be happy to submit a statement from her physician as to the condition of her body if that indeed was necessary).

Comment

The cases illustrate the need to proceed with investigative techniques that address the problems as they emerge. They also, regrettably enough, show the potential of cases to mutate over time and to emerge from one phase to another with newly shaped allegations requiring attention. Furthermore, in this real world of people whose "worst selves" could be said to have been liberated by their struggle, there is no clear path to a safe and healthy solution that easily presents. Although it is often possible to rule out one or more assertions, it is also true that the data often fail to eliminate all abusive possibilities and clearly usually rule in the presence of significant problem areas on both sides of the ongoing warfare.

The Expert in the Courtroom

4

Atty: Now, Doctor, you have indicated the father to be a mentally ill person. What is the nature of that illness?*

Expert: Paranoid schizophrenia.

Atty: And what have you recommended as to parenting time with his son?

Expert: Only the most closely supervised, preferably at a professional setting.

Atty: And why is that important?

Expert: Because his illness could cause him to become violent and harm the child. There are times when he does not understand the difference between what is real and what is not.

Atty: How did you become aware of his condition?

Expert: I interviewed him and I administered the MMPI. When I analyzed the MMPI results, he was very defensive and tried to hide what his symptoms were by denial, but there are critical items and he indicated on one of them that he has hallucinations.

Atty: Exactly what was that item?

Expert: "I see things that other people do not see."

What's wrong with the (above) picture? Well, among other things, when he was seen for a second opinion, the father presented as a 42-year-old, consistently employed, never violent individual with no history of interpersonal difficulties except with his soon to be ex-wife. He had never had any symptoms of schizophrenia according to himself and those who knew him well. The referenced Minnesota Multiphasic Personality Inventory (MMPI) protocol was within normal limits albeit with relative elevations on Scales L and K (a typical pattern for Domestic Relations [DR] profiles). And the remarkable Critical Item that gave away his illness? Questioned about the endorsement, he stated he was a hunter and very good at it; in fact, his hunting buddies had told him that he often saw things they didn't see, which put a lot of venison on his winter table.

---

* The testimony excerpt is a reconstruction based on the actual facts of a case where McPherson served to provide a second opinion and the basis for a motion for reconsideration of the temporary order restricting contact of a father with his child.

Types of Witnesses in DR Court Cases

The place of the expert witness in the court systems has been the focus of much discussion and for that matter a fair amount of research and observation. The use of questioning as presented in Wellman's (1932) redoubtable *The Art of Cross-Examination* nicely illustrates how the proper employment of procedure can effectively winnow out the helpful from bogus presentations. Our expert above, in the hands of a cross-examiner knowledgeable about the MMPI and mental health (and possibly aided by a professional consultant), could easily have been discredited. In fact, issues could have been raised by the father as to incompetent practice that would be sufficient to result in state board action. However, with the explosion of knowledge and its dissemination in this information age, the courts clearly cannot dispense justice without expert assistance from time to time because cases reflect an astonishing variety of factors. For the most part, the domain of a witness and his or her usefulness can be pretty well circumscribed and the court can focus on law, precedent, and case facts. However, in the realm of domestic relations cases, clarity of the fact picture is arguably much more difficult to achieve than is likely to be the case in most criminal or even many other civil proceedings. Almost all DR cases rest substantially on the shifting sands of perception and memory stirred by the tempests of emotion. However, the helpfulness of the expert depends on the quality of the input and the expert's capacity to identify that which can and that which cannot be presented; if the expert does not properly discriminate in this regard, he or she becomes part of the unstable and constantly reinvented presentations to which the court is subjected.

As with other court venues, an individual may be a fact witness or be qualified as an expert (see the section "Rules of Evidence"). In the DR court, fact witnesses might testify as to employment of a party or compensation or some other factual information that is considered relevant to the proceedings at hand. In relationship to issues regarding the children, there might be factual testimony about bringing the child to school on time or attendance at parent conferences by teachers or school aides. There could be testimony by neighbors as to observed participation between child and parent. An expert is needed, however, in areas where special knowledge and a trained opinion are necessary. Thus, expert witnesses may be brought in on matters of property and finances. With respect to children, an opinion as to whether parenting behaviors meet some designated standards defines an area within the realm of expert testimony. Certain categories of witnesses are commonly presented when unresolved custody disputes reach the level of court hearings.

Evaluators

Custody visitation evaluators are appointed in several ways, but all have essentially the same duty, which is to develop information pertinent to questions of custody and visitation. Evaluators are expected to follow published guidelines, such as those of the American Psychological Association or other authoritative professional sources. In all cases, such experts, in order to meet minimal expectations, would see the children and each of the parents and do evaluations of the youngsters in the context of their relationship to each parent. The preferred mode for appointment for most psychologists doing this type of work is a court order providing for an independent expert, which sometimes is achieved by what is known as an agreed judgment entry in which both sides jointly petition for the appointment. Sometimes courts issue orders for an evaluator on the motion of a party unopposed by the other party. However, it is possible, particularly in cases that become complex and highly contested, for each side to petition for its own expert. Under those conditions, a variety of expectations may pertain. The court may approve that each expert shall share results of the evaluation with the other or may expect that each expert will file reports with both parties or may approve an arrangement in which each expert files his or her report only with the retaining attorney, who then has the option of calling the expert as a witness. In the case of a neutral appointed expert, it is still possible that neither side will call the evaluator as a witness, although conceivably the court might on its own motion ask the evaluator to be present as might the guardian *ad litem* (GAL). Procedures and specifics vary on a state-by-state and even local jurisdiction-by-jurisdiction basis, as well as on a case-by-case basis.

Guardians *ad Litem*

Another kind of testimony that is sometimes given by mental health professionals or attorneys involves the presentation of evidence by the GALs. The GAL is appointed in cases where the court on its own or responding to motions by one side or the other asks an individual to represent the best interests of the child or children (the wards). In Ohio, statutory law defines that both lawyers and mental health professionals may be appointed. In courts where litigation too often becomes complex, there may be local rules favoring appointment of lawyers. If a lay (mental health professional) guardian is appointed, and it becomes necessary to file motions and otherwise engage in the practice of law (not including questioning of witnesses at trial), it can be the case that a lawyer is appointed to represent the guardian. In such situations, even more complex layering of communication occurs with the GAL speaking some but not all of the time through the attorney.

The GAL role has evolved over time. At one point, the GAL was viewed as having a confidential relationship with the wards excepting the usual mandated reportage. However, it soon became apparent that the GAL on occasion would develop information and a conclusion as to best interests that conflicted with what the child might him- or herself articulate as a preference. In cases where the court viewed the children as having the capacity to make reasoned statements of preference that were independent of coercion or undue influence, and such a conflict existed, there could then be appointed a lawyer for the child. That attorney would have the same confidentiality/ privileged communication with the child as with an adult client and would advocate for that child's position. The GAL's role became more strictly defined as an extension of the court's goal of a best interests solution. Confidentiality no longer pertained for any aspect of the GAL's investigations and data, all of which became subject to discovery by both sides (as well as any attorney representing the children's wishes). In Ohio, new guidelines reflecting these complexities came to require that the GAL issue a report in advance of court (in the usual spirit of discovery), *except* where the judge might specifically order otherwise. However, a report had to be in the hands of attorneys prior to the testimony of the GAL. (Some judges prefer to have the GAL's report reflect the impact of any evidence that comes out in the course of the hearing and on that basis order a delay of the report until after all other witnesses have been heard, excepting the GAL. Perhaps more commonly at this point, the judge may specify that the GAL render a preliminary report and opinion prior to the final hearing but supplement that report with a final statement after all witnesses have been heard and before GAL testimony.)

Testimony involves what is largely fact based (what was done, what was learned from what was done) but also involves the presentation of recommendations that essentially are of the order of expert opinion although not designated as such. However, those recommendations cannot be excluded on the basis of fact witness status. In effect, the GAL role occupies some kind of witness category that has similarities to evaluator status and lives in a no-man's-land between fact and expert. Furthermore, it is not uncommon for the GAL to be specifically requested to work toward resolution of the case, becoming an active negotiator sometimes at the hearing door (or even inside the courtroom with the judge absent and waiting in chambers—one hopes— for a positive outcome). A lack of success of the effort then may be replaced by an immediate move into trial mode.

Following release of the GAL report, whether before or after the plaintiff/ respondent witnesses are heard, each of which may be questioned by the GAL for the record, the guardian becomes a witness. His or her report is entered into evidence, and cross-examination occurs by all attorneys excepting the one who initiates to present the GAL's direct testimony.*

Treating Professionals

Another kind of expert testimony is provided by treating clinicians. A major problem source for both clinicians and the court has occurred when treating mental health professionals step over the line from an opinion regarding the capacity of a client to provide parental input (for which the professional may have observations or other data) and come to an unwarranted and unsubstantiated conclusion as to which party should be custodial and what should be the proper visitation arrangement. It is not unheard of for counsel deliberately to refer clients to therapists, ostensibly to assist with the stress of the situation or to address child issues that have emerged, but actually with the intention of using the professional in an expert capacity at trial. Once the therapist accepts the case, the counsel then lists the individual as a witness and provides a subpoena with the plan of not only providing the court with testimony about the therapy and how well the client is doing but also asking for an opinion about the ultimate issue as well. The duty of the testifying therapist is to avoid the mistake of answering that question, which can occur unfortunately and unwittingly as a function of the court itself or counsel in the approach to questioning. It is not uncommon for persons trained and expert in law not to have a clear insight into the reasons why treating professionals cannot function as forensic experts.

Clinicians need to understand the importance of telling the court or counsel that they are unable to answer a question because it is beyond the purview of the data they have collected and would place them in an ethically hazardous position with their State Boards. Treating clinicians can provide the court with an expert opinion as to the mental status of the particular person whom they have treated, the basis on which they came to that conclusion, and the implications of that diagnosis, as well as a description of the treatment and response that they have observed. The further hazard, however, specifically raised by cases with unproven and potentially unprovable allegations, occurs when treating clinicians, basing their diagnoses on the information from one side of a dispute, come to a conclusion that directly or indirectly implicates that the other side has committed some kind of inappropriate or inadequate parenting. Sometimes the error that can occur in

---

* The reasons for some of these distinctions are clarified in the section below on rules of evidence.

Table 4.1   Areas for Cross-Examination of a Clinician Expert

Area	Questions to be Raised
Reason for treatment	Was the case referred by an attorney for a party or by a party, on advice of counsel? Was the presenting picture from the child's statements and behavior consistent with the presence of the stated problem? Were you told you would likely be a witness in litigation regarding the divorce? If so, what were you given to understand would be the purposes of calling for your testimony?
Parental contact	Was there an effort made to contact the other parent? If not, why not? Was there any representation made as to custodial status? (In most jurisdictions, regardless of legal custody, each parent is entitled to know about treatment.)
Diagnosis	What is the *DSM* diagnosis? What are the specific bases for that conclusion? (Have a copy of the *DSM*, current version, available.) If the diagnosis is an Adjustment Disorder, go over the particular symptoms and the specific stressors to which the symptoms represent a response. If the diagnosis is post-traumatic stress disorder, go into whether the clinician inferred the traumatic event from the symptoms and then impeach on lack of knowledge of the requirements of the category. (Note: it is acceptable for the clinician to say he or she accepted the word of the child or parent; if that is the case, ask whether the diagnosis could be maintained if the facts were false.)
Course of treatment	What were the stated goals of treatment? Is or was the treatment activity consistent with those goals? What are the criteria for success or conclusion of treatment?
Improper testimony	If the clinician has provided an opinion as to parenting time or custody, and objections to that opinion have not resulted in exclusion, a question of knowledge of guidelines is in order. Are you aware of the ethical guidelines for doing child custody evaluations? (The area can then be further explored depending upon importance and degree of credibility involved.)

such an instance is correctable through the judicious and appropriate use of incisive cross-examination (see Table 4.1). However, the highly responsible clinician does not present him- or herself or the records without clearly indicating knowledge that the scope of information that has been provided is limited and the opinion is therefore only as good as the quality as that information may be shown to be. A further error of both science and law, which is discussed in detail below, goes to admission of testimony about the credibility of a source.[*]

---

[*] Traditionally, psychotherapy has rested on a premise of the therapist's acceptance of the patient's world as seen through the patient's words. The expression of skepticism with respect to what the patient says has not been high on the list of therapeutic responses. However, the most validated form of therapy to date, cognitive behavioral therapy, does include the importance of awareness and challenge to distortions in the patient presentations (Dobson, 2010). We would argue that that skepticism, which is the mark of science and the foundation of good psychological practice, should be especially in evidence when considering a diagnosis of post-traumatic stress disorder based only on the verbal reports of a parent in a custody situation or on the reports of a vulnerable to influence child.

Admission of testimony by a treating child therapist with only one-sided contact needs to be qualified and limited. Although the testimony can be considered expert in the sense of pertaining to diagnosis and treatment, it should never include opinions as to the forensic questions (custody and visitation). Furthermore, "back-dooring" unwarranted assumptions as to unproven realities looms when child therapists have post-tramautic stress disorder (PTSD) as a current diagnosis. The *DSM–IV* and the upcoming *V* specify that a PTSD requires that a traumatic event has occurred in fact and the symptom picture is the result of that trauma. No treating therapist, however, is in a position in these cases to independently confirm the presence of such trauma, and opinions based on the presumption of same (usually accompanied by a presumption of the identity of the perpetrator of abuse) are scientifically and clinically unacceptable, implicitly involve advocacy, and should be excluded from legal testimony. The carefully practicing therapist would indicate an Adjustment Disorder diagnostic category in recognition of the unknown factual foundations. In some civil court cases, treating therapists might be called to present evidence of their PTSD treatment based on their acceptance of a patient's statements as to events the patient experienced. With proper and careful indications of the sources of their data, such professionals could provide information about their treatment but not opinions as to causality and injury, which are the forensic issues and require the independence of a forensic evaluation. However, in the context of high-conflict divorce cases, it borders on malpractice to presume that evidence of events and perspectives presented by one party can be viewed with any confidence as having factual reality and then to further provide a diagnosis entirely dependent on such data. It *is* malpractice to then have opinions as to custody/visitation (see Chapter 5).

Rules of Evidence

U.S. Tradition

Statutory law, both federal and state, provides definitions for who may be considered an expert versus a lay witness. In general, the Federal Rules of Evidence (FRE) (2009) have become models on the basis of which state law has been drafted. Obviously, when it comes to being informed about the applicable standards in a given jurisdiction, practitioners must look to their state statutes. However, the general principles articulated in the federal rules are worthy of consideration in this context.

Rule 702 (Federal Rules of Evidence, 2009) sets forth the difference between an expert and a lay witness. When an individual is not qualified as an expert witness before the court, the testimony given is expected to be

"rationally based on the perception of the witness...helpful to a clear understanding of the witness' testimony or the determination of a fact in issue,
and...not based on scientific, technical, or other specialized knowledge." In
other words, the individual testifies as to what he or she knows and has per-
sonally seen and heard (but for the most part not including the statements
about what another has said; see the section on hearsay).

By contrast, Rule 702 defines that a witness may be qualified as an expert
on the basis of "knowledge, skill, experiences, training, or education" and
may then have an opinion as to the nature of the subject matter being presented. The defining functional difference between lay testimony and expert
testimony is the providing of expert opinion. The expert opinion is supposed
to be based upon "facts or data...the product of reliable principles and methods," and further it is expected that "the witness has applied the principles
and methods reliably to the facts of the case." The substance of Rule 702 in
many respects mirrors the implications of the *Daubert* (1993) decision and its
progeny (see below for elaboration).

Rule 703 (Federal Rules of Evidence, 2009) then goes on to allow experts
to rely upon not only particular facts that have been gathered by them in the
instant case, but also on those matters which are "reasonably relied upon by
experts in the particular field." It is in Rule 703 that an important provision
is articulated: "Facts or data that are otherwise inadmissible, shall not be
disclosed to the jury by the proponent of the opinion or inference, unless
the court determines that their probative value in assisting the jury to evaluate the expert's opinion substantially outweighs their prejudicial effect." That
same principle is also applied in bench trials where there is no jury and both
administration of the court process and fact-finding are conducted by the
judge or magistrate.

Rule 704 (Federal Rules of Evidence, 2009) goes to the issue of ultimate issue, a matter that has been a subject of debate in forensic practice.
Melton, Petrila, Poythress, and Slobogin (1997) generally have maintained
that the ultimate issue should be off limits to the expert. However, Rule 704
actually indicates that testimony may include an ultimate issue, unless the
issue goes to "mental state or condition of a defendant in a criminal state"
where that condition constitutes "an element of the crime charged or of a
defense thereto." Obviously, that exception to having an opinion on the ultimate issue does not pertain to the DR court testimony of evaluators or other
expert witnesses. This exception, and state rules that incorporate it, would
allow the generally expected opinion and testimony as to at least elements of
best interest that may be considered to be part of a psychological assessment.

In Rule 705 (Federal Rules of Evidence, 2009), it is indicated that an
expert can testify as to an opinion without providing the facts or data
upon which the expert has been relying. However, the court can require
otherwise and "the expert may in any event be required to disclose the

underlying facts or data on cross-examination." In approaching these cases, when experts are involved in assessment of either children or families and brought to the family court in order to provide the results of their inquiries, we would take the position that any and all data must be presented to the court as part of the testimony and should be made available to the opposing counsel in whatever is the expected timely submission. Equivocal cases provide a particular challenge to these courts. To do other than to provide fully the basis on which any conclusions are articulated is to potentially defeat the purposes of open court hearings and the testing of the information that is submitted thereto. Furthermore, the stance of providing opinions without accompanying foundation in effect amounts to arrogance on the part of an expert who in so doing operates as if professional experience should be sufficient basis for conclusion. Current research in psychology and psychiatry clearly has demonstrated the fallacy of relying on clinical opinion over more objectively generated data (see especially the Chapter 5 section on prediction of dangerousness).

Expert Evidence in Canada

Canadian law in regard to experts and testimony is fairly similar to that of the United States. Expert evidence to be admissible must be relevant. In the case of scientific testimony, there are concerns that the jury not be misled by credentials and apparent expertise such that inaccuracies are accepted as true (the issue of prejudicial outweighing probative value), and the opinion must reflect commonly held positions in the scientific community. In the course of the last 18 years, the Canadian Supreme Court has provided that expert evidence must be relevant, necessary to the work of the court, and not subject to some other properly applied exclusionary rule (*R. v. Mohan*, 1994). In the years after *Mohan*, that Supreme Court also came to include the *Daubert* criteria as well *R. v. J. (J.-L*, 1999).

The *Mohan* case is instructive as it abuts the arena under consideration in this volume. A physician named Dr. Mohan was on trial for four counts of sexual assault perpetrated upon female patients. The defense included a desire to admit the testimony of a psychiatrist named Dr. Hill, who was prepared to state that the acts committed required a certain kind of personality configuration and specifically that the commission of the four different acts described required that an individual be a sexual psychopath. He was further prepared to state that the defendant did not possess those characteristics. There was an appeal that reversed, and a second appeal to the Supreme Court that reversed the reversal and added the criterion that expert evidence must not only be relevant but also *necessary* for the trier of fact to apply the relevant law. In further elaboration, the Court indicated that for the expertise to be brought into the forum, the scientific community must concur about the standard profile, there must be research that supports that stance, and there must be concurrence about how the defendant is identified within or outside of the group described (Glancy & Bradford, 2007).

Of particular importance for purposes of domestic relations cases, the issue of ultimate issue has been considered as well. The current stance of Canada's Supreme Court is not to oppose in general the testimony of experts on the ultimate issue but to expect that the threshold of admittance will rise as the testimony gets closer to providing opinion on the primary issue before the court (Glancy & Bradford, 2007). (As is detailed below, in the United States there is a definite tendency for DR and family courts to rely heavily on experts who are not infrequently appointed by the court itself. However, it is our impression that application of increasingly rigorous consideration as to the appropriate limits of testimony has not been characteristic of the process of making decisions to admit or exclude proposed evidence from those experts.)

Finally, as is also true in the United States, the definition of an expert is sufficiently broad to include various kinds of specialized knowledge and background. Specifically, Canadian decisions have referenced a model artic- ulated in the 1993 U.K. case known as "The Ikarian Reefer." In that deci- sion it was opined that an acceptable expert must not assume any advocacy role in the case at hand. He or she must come from a position of neutrality, must provide the basis in fact and theory or assumptions that is the foun- dation for the opinion, and must not exclude any data that might be nega- tive to the position taken. It is also expected that experts will respond to questions asking for opinions beyond their area of expertise or information by indicating inability to provide an opinion, thus acting to limit what they present (Bogoroch & Goldstein, 2010).*

The Problem of Expert Opinions on Credibility

It is fairly well established that an expert may not invade the province of the court by having an opinion on the credibility of a witness. In the DR court, however, where generally speaking the judge functions as the finder of fact, and where significant latitude has been afforded to expert witnesses, walking over this line has been known to occur. At the same time, in appeals cases it

---

* The Ikarian Reefer case (Ikarian Reefer, The 1993 2 Lloyd's Rep 68 [Comm.Ct.Q.B. Div.]) involved a ship that ran aground and caught fire. In the ensuing litigation, insurers based their defense on a challenge to the assertion of arson by owners for which the founda- tion was provided by plaintiff expert, a Dr. R. Meadow. His advocacy, rather than objec- tive expertise, led to an appeals decision that articulated specific rules of conduct and testimony for experts. He was subsequently removed from the British medical register (Friston, 2005).

has been generally indicated that experts should not be making those kinds of statements. Interestingly, however, one can find instances of the breach of this principle with caveats. Thus, in *Brown v. State* (1987), the Wyoming Supreme Court provided an extended discussion of this general area of the credibility of a witness in the context of a recantation case. One of the things that was found in this case was a statement to the effect that the trial judge "did not consider any of their (expert witnesses) testimony that sounded like they" were vouching for the credibility of witnesses. A number of points need to be considered in this context, which we believe lead to some guidelines for DR court cases.

1. In the absence of any empirical foundation, it has been generally felt that when a witness recants, there is more likelihood that the recantation is false than that the original testimony was.
2. It has been generally upheld that judges, at the trial level, have been able to observe a variety of factors including other evidence, the demeanor of the witness, and indications of duress or coercion, such that making the decision to admit the witness's testimony is on sounder ground than is likely to be the case at the appeals level.
3. It is a matter of record, as the below extended description of the *Brown* case indicates, that credibility testimony has been admitted not only going to the testimony of a witness in sexual abuse cases, but also going to the recantation of said witness in the subsequent appeals action.

In regard to any of the points above, we will argue there is no scientific evidence to support that an expert witness has a basis for bringing such an opinion to the attention of the court.

The Brown *Case*

In this case (*Brown v. State*, 1987), there were apparently two daughters who indicated the father had sexually molested them up to and including sexual intercourse. Other facts were also in evidence. The father had indicated in the course of counseling sessions that he had molested the daughters and the father testified that he had performed certain acts that he justified as sex education. Those acts included presenting his own erect penis for the daughter to touch so that she would understand that function of the organ and would be prepared for adulthood and that he massaged her nipples in order to teach her how emotions can get aroused by such activity. It was further developed in the course of this case that he began this activity after she indicated she had lost her virginity while babysitting, and it was also indicated that she was 12 years old at the time. Both she and her sister were placed in the care and custody of the social services agency, apparently due to the mother in the case being unable to accept what the girls were saying and unwilling to protect them from contact with the father. The recantation occurred under conditions where the child denoted as MCX wanted to leave foster care and wanted to return to her home with her mother, but it was indicated that in order to be welcome by the mother, she had to effectively ask for the release of the father on the basis that she had falsely testified in the initial case. Her recantation petition was subsequently filed. Her sister, however, was unwilling to testify in a recantation. As is not entirely uncommon in cases of this sort, there were some problems with dates of occurrences, and at least one of the alleged instances could not have happened at the time it was charged that it occurred. That fact provided some support for the dissent that was registered in the decision. However, the majority voted to reject the motion for a new trial.

In the context of the appeals process, testimony by a psychiatric nurse to the effect that recantation often occurs because of family pressures, and the original transcript of testimony by the clinical psychologist was admitted in the appeals effort, supporting the position of the state. The psychologist's testimony at trial included that MCX's recantation "was consistent with her having been the victim of sexual abuse."

The legal discourse in this case reviewed the significant number of cases that have considered issues of recantation in witnesses. A variety of standards has been articulated and followed. Apparently, in the jurisdiction of the case there was no controlling precedent, although a number of cases provided a basis for guidance. Three cases of particular interest were *Larrison v. United States* (1928), *Berry v. State* (1851), and *Opie v. State* (1967). The *Berry* case required that the judge feel certain that if the recantation were heard by the jury, it would be likely to lead to reversal of the original case. However, the judge does not have to be certain as to the truthfulness of the recantation itself. *Larrison*, on the other hand, has a lesser standard as to the importance of the recantation to a reversal, but the judge has to "be convinced of the truthfulness of recantation."

Implications

The *Brown* case, on the face of the facts alone, supported the original jury's response of the finding of guilt. The alleged perpetrator admitted in more than one context to behavior that clearly would qualify as sexually abusive involving two of his daughters. The testimony of these children at the trial was obviously a part of the record and was considered by the jury in coming to its conclusion. That testimony was conducted under the usual court process of examination and cross-examination. The need to bring forth, at either the trial level or the appeals level, a professional expert who would have an opinion about either inaccurate (see below) profile evidence or credibility of statements made themselves was unnecessary and unwise and, to our mind, should have been excluded on the basis of its scientific unworthiness.

Scientific Evidence

Eyewitness memory has been shown to be unreliable in many situations, a point that was recognized in the *Brown* decision. However, the detection of deception, using behavioral clues, has been extensively researched with consistent findings to the effect that professional witnesses and observers are incapable of reaching any kind of reliable standard such that their testimony should be permitted as to the truth of an assertion. Over time, a variety of relatively subtle clues has been investigated using very precise measurements, and some improvement in the ability to detect truth versus falsehood has been observed (Sporer & Schwandt, 2007; Vrij, Granhag, & Porter, 2010). In the specific case of child sexual abuse, research has identified some markers that are more likely associated with truth-telling versus the lack thereof, and the long-term work with the Content Based Criterion Analysis (CBCA) has been consistent. However, the level at which identification can be made of truth versus falsehood is such that there is no basis for admitting such testimony into court where a matter of guilt versus innocence in a particular case is at stake (Vrij, 2005; Vrij & Mann, 2006; see also Chapter 3). In fact, the ability to discriminate between truth versus falsehood is a function of not only characteristics of the interviewee, but also characteristics of the interviewer. The bottom line that can be derived from this complex information is that neither historically nor up to the present day is there any basis for taking the position that experts in the field of child sexual abuse can provide the court with reliable statements as to the veracity of the children or others from whom they have gathered information.

"Consistent With"

The phrase "consistent with" has been found in testimony periodically in these kinds of cases. It is the kind of testimony that was referenced in the *Brown* case where the judge indicated that no importance was attached. It has long been known that when evidence enters the courtroom and then is excluded on an objection, in fact, it still has an impact on thinking, even though in the case of jury trials the panel may be specifically instructed to ignore what was stated. It is possible that judges trained in law and adhering to the principles of legal discourse may be able to insulate themselves more than lay jurors from that tainting by the articulation of subsequently not admitted and therefore presumably not considered evidence. But most of the research in psychology has not found that particular professional identification and training adequately ensures against the normal processing of information that is typical of human beings. (In a somewhat similar mode, reference can be made to the studies of Milgram [1974] that were prefaced on the notion that growing up in American culture would insulate against obedience seen in the Nazi atrocities, research that, of course, demonstrated the opposite. Neither experience nor training is likely to inoculate effectively against the more basic mental processing of information that is more or less characteristic of human functioning.)

In any event, the use of the phrase "consistent with" has been the way in which witnesses have presented information that ostensibly was not a statement as to the veracity of the witness or the actuality of the crime, but rather was simply a scientific or clinical—more often the latter—opinion that the facts fit with the conclusion of guilt. In effect, this is a kind of profiling generally considered to be not inappropriate as a way to proceed with an investigation but highly inappropriate as a basis for conclusory testimony in the courts. Fundamentally, any kind of profiling evidence is at its heart a statistical statement. In the case of recantation behavior, even the statistics, however, are not researched and known. There are no adequate studies that would allow a statement to be made that some specific percentage of cases are true cases versus false ones, much less any data on false positives and false negatives. Moreover, as can be seen in the discussion elsewhere of risk assessment, the current concern being raised about any kinds of actuarially based conclusions in forensic work relates specifically to the impact that false positives and false negatives have on the conclusions about an identified person. The court seeks to know whether in the specific instance case a defendant or a petitioner has done a wrong act to a child. The court does not seek to know whether, in the group of people with some set of characteristics similar to that of the defendant, some percentage of them have done wrong acts. The latter statement has research value and potential theoretical importance, but it does not have probative value for determining innocence or guilt and is highly prejudicial.

Recommendations

It is our strong recommendation that DR courts, in dealing with these kinds of cases, should exclude any and all testimony by experts who are conducting assessments as to the credibility of any statement made by any of the participants in the assessment process (excepting where based on starkly objective facts). Such statements would include credibility of an allegation, credibility of a recantation, or credibility of any other person's statements that may be gathered, such as parents or other observers. The proper province of testimony, however, would include the conditions under which statements were elicited, the presence or absence of motivated influences that have been documented to be present, and the presence or absence of statements that can be falsified by the data that have been collected. In other words, it is strongly suggested that, in effect, the expert should follow the wisdom of *State v. Boston* (1989) wherein it is allowed to make a statement as to procedures followed and whether those procedures meet reasonable scientific standards for assessment, as well as what was the content of data collected, but the notion of the credibility should remain strictly the province of the judge.

Hearsay

It is an established principle that statements classifiable as hearsay usually are not admissible as evidence in the courts. As with law generally, however, that which is a usual process has its exceptions, which themselves are defined as to their scope. The FRE provide a generally accepted model for the definition of hearsay: "A statement, other than one made by the declarant, while testifying at the trial or hearing, offered in evidence to prove the truth of the matter asserted." The basic reason for disallowing hearsay is that the originator of the statement cannot be subjected to the examination/cross-examination process, which is the means by which the court determines limitations and credibility of evidence presented to it.

Just within the federal rules, there are 24 exceptions to this established principle, among which include in part the following: certain public records and reports, excited utterances or spontaneous statements, evidence of the absence of a business record or entry, family records concerning family history, and judgments of a court concerning personal history, family history, general history, or boundaries, where those matters were essential to the judgment. Other exceptions listed include:

Recorded recollections
Records of religious organizations concerning personal or family history
Reputation concerning boundaries or general history
Reputation concerning family history
Reputation of a person's character
Statements about the declarant's then-existing mental, emotional, or
    physical condition
Statements made by the declarant for purpose of medical diagnosis
    or treatment
Finally, there is a "catch-all" category

A brief exchange on this point illustrates the essence of the hearsay domain. A respondent to an Internet legal site wrote as follows: "We are facing a battle with my fiancé's ex-wife. She has been cohabiting with someone and has denied these issues. Can I be subpoenaed to testify if one of the daughters, whom (sic) lived with her and the new boyfriend, has told me about these two living together, or will this be considered 'Hearsay'?"

A response was provided by the moderator of this open forum, which was as follows: "That would probably be hearsay. You can only testify to what you know, not what you claim other people have told you. There is no way the other side can cross-examine people who are not there."

This exchange encapsulates the whole purpose of the hearsay rule, which is to avoid the court being subjected to unverified and unverifiable and, in fact, potentially quite false information. At the same time, a review of the above exceptions should make it clear that there are many doors by which hearsay evidence may come into the court system.

Some of the exceptions are designed to allow into the court evidence that cannot be obtained any other way and may be particularly pertinent to the issues at hand. One of the exceptions, excited utterance, was specifically created in the face of children's spontaneous reportage, often under some emotional duress, regarding victimization, with persons hearing their statements allowed to report on what was heard in the court system, even though the child making the statement would not be, him- or herself, competent to testify.

An illustrative decision is *Charleston County D.S.S. v. Father, Stepmother, and Mother* (1995). This family court case involved an accusation that the mother had engaged inappropriately with the child, but that the child recanted on the statements he had made to therapists. The therapists were permitted to testify to the out of court statements and were also allowed to testify that such recantation is common in intrafamilial abuse (we have some problem with the latter as below detailed). The caveat that was part of this decision was that "Out of court statements must be shown to possess particularized guarantees of trustworthiness."

In a consideration of prejudicial versus probative value, issues in this arena should go to the capacity of professionals to identify "particularized guarantees of trustworthiness." As has been already detailed, the weight of all research findings on the ability of mental health professionals and, for that matter, other professional groups to identify successfully that which is accurate and truthful from that which is not in children or adults interviewed has not sustained such capacity. In fact, it is an affront to scientific findings for anyone to testify in a court of law that an interview allows a conclusion that there is any guarantee of trustworthiness of the statements made within that interview. Furthermore, as was illustrated in the *Charleston County* case, the allowance of a statement that recantation is a common occurrence in a particular category of abuse amounts to allowing a highly prejudicial impact to occur in which the court is influenced to feel that in this particular instance a profile of trustworthiness has been achieved by virtue of the context in which the statement took place.

Comment

It would be our argument that the admission of out of court statements made by children under spontaneous conditions may well serve the purpose of giving consideration to their best interests and indeed their essential welfare and safety, but the further allowance of any statements having a bearing or implication as to credibility exceeds any reasonable scope of testimony by mental health professionals on both scientific and legal bases. Furthermore, it is the province of the fact finder, whether jury or jurist, to come to the ultimate issue conclusion as to the credibility of a witness. When the witness cannot be evaluated by the court through the legal process for purposes of eliciting at the very least behavior on the basis of which the court can come to its own conclusion, and then the unreliable and scientifically indefensible opinion of a mental health professional is allowed as evidence as to the credibility of this unavailable witness, we have a compounded situation that is fraught with error. In the particularly ambiguous situation of equivocal abuse in contested domestic relations situations, the admission of evidence of this type is likely to perpetuate serious error. However, its attractiveness to the courts may well be that it allows some kind of comfort of relying on ostensible expertise in coming to a difficult conclusion that could precipitate the child to ongoing victimization or conversely to the loss of a parent and a life that includes being (falsely) defined as of so little value to that parent that abuse was perpetrated.

Ohio Case Law Illustrations Regarding Hearsay

The hearsay exception of excited utterance refers to the situation in which a child makes a statement usually spontaneously or in the midst of emotional reactivity in the hearing of someone who is then presented in court to provide evidence of the statement. Such testimony is acceptable in court because the spontaneous and heightened emotional conditions under which the statement occurred are viewed as securing its likely truthfulness. The further aspect includes that the child involved is too young or not competent to provide evidence. That hearsay exception, however, is to be limited to what the child said and under what conditions the child said it. What is not supposed to be permitted are statements, particularly from persons engaging in evaluation (which more often than not reflect contrived rather than spontaneous interactions), that not only reflect what the child may have said, but also include the evaluator's assessment of the child's credibility. Consistently, the courts have viewed such statements as invasive into the arena of the ultimate issue, which is the province of the trier of fact (jury or judge). The referenced case in Ohio for such unacceptability is *State v. Boston* (1989), a criminal case. In that case, the court stated as follows: "An expert may not testify as to the expert's opinion of the veracity of the statements of a declarant." The court went on to reverse a gross sexual imposition conviction because of the expert testimony as to the credibility of the alleged victim. Specific to the cases under consideration, the *Boston* case involved a father of a very young child in the midst of a high-conflict custody case where the father was alleged to have engaged in molestation during weekend visits.

The expert witnesses involved had opinions to the effect that the child did not engage in fantasy regarding the allegations and that she was telling the truth, which the court characterized as "egregious, prejudicial, and...reversible error." Cases following *Boston* affirmed the position. For example, *State v. Burrell* (2011) involved reversal of conviction because of expert witness statements that were prohibited under *Boston*.

On the other hand, in at least one case where the expert apparently inadvertently made the statement, "She was very believable," the conviction was upheld. However, in that case, the judge immediately provided an extended "curative instruction" in which the jury was provided information about the kinds of statements that are not allowed and which must be disregarded.[*] In addition, there was substantial evidence that allowed confidence in the conviction that was entirely independent of what this expert said the child stated in the hospital. Because of that judicial effort and the accompanying independent evidence, the conviction was upheld (*State v. Cornwell*, 1998).

Implications of the *Daubert* Decision

The *Daubert* (1993) decision needs to be considered in context and with an understanding that its applications are not standard throughout all jurisdictions. In fact, some states are *Daubert* states and some are not. In the case of Ohio, it has been characterized as both by at least one writer who analyzed relevant decisions throughout the state and their implications. Ohio is not a *Daubert* state in the sense of having specific legislation or precedent articulated as such, but it is a state in which there have been decisions rendered that favored considerations of a *Daubert* type (Fridman & Janoe, 2011). Consistently, Jurs (2008) offered Ohio as having model legislation because of its flexibility in allowing a civil standard of probability but a criminal standard of possibility for expert opinion.[†] As of 2006, 30 states were considered to be *Daubert*, or consistent with that standard, and 14 had rejected endorsement in favor of alternative criteria (Kaufman, 2006).

---

[*] As already discussed, it is generally recognized that telling a jury to disregard some testimony is an exercise in futility. The operation of memory does not include erasure of information already in long-term storage and the exercise of the reasoning process always includes reference to anything the individual may have classified to him- or herself as important. Although in this case, the "curative instruction" was indeed carefully crafted, it is highly unlikely that it would actually allow the jury to disremember the information.

[†] Most experts understand they must provide opinions based on the standard that the testimony is more likely than not to be accurate; however, it has been reasoned by some (not all) that the lesser standards of "it could happen" (versus it could not occur) allows information of potential value to be provided. Such a standard for the most part favors the state's need to limit the scope or emphasize conditionality of an expert's offering.

Daubert considerations, however, have arisen out of a concern about the nature of the evidence that is admitted and upon which the court makes decisions. If any and all data are admitted as if equally adequate, the door is open for the most frivolous of theories to become a basis for very serious and far-reaching decisions. The case of the so-called Twinkie defense is a model for such frivolity and distortion (Pogash, 2003).* At the same time, the original Supreme Court decision in *Frye* had as its purpose both limiting the kind of data that came into the court to that which would be generally accepted by well-informed scientific experts and, at the same time, specifically allowing that scientific evidence become part of the court process. The issues that led into the *Daubert* decision, however, reflect another set of factors in the development of the society and in the development of science. With the information explosion and with the increasing capacity to develop and test theoretical ideas and publish new findings, to wait for a published set of general endorsements would restrict the court from considering findings of relevance and importance in instant cases. Therefore, the problem for the court system is one of what might be construed as separating the cream from the whey of the milk of evidence.

It is somewhat important to consider the nature of science in the context of this discussion. Science aims to provide explanation and does not have as its primary purpose the prediction of behavior. Law is at least construed as categorical, but most science, and particularly social science, is continua based. Answers are found in degrees of presence rather than in a confident assignment to Box A or Box B. The scientific underpinnings in such a domain involve the application of statistical probabilities, the development of norms, and the comparison of specifics to normatives with resulting statements that allow some kind of reliability and validity. Social science is sometimes referred to as nomothetic in that there is a theory, there is the development of generalized findings across a representative population group, and there is generation of statistical statements that describe that group and allow some kind of confidence in assigning individuals to a likely place within that group. However, the *application* of psychological and other social science methodology to particular situations is best described as idiographic. The individual becomes the universe of data. The importance of findings are

---

* As Pogash pointed out, the defense in the Dan White case involving his murders of Mayor George Moscone and Supervisor Harvey Milk never really argued that blood sugar levels were responsible for his behavior; they did present that his depression should allow a finding of diminished capacity and his change in eating habits from healthful to high-sugar snacking was presented as a depression symptom along with other details. The "Twinkie defense" words were coined by a reporter, caught on, were viewed erroneously as causally cited, and entered even the legal lexicons. Defense argued that depression so altered Dan White's thinking and emotional stability and that other stressors in his life were so high that he should be found guilty of the lesser crime of voluntary manslaughter.

related not only to their placement within nomothetically designed populations, but also in the degree to which the interrelationships among a variety of measurements allow some kind of decisions about the status of the individual in the particular context, none of which are exactly represented at the nomothetic level.

In the particular case of child custody evaluations, the kinds of data that have been brought to bear have included personality testing of parents, usually involving the MMPI-2 but sometimes also involving other methods such as the Millon Clinical Multiaxial Inventory III (MCMI III), Rorschach or other projectives, as well as in some extended procedures the use of intellectual assessment. The first question that has to be raised in the application of psychological measures to custody issues is whether that application will answer any questions relevant to the matters before the court. Except where there is a significant deficit of intelligence such that judgment and capacity for decision making might be negatively affected, there is usually little or no justification in extended cognitive assessment of parents. If parents are within the generalized average range of functioning as represented by their having completed high school, perhaps having attended college, having successfully managed job situations, and being able to present themselves in interview in a coherent fashion, there is no reasonable purpose for assessing their intellectual functioning.*

As already indicated, however, improperly founded theories and logical fallacies applied to specific court cases are and should be anathema to the court system and should be excluded as scientific evidence. Table 4.2 provides some guidelines to the kind of psychological evidence that should or should not be considered for admission. The table includes an analysis using the *Daubert* criteria. As the table illustrates, psychological assessment procedures vary when considered in relationship to the criteria that have been used to evaluate adequacy of evidence. Given the significant use made by the DR courts of mental health expertise, the limitations that currently exist need to be more fully appreciated and included in the thinking of the jurist whose responsibility is to make final categorical decisions.

---

* A specific case can lead to exceptional procedure. For instance, we were once referred a case where it was alleged that an individual had a severe deteriorating condition of dementia on the basis of which the children of this May/December marriage should be placed with the alleging parent with limitations on visitation. In that case, a complete battery was administered to counter the theory that the individual was impaired and the nomothetically based outcome presented to the court as substantially proving presence of quite adequate mentation. (His ongoing currently nationally recognized excellence in his professional work was also presented as consistent with test results and may have been more effective.)

Table 4.2 Analysis of Psychological Assessment Procedures from the Standpoint of Applicable Legal Standards in the Domestic Relations Court

Process	Scientifically Tested	Peer Reviewed	Known Error Rate	General Acceptabilty	Relevance	Probative/Prejudicial Value
Intelligence testing	Yes	Yes	Yes	Yes	Limited to only cases when questions exist as to the decisional capacity based on cognitive limitations.	Has significant value not only in the questions regarding mental capacity. Probative > Prejudicial
Objective Personality Assessment	Yes	Yes	Yes	Yes	Results are limited to descriptions of personality factors and the presence or absence of likely mental illness, all of which may be important to questions at hand.	May assist in designing outcomes that enhance strengths of parents for the children. May increase an under-standing of interparental dynamics. Probative > Prejudicial
Interviewing						
(a) structured and semi-structured interviews	Yes	Yes	Unknown	Yes	Only highly structured approaches have been subjected to scientific analysis. These methods, however, are not useful in investigative and custody evaluative procedures.	Prejudicial > Probative
(b) idiographic case driven interview	No	No	No	Yes	High relevance because the entire focus is on the particularities of individual family dynamics and history.	If interviews become the vehicle for unvalidated and excludible hearsay, are problematic. Are substantively valuable as basis for inferences to attitudes, knowledge, and interpersonal factors. Probative > Prejudicial

Continued

Table 4.2 (Continued)   Analysis of Psychological Assessment Procedures from the Standpoint of Applicable Legal Standards in the Domestic Relations Court

Process	Scientifically Tested	Peer Reviewed	Known Error Rate	General Acceptabilty	Relevance	Probative/ Prejudicial Value
Risk Assessment						
(a) SARA (Spousal Assault Risk Assess)	Yes	Yes	Research is ongoing	Not yet	High. Domestic violence is of substantial importance to best interest questions.	Methodology is unproven for identifying domestic violence in the absence of admission or other independent confirmation. Prejudicial > Probative
(b) Abel	?	?	No	No	The theory is not confirmed independently and has significant flaws based on prior scientific work. Therefore, development of objective scientific evidence has not been facilitated.	High, but there is no no basis for validity.[a]	Court decisions and scientific findings do not support the use of the Abel to identify sexual abusers among the population of those who deny any acts of same. Prejudicial > Probative
(c) STATIC 99	Yes	Yes	?	Yes	High in that sexual abuse is a major conern.	STATIC99 does not allow prediction from among the population of those not found guilty of a sexual crime and is currently under some scrutiny with that group as well. Prejudicial > Probative

[a] The database is suspect with refusal to share on the basis of proprietary concerns.

Specialized Forensic Instruments

In many applications of forensic work, there are specialized instruments designed around the legal definitions. The Grisso (1998) Understanding and Appreciation of Miranda Rights would be one such; the Evaluation of Competency to Stand Trial–Revised (ECST-R) (Rogers, Tillbrook, & Sewell, 2004) is another. Several standardized approaches have been used in assessing for different kinds of malingering. These methods have the advantage of being specified for the particular forensic questions and having a normative structure that allows some formal scientific confidence in the results. In the case of DR work, some attempts have been made to systematize assessments and to develop instrumentation. However, because the primary legal principle involves best interests, because that principle is variably defined across North America, and because it includes items that can be approached from the standpoint of psychological measurement and items which cannot be subjected to same, it is no surprise that highly specified and normed instrumentation has yet to emerge.

Presentation of Expert Evidence

There is a literature that instructs experts on how to function in the courtroom. In the particular area under consideration, some specific advice, above and beyond the general expectations that are held out for experts, would include the following:

1. Be aware and present as part of the report any insecurities of data that pertain.
2. Conclusions and recommendations need to be worded conditionally.
3. It may be appropriate to present more than one set of specific remedies predicated on the ultimate findings of the court as to certain unknowns.

Preparing Evidence as an Expert

When conducting a psychological evaluation on custody matters a systematic approach to preparation can enhance testimony at the time of the court hearing. Although in most cases the expert's report is utilized to settle the matter before the court, there are occasions when testimony is required. It is important to prepare each case in a fashion that enables the expert to do a competent job during his or her testimony. For those psychologists who plan on providing these types of services, it is important to have a basic standard protocol that is followed for each case. Our standard protocol is outlined elsewhere in this book. However, as we also have indicated, the investigation needs to be case driven. The data collected must be maintained in a form that lends itself to an organized file.

An expert can be called to testify by one party or the other or the court. As part of this process he or she will be subjected to direct and cross-examination by the attorneys for the parties as well as the GAL if one has been designated. A great deal has been written about expert testimony in cases where psychological evaluations are conducted. In testifying in custody matters it is important to have the material that formed the basis of the evaluation organized and accessible to facilitate requests by counsel or the court. Afsarifard has a folder that contains several sections that include his own handwritten notes, psychological test results, collateral information such as material provided by external sources, administrative paperwork such as consent forms, releases from the different clinicians and parties, and the report.

It is important to review all material prior to appearing in court to testify. At times the records are requested by parties and copied in their entirety. Although not commonly practiced, some attorneys who have subpoenaed the expert as their witness may want to have a conference prior to the testimony. However, when the witness has been appointed by the court to be an independent expert, it is not appropriate to discuss the content of the expert's testimony without both counsel and guardian (if there is one) as part of the conference. If the mental health professional has been appointed to be one attorney's expert and there is another expert on the other side, pretrial conferencing that includes the expert's testimony may take place (and may be a basis for either bringing the expert in to court or deciding not to do so).

There are occasions where counsel for a party will use the procedural aspects of the testimony to create confusion in order to get the expert to contradict him- or herself (usually when what the expert has to say does not favor that client). In one such case, the counsel for one of the parents used a copy of the expert's handwritten notes and numbered the pages differently than were in the originals. Referring to material with the new page number he created for his record, the lawyer began asking the expert to make comments about specific items, creating a problem for the expert who would have difficulty finding this information due to the page change. This strategy gave the appearance that the expert was taking a great deal of time answering simple questions. In due time, the magistrate became aware of this situation and advised the counsel to provide the expert with a copy of the renumbered material, thus preventing further confusion. (It can be noted that a quiet and respectful demeanor particularly when under attack is more likely than not to result in the court coming to assist in a situation that gets out of hand.)

Summary

Witnesses before the court are expected and are sworn to tell the truth, the whole truth, and nothing but the truth. The swearing of the oath places the witness in a position where any known falsehood is grounds for a charge of perjury, a serious criminal offense. To the extent possible, the court wants to know the truth of the matters before it so as to make decisions based on the best foundation of fact and opinion available (when considered in the context of legal precedent). In these cases, truth is an elusive quality when it comes to perceptions and fears and the emotionally enhanced responding that is characteristic of these kinds of domestic relations cases. Memory is known to be constructive, and it is now an established fact that memory changes as the time from the event elapses. Postevent information gets incorporated into the memory system and becomes for the individual testifying a fact, honestly presented but distorted. The perception on each side of these kinds of disputes comes to be in many cases reality for the witness. Expert witnesses can assist the court in this task, but they also must operate with appropriate humility and ongoing scrutiny for the limits of what they can reasonably provide that is scientifically founded. The whole purpose of expert activities and testimony is to assist the court in more adequately sifting through the information and, it is hoped, leading to final decisions that in fact implement the best interests standard while protecting the children involved.

Practitioner Hazards

5

Arlene may have been upper middle class in her lifestyle and suburban setting, but her roots were more solidly working class and the manners and behaviors that are characteristic of the upper levels of society had been assumed in consequence of her husband's financial success and their ultimate location in a pricey suburban area. Her judgment and personality structure, however, were a function of personal history and probable biological foundations rather than reflecting either her class origins or attainments. As the case progressed, and her rage grew more and more focused, and as she continued to experience setbacks in the various attempts made to convince the guardian, the evaluator, and the court that her children were either abused or would be by her soon-to-be ex-spouse, her ability to exert control over her own behavior deteriorated. There was documented physical abuse of one child, resulting in supervised visitation with both. While under observation, she proceeded to behave seductively in a visit with the younger male child and had to be redirected. Subsequently, other out-of-boundary behaviors emerged, including a reported attempt to run over an individual whom she viewed as an enemy.

Ultimately she was charged with harassment of public officials that led to her incarceration. By this time, the case was post decree and her parental rights were lost. From the prison, she contacted the daughter's therapist and accused the father of likely sexual abuse of the preteen, insisting that the child be subjected to an internal physical exam to get the proof. She threatened to make a licensure board complaint against the child's therapist unless that procedure was accomplished. The therapist called the evaluator asking what she could do to protect both the child and herself. The father was notified but told only that the mother had made a complaint. He agreed to bring the daughter in for a forensic interview and further agreed only to say that the session was a follow-up to the earlier evaluation. The evaluator explained to the daughter the importance of telling the truth and further detailed that there was a safety plan in place such that if anything had happened to hurt her and she needed protection, there was another door through which she could go to safety. Provision was made in advance for someone to take her to police protection if necessary. Upon hearing this preparation, the daughter looked at the evaluator and said (on camera), "What has my mother said now?" That mother's behavior was extreme, even for this context. It finally included a message left on the voicemail of the evaluator that included the words, "You better watch your back." (Although the immediate goal of shielding the children from parental pathology was achieved in this case, the loss of their mother in the process would also have cost them dearly. The mother's behavior had included many positive contributions to their growth and development; the rituals and happy times of the past that could have continued were sacrificed to achieve protection from the present.)

Extreme cases of this sort represent personal psychopathology, usually characterized as a severe borderline personality condition. Individuals in this subsection of the divorcing population, with this kind of personal pathology, can easily move to a number of destructive levels in their interactions with those who come to be involved in their custody cases, and they have not only the perceptual distortions and the emotional drive in the form of built-up rage over the course of their lifetimes, but also a comfort with taking legal and perhaps even physical action to implement what they see as their rightful goals.

It is generally agreed that custody evaluation in general is a high-risk area of practice. Certain factors are present that contribute to the risk levels, among which is that the population affected is a group comprised of persons who have at least some willingness to be engaged in the legal system and who have experience of how that system works. In addition, the matters at stake in the decisions made in the domestic relations court are of personal and extreme significance inasmuch as they involve the ending of a relationship which at least at one point was usually believed to be a permanent commitment and now is equally evidently a broken arrangement. People generally do not wish to take responsibility when things go wrong and will find ways internally and externally to shift the blame. The dynamics between partners who are divorcing and are litigating, as opposed to having come to some mutual conclusion and then created a dissolution, involve intense affective levels, most of which are negatively tinged. When litigation comes to involve outsiders in the form of guardians and evaluators, the first line of defense for a parent is for each to try to convince others of the legitimacy of his or her position. Failure to do this activates all of the underlying negativity and leads to an intense search for some fault on the basis of which the expert can be found lacking. The motivation to find those faults and then to use them to punish or eliminate the influence of the professional is high and is often driven by other interests.

Among those other interests are attorneys themselves, whose livelihood depends upon effective litigation on behalf of their clients and whose ethics demand the full force of committed advocacy. Attorneys, motivated by the combination of training, financial gain, and ethical canons, can in many cases be prevailed upon to initiate actions against the professional who does not meet a party's expectations. (Furthermore, although improper or unwarranted use of the legal system to punish a professional who failed to please someone is regrettable, it needs to be noted that the options of license complaints and civil suits exist as part of justice to offer individuals a chance to redress grievances that arise from improperly practicing professionals.)

In this chapter, there is an inquiry into just what the realities are of complaint levels and management of same considering both license actions and malpractice suits. Ethical constraints and guidelines are reviewed and some models presented for practice that may allow the wary professional to steer effectively through the quite troubled waters of high-conflict couples and allegation-laced case presentations.

There was a point when psychological-psychiatric-therapeutic practices were not among the high targets for malpractice suits (Conte & Karasu, 1990). That fact is perhaps understandable in view of factors such as the use of the talk therapies did not result in physiological damage and the early reliance on rather extended relationally based therapies meant that patients had a strong positive bond with their therapists regardless of whether they actually improved symptomatically.[*] Under such conditions, the motivation to engage in suit action would be relatively low. Over time, as psychiatric practice came to involve more and more biological measures, and therefore more and more potential for biological damages, the potential for the malpractice suits increased. Furthermore, to the extent that psychiatrists in particular came to rely primarily on a medication-based practice, their relationship bond with their patients may have lessened somewhat over what was the case when they were doing, for an extreme contrast example, five-day-a-week psychoanalysis. The litigiousness in the psychiatric field is reflected in the fact that a national survey of directors of residency programs conducted in 1993 showed that 14% of that population had at least one malpractice suit lodged against them. The basis for such suits, however, was largely suicide of patients viewed by family as indicative of a lapse of practice and sexual abuse of patients. The highest settlement in the cases surveyed in this research was $500,000 in the case of a patient who was discharged from a hospital as safe for society who then proceeded to kill his mother (Wagner, Pollard, & Wagner, 1993). A little less than a decade later, psychiatric malpractice suits and board disciplinary actions were more prominent and especially reflected sexual involvement with patients. There was vulnerability noted for child over adult psychiatrists. Consistent with the above comment regarding psychotherapy practice, psychoanalysts were less represented (Morrison & Morrison, 2001).

Mental health practitioners know that they have vulnerability when they agree to serve a population where emotional and cognitive stability is lacking. In a purely clinical practice, there are periodically situations that represent some danger. In a forensic practice, the lack of protective impact of the therapy relationship and the legal exposures create further risk potentials.

---

[*] Even so, as documented in 1982, some liabilities existed with legal consequences when boundaries were transgressed as in sexual victimization of patients by therapists (Kermani, 1982).

Practitioner vulnerabilities can be categorized into three sections:

1. License actions in which a disaffected patient or client decides to make a complaint to the state board and thus initiates at the very least an inquiry from that body and sometimes a full-fledged investigation.
2. Civil suit actions in which it is alleged that standards of practice are not met and that harm has been done in consequence. As soon as such suits are filed, the malpractice insurance carrier is informed and legal representation of the insurance company is afforded to the practitioner. Depending upon the situation, the practitioner may need to get his or her own attorney to represent his or her interests. It is not uncommon for malpractice insurance attorneys to negotiate a settlement, which can leave the practitioner without both satisfaction and a record of vindication.
3. Personal safety. As the case above illustrated, a serious deterioration in control systems and rage-driven behavior can move to the level of a personal assault or threat thereof against a practitioner or other persons. Personal safety issues become difficult for anyone who is by virtue of the work setting, both visible and to some degree predictable and often alone or poorly protected in any physical sense. At the worst level, not only the individual practitioner, but persons close to him or her such as family can become targets.

In the case of divorce custody work, as seen below, the potential for actions to take place in the first two categories (licensure board and civil suit arenas) is seen by many forensic practitioners as higher than for any kind of ordinary clinical practice. (However, litigation in the area reflects that clinical practice has been particularly affected by the development of attitudes and case decisions that pertain to inappropriate boundary behavior by mental health professionals, notably involving sexual contact with patients.) Fortunately, there are also some protective measures and responses that are available to practitioners, which are detailed below.

Legal Risks

Licensure Board Complaints

One view of the particular hazards of the custody evaluation area, including the cases where allegations have surfaced, was obtained by a survey of Ohio State Board Domestic Relations (DR) cases. When a complaint is made to the state board that eventuates in a charge being filed by the board, a public record is created. The full public records of domestic relations cases from the Ohio State Board of Psychology were reviewed. In all, 23 records were found that spanned the period from 1991 to 2010. Most of them represented the past 10 years. Table 5.1 shows the distribution.

Of these 23 cases, 18 involved providing an opinion regarding custody or visitation without having done a custody evaluation. Not atypically, a psychologist who was acting as therapist for either a party or the child of the parties provided either to counsel for one of the parties, to the court directly, or to the guardian an opinion as to what the best interests of the child might be. Three of the cases involved a violation of the supervision rules but also implicated a role conflict problem. In one case, however, the dual role conflict was that of setting up a business with a supervisee, rather than directly reflecting work in the domestic relations context, although the work being done was in that area. One of these cases involved an extended and highly improper way of proceeding for doing custody evaluations, such that it was well below the standard of care that would be acceptable. In another, there was what might be termed inappropriate role diffusion with a minor client, not involving any kind of direct abuse but, in effect, creating a dependency on the basis of which the therapist then allied with the child against the father and against the child's having a relationship with the father. Finally, there was one case that simply involved a violation of rules regarding how records are to be kept and how billing should be handled.

Six of the 18, or truly a third of the custody visitation context cases, also included a context in which there were abuse allegations, either physical or sexual, the latter being the more common, and biased information was supported without proper investigation.

Almost all of these cases were handled by consent agreement, except three, wherein it was somewhat unclear and one that was clearly an adjudication following a hearing. The penalties included reprimands, suspensions for either a designated or an indefinite period of time with requirements for reinstitution, and complete loss of license. Many involved a permanent restriction against any further work in the domestic relations context, with only fact testimony allowed where the psychologist might be subpoenaed. In other words, the psychologist could respond to the subpoena without violating the restrictions but could not present any kind of expert witness reportage nor have any expert opinions for the court. Remedial continuing education (12–30 hours) was prescribed in many of the reprimand or time-limited suspension cases, with the proviso that none of the hours would be applicable to license renewal. In addition, there might be tutorials with a licensed psychologist approved by the board, or monitoring of practice by a licensed psychologist with reports to the board, essentially a form of supervision.

Table 5.1   Review of Ohio State Board of Psychology Actions in DR Cases by Year

Year	$N = 23$ f	Practice Issue	Outcome
1991	1	Supervision violation	Consent agreement
1992	1	Dual role involving business relationship with supervisee	Consent agreement/Suspension 4-1/2 months
1999	2	a. Improper billing and records maintenance	a. Consent agreement/Reprimand
		b. Role conflict: therapist to negotiator to mediator	b. Consent agreement/Tutorial
2001	1	*Report and testimony regarding mother without any contact, based on work with father; prior complaints of custody evaluation as treating psychologist	Consent agreement/No further work in DR
2002	4	a. Custody opinion as a therapist	a. Consent agreement/Permanent restriction from DR work
		*b. Dual role, encouraged children to reject father	b. Consent agrement/Reprimand/6-month suspension/Education
		c. Supervised psychology assistant to treat and then do evaluation of children; wrote custody recommendation letter	c. Consent agreement/Reprimand/Restriction from DR work for 24 months
		d. Violation of consent agreement: continued testimony and work on DR cases	d. Consent agreement/Suspension 4-1/2 months
2003	6	a. Therapist made recommendations without doing custody evaluation	a. Consent agreement
		*b. Therapist gave custody/visitation opinion with no contact with mother/report and testimony	b. Consent agreement/Reprimand/Permament restriction from DR work
		*c. Opinion re: custody was family therapist/wrote letters and testified	c. Consent agreement/Reprimand
		*d. Inappropriate alliance with child therapy patient	12-month suspension/12-month restriction from all DR work, course on report writing

Table 5.1 (continued)   Review of Ohio State Board of Psychology Actions in DR Cases by Year

Year	N = 23 f	Practice Issue	Outcome
		e. Custody opinion as a therapist/ worked with mother to support allegations regarding 3-year-old; no contact with father; testified	e. Consent agreement/ Reprimand/9 hours of continuing education in child custody
		*f. Therapist provided opinion as to custody; improper foundation for a diagnosis of Dissociative Disorder and PTSD	f. Adjudication order/Indefinite suspension, with possible reinstatement/Continuing education and monitoring
2004	1	Supervision offense in a DR context	Consent agreement/Monitored practice for 12 months
2005	1	Was couple's therapist/provided alternative opinion re: custody based on review of court evaluator's report/breach of confidentiality	12-month suspension/Permanent restriction from all forensic work/24 hours of continuing education
2006	2	a. Therapist provided opinion re: custody	a. Consent agreement with license surrender
		b. Marital and individual therapist/provided opinion re: custody	b. Suspension/Practice restriction/Education requirements
2007	1	Therapist for child/provided opinion as to father's problems based on mother's report/sent letter to GAL	Consent agreement/Reprimand/ 24-month restriction from DR work/30 hours of remedial education
2008	2	*a. Improper custody evaluation practices	a. Voluntarily ended Ohio practice and did not maintain license
		b. At request of attorney, evaluated child's capacity to refuse to visit with a parent/ wrote report recommending child could refuse	b. Consent agreement/Reprimand/ Indefinite restriction from DR work/24 hours of remedial education after which could apply to have the restriction removed
2010	1	Provided visitation recommendations without evaluation of anyone, on the basis of attorney input only	Consent agreement/Restriction 12 months from DR-related work/12 hours of continued education

* Cases where allegations of abuse, sexual or physical, and alienation were recorded.

Consent agreements always contain a provision that the board will make the licensee and the nature of the offense and the agreement available to Ohio licensed psychologists, any requesting records of board actions, the Healthcare Integrity Protection Data Bank (HIPDB)[*] and any other federally mandated sources, as well as it being part of the board's permanent and public record. These outcomes represent a more severe picture of penalties than may be apparent, in that any psychologists who are doing clinical in addition to their forensic work (and most do) may find themselves either having difficulty maintaining their malpractice insurance, paying a great deal more for that insurance, or losing their status on clinical panels, thereby becoming ineligible to receive insurance reimbursement. Thus, a foray into forensic work that is ill considered or poorly handled can essentially cost a psychologist a substantial portion of any independent practice that he or she may have.

Another sample of cases with some overlap with the above sample were available from the biennial enforcement report for June 2008 to June 2010. That report, not limited to divorce/custody related situations, indicated that 14 cases were processed, 5 involved permanent license surrender as a penalty, and 6 involved a loss of license with possible application for restoration after 3 years. Reprimands were issued in 4 cases. The offenses, which were not detailed as to content, included negligence, competence issues, violation of confidentiality, and 5 in which no reason was stated except that the psychologist agreed to the loss of license rather than see any further investigation go forward.

An attempt was made to develop information across the country. All licensure boards were contacted by e-mail using a brief questionnaire (see Appendix C). Responses were sufficiently limited (five states: Minnesota, Missouri, New Hampshire, North Dakota, Rhode Island) that no claim can be made for national representation. However, the information collected was fairly consistent. Complaint levels were far higher than actions taken. Most actions involved probation, suspension, or rehabilitation/education/counseling/supervision. Revocation, the most severe action, was rare. Respondents indicated variations of consent agreements as the vehicle most common for case resolution where other than dismissal was involved. Although there was impressionistic concurrence that custody cases represented high potential arenas for complaints, the statistical basis was usually not available (boards were not tracking by content area of complaint but

---

[*] The HIPDB was established pursuant to the structure created by Title IV, Public Law 99-660, and mandated by the 1996 HIPAA regulations. It is a national databank that maintains a record of all adverse rulings by licensure boards in the healthcare fields (retrieved Jan. 29, 2011 from http://www.npdb-hrsa.gov/topNavigation/aboutUs.jsp).

rather by ethical or legal category). Where some factual knowledge existed, the problem areas for custody complaints included accusations of bias, dislike of recommendations, misuse of tests, dual role (therapist to evaluator), problems regarding either the release or nonrelease of records, and even "being rude."[*]

When Bow and Martindale (2009) surveyed a national sample of 138 psychologists doing child custody work, their overwhelming perception was that this area did represent hazardous practice and that the likelihood of malpractice actions and ethics complaints was significant. Most of these practitioners indicated they were doing this kind of work less than half the time. (Given the very limited findings from the state board responses, it may be that there is some overperception of hazard, which is consistent with the finding that highly experienced specialists were usually successful in defending complaints made against them; see the following).

In a slightly different approach, Bow, Gottlieb, Siegel, and Noble (2010) recently published a survey of practitioners for their perspectives on the experience of licensure board complaints. The participants surveyed represented 27 states. Almost all were doctoral-level practitioners who indicated an average of 45% of their cases involved child custody activity. In other words, this respondent sample represented a highly qualified and experienced group. Sixty-three percent indicated experience dealing with a complaint to a licensing board regarding the child custody area. The complaints importantly featured allegations of bias, poor procedures, failure to investigate a relevant issue, and financial problems. Less common were allegations of inappropriate involvement with children, dual roles, inadequate training, informed consent, perjury, misrepresentation of collateral information, and exceeding the scope of the original court order. What is also important is that in 84% of this respondent sample, no action was taken against their licenses.[†] Perhaps consistently, 73% endorsed that the licensing board operated on the basis of fairness. However, in general, there was an acknowledgment that the experience was stressful. The high-risk, red-flag indicators for cases likely to cause complaint actions suggested by this sample included the presence of personality disorder and history of litigation against professionals.

---

[*] The protective function of human courtesy and respect has already been demonstrated in medical practice, where malpractice rates dropped when physicians acknowledged errors and apologized rather than using denial and avoidance (Goodwin, 2010).

[†] The general lack of action taken in the case of highly qualified and experienced forensic practitioners contrasts with the case resolutions reported for the Ohio Board sample. It would appear that those who are practicing carefully as forensic specialists are accurately discriminated from those who have unwisely and incompetently ventured into this arena.

Given the prominence of alleged bias as a basis for complaints, Bow et al. (2010) listed the following categories:

1. *Personal Bias.* An example is seen below in the reference to Israeli social worker evaluations (Cohen & Segal-Engrelchen, 2000). In personal bias, the evaluator operates on the basis of values and attitudes for which there are no substantial scientific bases.
2. *Confirmatory Bias.* Investigations do not proceed adequately to look at all possibilities.
3. *Confirmatory Distortion.* This source of bias reflects deliberate selection of evidence that is supportive of a position and nonreportage of evidence that is not.
4. *Countertransference Bias.* Evaluators respond on the basis of personal issues and experiences rather than to the case characteristics, a well-known hazard in doing intensive psychotherapy.

On the basis of their work, Bow and colleagues (2010) suggested that by avoiding cases with characteristics known to increase vulnerability to complaint, the practitioner can proceed with more comfort. However, this book is about the cases that in fact are highly hazardous. We would argue that contrary to the Bow et al. recommendation, it is exactly in these kinds of cases that the courts most need the balance and scientifically informed process that a competent professional can bring to bear. It is because of that need of the courts that we are presenting ways to handle these cases that will be both protective of the process, and therefore the population served, and protective of the professional who is willing to undertake this work.

Civil Suit and Malpractice Actions

Strategies for practicing defensively from sources such as malpractice insurance representatives as well as experts in legal and ethical matters are often communicated to health delivery professionals. Clearly, in forensic work, defensive and proactive practice procedures assume significance. The most hazardous situation in DR work, from the standpoint of having a successful action filed by an individual, occurs when a practitioner is not following the articulated standards and expectations that pertain to custody work. Interestingly, there remain individuals who will assert that a treating therapist can also function in a custody evaluative capacity, which is clearly the category that gives rise to successful actions. In addition, there are those who make statements when called upon to do so about matters of custody and visitation based on their experience of having provided treatment to one or more persons in the family but not having the foundation necessary for those statements. Sometimes errors in this regard are inadvertent or at least reflect being led into error by lawyers whose focus is on the end product of winning their cases and who may or may not appreciate that they are precipitating the witness to ethical error. Especially where the process is intended, it may approximate a kind of entrapment. The mental health practitioner who is not doing a custody evaluation in a given case needs to observe extreme caution when called into a court action, because an adverse finding by a state board or ethics committee can lead to significant vulnerability in a subsequent malpractice action.

For example, consider the following case and testimony:

It was established that the psychologist was hired to consult with counsel regarding the methodology and information available in a court-ordered custody evaluation. The psychologist correctly identified that role. However, in the course of elaborating during direct testimony, he made many statements about the conclusions and recommendations that were drawn from the work done. He correctly identified some areas where questions could be raised as to procedure. Some objections were raised and overruled, and then the judge directly addressed the witness, asking:

Judge: Doctor, it seems like you are recommending that the mother have sole custody. Is that what you believe to be in the best interest of the children?
Psychologist: Yes.

The witness went on to provide his reasons for that conclusion, again in response to the judge's question.

The ensuing cross-examination focused on the APA guidelines, established that the doctor was not familiar with them, and proceeded to obtain in excruciating detail the degree to which his testimony exceeded the limits contained therein. Cross also elicited multiple opinions as to meanings and implications of the data in the report, most of which would offend against the requirement that a custody recommendation must be based on a properly completed custody evaluation.

What is particularly important in the above case is to realize that the judge had no intent of trapping the psychologist but in effect did so. The psychologist, perhaps under the misapprehension that responding to the judge was a protected process or a mandate, wound up on record making a best interests recommendation in a case where by doing so he gravely exceeded the boundaries of his role as a case consultant. He was led into this error by the lawyer who called him as a witness, by the judge who followed up with his own questions, and also by the cross-examination where there was clear intent to establish error. He subsequently had no effective defense in the licensure action that followed.

All that is required for a civil suit to be filed is that the plaintiff knows how to make a presentation in the civil court. In most cases, such actions are taken by an attorney representing the plaintiff, and the action is easily accomplished. The usual process entails the following:

1. The suit is filed in the civil court.
2. An official notification involving the serving of papers is made. Even if there is not "proper" service, the practitioner must not ignore the situation.
3. The practitioner, if he or she has been listening at any of the continuing education seminars or reading any of the available information, immediately calls his or her malpractice insurance and sends the notification to the attention of the recommended person. The practitioner is told not to engage in any contact with the attorney or the individual filing the action.
4. The attorney from the malpractice insurance contacts the now defendant psychologist or practitioner and either by phone, in person, or both reviews the case and establishes the initial foundation for defense. The practitioner is warned that if the insurance does not cover all aspects of the complaint that has been made, the psychologist may need to have personal representation for that aspect. Negotiations then ensue.

In the case of an evaluation conducted pursuant to a court order, in most jurisdictions there is quasi-judicial immunity. As long as the work of the psychologist has met prevailing standards and has been carried out under the purview of that order, the psychologist takes on the same kind of legal protection that judges have and suits are dismissed, often with prejudice, thus preventing a refiling. This protection, however, itself has come under attack in one quarter where two attempts by the same legislator have been made to strip evaluators of the immunity. The loss of that protection would likely curtail if not eliminate the services of psychologists and others providing for the family courts. It needs to be noted, however, that inappropriate exploitations and incompetent practice have invited this kind of legislative assault. On October 26, 2010, *Judicial Council Watcher* posted the story of Stephen Doyne, characterized as a "clinical psychologist," who by virtue of false credentials, including diploma mill degrees, has made "over a million dollars in billings a year in La Jolla (San Diego) California…being appointed by the courts" to do custody evaluations. At the same time, the first attempt to strip immunity from almost everyone who serves the courts was a vehicle to make it nonlegal to find "parental alienation" (PA) (regardless of the data); this second attempt has exempted some persons, notably social work investigators, and eliminated any reference to PA, but it still would paint all custody evaluators with the same brush that Dr. Doyne's case represents. In effect, it would make it infeasible not only to do custody work, but to serve in any forensic mental health reportage capacity (see Assembly Bill 2475). Some of the motivating force in the background comes from a special interest group called the California Protective Parents Association, a group within the sphere of influence of the Battered Mothers Custody Conference (see http://www. batteredmotherscustodyconference.org) and other like-minded organizations. Greenberg, Shuman, Feldman, Middleton, and Ewing (2007) provided a discussion noting both the presumed advantages and disadvantages of quasi-judicial immunity, the limitations of its scope, and the existing mechanisms and remedies that exist to address poor practice.

In an article that reviewed concepts of standards of practice and standards of care, Heilbrun, DeMatteo, Marczyk, and Goldstein (2008) detailed the difference between the two concepts and pointed out the need of the profession to clarify and clearly provide standards of practice on the basis of which judicially determined standards of care would ultimately be founded. They noted that by developing such standards, the scientific basis, as it has matured, as well as the ethical foundations of the profession, can inform case law decisions. In that way, the interaction of practice and law will allow the emergence of a much more robust structure to guide the efforts of those in the field.

The following case history details a civil suit action filed against an evaluator, and others:

> Although not all troublesome cases include the presence of significant money and status, and are usually driven more by psychological than financial considerations, the availability of funds certainly allows litigation activity to expand. The father was a member of an old-line family where several generations had benefited the community at large. The wife also came from the upper class. Unlike some others in the family, he was not oriented toward business and preferred to pursue a teaching career. That he was independently wealthy certainly allowed him the latitude to opt out of the pursuit of financial success. The mother's family was notable for some indications of significant dysfunction, much of which had been hidden from view. After the birth of their son, she became more and more dissatisfied with their life and elected to involve with a lover. At the same time, she grew more and more possessive of the child and acted to restrict contact with his father even while the couple was still living together. Ultimately, she became convinced of sexual abuse potential or actual and filed the first of several reports with Human Services. She hired an attorney, acted to freeze financial accounts, and filed for divorce asking for sole custody and supervised visitation for the father. In the course of the case, a guardian was appointed and a custody evaluation was completed. The child's temporary custody was placed with the father after the mother's behavior in court gave rise to serious concerns about her stability. Supervised visitation was provided for her; part of the evaluation included being present at one of those sessions, during which she attempted to take the child aside and get him to agree to accuse the father of sexual advances. The case went to court, recommendations included sole custody to the father, treatment for the

mother, and a graduated program of supervised to unsupervised visitation dependent on response to treatment. Following the court's order, she and her now fourth attorney filed suit against the evaluator, the judge, the attorney for the father, the guardian, and the therapist who had been seeing the child to help him adjust to all the ongoing changes in his life. In all cases, the suits were dismissed with prejudice, meaning they could not be refiled. These court actions, however, were active for over a year. Furthermore, when malpractice insurance was renewed for the next five years, the psychologist-evaluator had to attach a description of the case and the outcome. (To some degree, it was helpful to be sued in a group that included a sitting judge.)

Personal Safety and Physical Risks

Personal Risks

In general, psychologists are aware that there can be some risks in the practice setting, even where the focus of most if not all of their work is on clinical matters. Persons who have difficulty with self-regulation or family members of patients who develop convictions about the therapy being harmful can in some instances decide to take action against a practitioner. Generally speaking, actual threats of physical harm are rare and actions even rarer. Other sources of danger include the vulnerability to robbery or other criminal acts where the office or psychologist becomes a target of opportunity. Most psychologists do some self-protective things, including locking doors when alone, especially when keeping late night hours. Some operate carefully when leaving a building at night and going to a car in a parking lot. Some cars have features that enhance safety, including the ability to unlock them at a distance, turning on the interior light before the individual enters the car, and the further potential to activate an alarm under threatening circumstances. Some psychologists obtain and maintain self-defense training. Forensic practice, where the outcome of work may often directly negatively affect the interests of one or more persons, has a higher potential to activate on the part of persons with disinhibition potentials an act or acts against the professional. Problems in this area for the mental health professional stem from matters of human thought processes, training, and personal capacity. It is almost axiomatic that humans have a sense of invulnerability which allows them to treat life in a somewhat cavalier fashion, most present in adolescence but remaining to some degree throughout adulthood. Secondly, training in mental health as with all service areas inclines toward trust and a sense of working with people rather than being first and foremost in an adversarial situation (which is anticipated more naturally by those in law enforcement, for example). Finally, such professionals are not selected for the presence of physical competencies helpful under threat or attack conditions; only some actually possess the ongoing readiness to deal under those circumstances.*

Very little, if any, research has been done on the physical risks that may exist for forensic practitioners in the child custody field. There is anecdotal evidence and there is significant information about how to engage in defensive practice from a legal/ethical standpoint. It has been clearly documented that practitioners do, sometimes on the basis of naiveté and other times on the basis of a presumption of being able to get away with boundary violations, engage in behaviors that are off limits. Based on the kinds of questions that have come to him, psychologist-lawyer Woody (1997) has provided guidance to professionals, but the areas covered have to do with the well-known ethical standards and guidelines and the wisdom of following them, and the usual cautions in the legal arena around how to respond to subpoenas or court orders. As was seen in the inquiries made into psychology board interactions, the failure to follow articulated standards and rules can lead to a substantial negative consequence for the practitioner.

Risks to Others

The well-known *Tarasoff* (1976) case not only represents what can occur when client behavior involves threat and action, but also illustrates an instance in which resulting legal actions come to affect clinical practice throughout the country, to say nothing of creating a confusing set of varying precedents for the legal community. In *Tarasoff* and subsequent related cases, the ethical duty to confidentiality is confronted by the legal and ethical duty to prevent harm. Complicating the situation is the ongoing finding that prediction of dangerousness is not an area where either science or clinical practice has allowed significant optimism (Dolan & Doyle, 2000; Fulero & Wrightsman, 2009; Monahan, 1993). In fact, Monahan's (1993) prediction that actuarial methods for making such calls would further develop has materialized. One example would be found in the work of Barnett, Wakeling, and Howard (2010) who reported on combinations of the Risk Matrix 2000 with Static 99 and other tools. Fulero and Wrightsman (2009) detailed by area available methods and the limited capacities of same including for domestic violence. Overall, the capacity for violence prediction to be provided to the courts is

---

* It is perhaps interesting to note that judges have always known they were possible targets given the work they do and its impact. New judges and magistrates in Ohio have mandatory training at the Ohio Judicial College that includes within the broader spectrum of judicial functioning a particular section on personal security. Spouses are encouraged to be present at this time so that they, too, can be aware of the vulnerabilities that exist and support the necessary precautions.

questionable due to the limitations of difficulties of criterion measures and problems of data collection that result in problematic levels of false positives and false negatives. Those findings create serious issues around contributing to decisions about the identity of some one particular person's potential for specified acts (and therefore become part of a decision to limit freedom). Given the ongoing findings of inquiries in this area, the further implication of the inadequacy of dangerousness prediction is the problem of managing personal security where the potential for vulnerability is not well known or anticipated. The question becomes, for the practitioner, at what point are specific strategies necessary, especially where those strategies have downsides that affect practice.

The *Tarasoff* case has certainly made for significant education and training and increased the awareness of the importance of reporting threats because of the legal hazards involved. Nonetheless, it is intriguing to note that although 50% of the threats against the president of the United States reported to the Secret Service involved persons with mental health histories, only 12% of those referrals actually came from a mental health source. A study conducted by Coggins, Steadman, and Veysey (1996), which looked at the situation from the perspective of protection of the president, confirmed that most practitioners do not have a clear understanding of the role of the Secret Service and the necessary importance of reporting such threats. Most operated on the basis of a clinical assessment of the threats that were made, with the notion that only those that were viewed as likely to involve "real" danger needed to be conveyed. They were not necessarily aware that reportage of all threats against the president, providing they proceed with documentation and follow any guidelines that may apply, are in fact legal. From the perspective of the Secret Service, having a list of possible as opposed to probable threat sources allows higher levels of protection. However, although it is a federal crime to threaten the life of the president of the United States, for clinicians the ethical obligation of confidentiality remains in place as well. Mental health professionals dealing with mentally ill patients are expected to use judgment and to balance patient rights to confidentiality and freedom from self-incrimination against the risk such individuals are perceived to involve. The usual response to this problem is to follow the guidelines that have emerged from the *Tarasoff* case and call for a documented clinical conclusion that a patient is a danger; then reportage must occur (Monahan, 1993). Obviously, such conclusions maintain the behavior of clinicians who engage in assessment and clinical decision making as part of dealing with patient threats against others, whether the president or their own family members. These expectations growing out of ethical obligations conspire to maintain professional behavior that is scientifically flawed and unfounded. The issue created by the inability of most clinicians and even most actuarial schemes to predict dangerousness well becomes clearer.

Not dissimilarly, Thelen, Rodriguez, and Sprengelmeyer (1994) inquired into attitudes relating to reportage of suicide, homicide, and child abuse threats made by patients. A significant subset of clinicians operated on the basis of absolute confidentiality, in spite of the laws to the contrary, and were, as a result, somewhat likely to experience significant practice-related stress in dealing with patients making such threats. There was, however, variation of the degree to which the expectations of reportage were generally followed. It is our experience that given the variable results of the involvement of social services and law enforcement when threats are reported, clinicians may well be reinforced for making judgments as to whether the law really applies in an instant case. Unfortunately, making those judgments precipitates to a higher level of overall risk, not only to the practitioner for any perceived procedural deficits, but also to the community in the form of the practitioner not being able to adequately predict who will and who will not act upon statements made.

Risks of Danger for the Practitioner—Professional Perspectives

When the father entered the court clinic ostensibly for a family-based interview, the purpose of which was to assess options in a conflicted divorce/custody case and to present recommendations to the court, no one there was prepared for the eventuality that he would come armed and would kill the mother of the child. After shooting his victim, he grabbed the child and tried to make an escape. An alert deputy, who happened upon the situation, shot the man and grabbed the infant as the father fell to the floor. That case led to the first installation in that court of screening equipment. Persons in the clinic indicated significant emotional reaction to the assault on their usual perception that they were in a safe environment. (In the juvenile court case that followed, in which due to Muslim cultural factors the family of the assailant sued for custody of the child, Afsarifard appeared to provide recommendations for the mother's family to have the baby on the basis of data collected using the best interests perspectives as a guide, rather than the religious precepts that in fact were part of both parents' backgrounds. The father was sentenced to life in prison for the murder.)

There is a substantial literature on the perception of risk in the general sense, often involving the general population or relatively specialized areas of health- or safety-related functioning. In general, the knowledge from studies in that area emphasizes a complex set of factors, notably involving perception of risk, perception of personal salience of the risk, and beliefs about efficacy and control (Cooper, 2010; Slovic, 1987). Management of risk in the workplace is considered to require the development of assessment of realities and promulgation of specific policy and procedure (Cooper, 2010). There are no studies exactly on point for professionals dealing with risky domestic relations situations. However, Traylor, Price, Telljohann, King, and Thompson (2010) did complete a survey study with a good response rate (67%), in which they found that 78% of clinical psychologists in the sample regarded persons with mental health problems as having significantly enhanced risk of violence to self or others if there was access to firearms. In addition, the study indicated that clinicians do not systematically assess for such access, do not maintain records of possession of same, and do not have any standardized approach for dealing with the area.

Three experienced clinicians provided some of their perspectives in response to questions about risk, both legal and physical. All were boarded forensic psychologists. One indicated no experience with board complaints, malpractice suits, or physical threats. Perhaps consistently, that individual did not have any special procedures in place to enhance protection or security. Two indicated they had had experience with nuisance complaints growing out of domestic relations work, one having considerably more experience than the other. Both of the latter made use of attorneys to assist in addressing legal situations. One noted that it could also be helpful to have a colleague review the situation and respond to it from the practitioner perspective. These two also reported having had to deal with overt threats of physical violence. Both indicated having some self-defense weapons available, significant personal training in self-defense, and the filing of police reports. One respondent has had some experience of Internet-based problems and has paid for consultation and technical assistance to identify persons responsible for anonymous hostile statements. That respondent noted that actually engaging with people who are making such threats was not considered productive or wise. Unless the identity of some threat was known, it was felt that making a police report allowed documentation of an "in case" variety, but asking for active investigation and contact with the individual was more likely than not to complicate and raise the potential for action.

The importance of prevention was seen in how these practitioners approached the area. One respondent noted that evaluators have to be aware of the relevant legal framework for what they do. It is common for warring spouses to use GPS devices, spyware, and phone taps to get information that is then brought to the evaluation. Before reviewing and using such information, it is important to obtain on the record how the information was collected or came into the possession of the person being interviewed. Only if the material has been acquired legally should it become part of the knowledge base of the evaluation, thus preventing an avenue for a potentially successful lawsuit from the other side. (The psychologist noted somewhat wryly that it is not entirely uncommon that the materials brought show more of the pathology of the bringer than of the other party.)

Another source of actions taken against evaluators involves other professionals whose work has been below par and then has been critiqued and not infrequently eliminated as evidence in a case. Public testimony to the effect that psychological work does not meet scientific or ethical standards can be viewed as detrimental to an individual (as well as constituting a narcissistic wound); motivation is thus created to get back at the testifier.

Some legal procedures and case management approaches suggest efforts to reduce unnecessary nuisance suits. Even if the evidence from these interviews and from survey literature indicates that careful practice usually allows survival in legal challenges, the wear and tear on the luckless practitioner can be significant, and the processing of a legal case is an extended matter. One respondent had recently read of a case where a spouse in a DR case was sentenced to real time for having illegally hacked into the soon-to-be ex-partner's e-mail. That same informant also noted that there are some jurisdictions where if parties in an active DR case intend to file board complaints, they must first provide the substance of those actions to the presiding judge. That remedy tends to limit significantly how quickly the weapon of a board complaint gets used.

Dimensions and effects of threats and acts of violence against mental health professionals is an underresearched area in general that has only recently begun receiving significant attention. Pope and Vasquez (2007) reviewed available studies that supported the presence of a widespread phenomenon: one out of five psychologists indicated a physical attack and over 80% feared such an attack; one out of four reported calling for police or security protection; 3% indicated having a weapon for self-protection. Pope's Web site (2010) listed 39 articles from 1986 to 2008, with an emphasis on the last 10 years, documenting aspects of the above, some of which contain specific advice for improving personal security, particularly from patients who engage in stalking or threats of violence. There has been inquiry into the psychological impact of such experiences on therapists. However, none of the research reported reflected the particular situation of the forensic practitioner.

One relatively recent study is not atypical. McIvor, Potter, and Davies (2008) looked at stalking behavior involving patients and their psychiatrists in London. Psychiatrists were queried in this mental health organization with the result that out of 198 doctors surveyed, 121 responded and 41 indicated they had been stalked. Most of the stalkers were personality disordered males, although a significant cohort exhibited major mental illness. The duration included from a few weeks to as long as 16 years. Interestingly, physical threats were made in the case of 14 of the respondents. It was suggested that special training programs and policies were needed in order to address the problem. Other studies (see Pope, 2010) have started to provide guidance for the development of personal and agency policies and procedures.

For the practitioner in private practice, a combination of low levels of hysteria, careful assessment of personal capacity, review of basic building/office security, and the increase of watchfulness when specific cases present with threat potentials leads to some enhancement of security. Even individuals with limited physical capacity can profit from some personal defense training tailored to the situation and the abilities involved. Good self-defense training emphasizes when not to take a personal defense action. (In a karate class some years ago, McPherson heard the instructor point out that all the techniques learned were likely only to increase danger if the opponent had a gun, in which case compliance with demands might be the better course of action where longevity is the desired end.)

Some professionals keep personal weapons on their premises, and some, depending upon the jurisdiction, legally may carry concealed weapons. In one case, a private detective on a death penalty mitigation case suggested that interviews at a certain address would be best attempted only if armed. The problem with such approaches to personal safety is the relative unlikelihood that having a weapon on one's person or in one's desk will help if the other person has a weapon out (and less inhibition about using it than would be true for the average clinician). There is also the problem that a weapon anywhere in the immediate environment may be pre-empted and used against the professional. Learning how to be hyper-alert in some situations is one strategy for increasing personal safety. Having the ability to lock doors and determine who is outside before the individual is allowed in when the practitioner is alone is an important defense measure. Secure locks that cannot be easily bypassed with a credit card or a small tool are important not only for personal protection but to protect the premises from efforts at breaking and entering with intent that could range from simple robbery to accessing confidential files. Finally, it is a good idea to arrange for the presence of another individual in situations where there is any apprehension on the part of the clinician. Such a presence reduces the potential for acting out and increases the potential for survival should there be decompensation.

At a lower level of personal danger, the behavior of clients including children can present a safety issue: one family therapist doing reunification therapy had to deal with children running out of the office and disappearing down an office corridor; another has had the experience of children engaging in destructive acts including while "supervised" by a parent. One parent allowed a 2-year-old to climb up on a high table with some intention of jumping off while the older sibling was being interviewed; the presence of the office manager and alertness to likely defective parenting saved that situation from a precipitous disaster.

Emergence of the Internet

Bow et al. (2010) noted that one of the ways in which actions get taken against custody evaluators is by way of the Internet, where public statements can be made about people and it is virtually impossible either to control or effectively mount an action that addresses false information. Even where a suit might result in some kind of negative outcome for the person who has been identified as doing the posting, the damage is done and the Internet, in effect, lives indefinitely.* Although Internet postings would not as such become a basis for the loss of license or a monetary settlement, both of which are punitive outcomes from license actions or malpractice suits, the psychological impact of seeing negative statements that are in the public domain, perhaps especially when those statements are false or misleading, is an unstudied area.

A survey of the scope of available Internet-based activities relevant to the plight of the forensic professional who excites the ire of one or more of the parties involved in these kinds of cases is beyond the scope of this volume. What can be noted, however, is that "cyberstalking" is a known phenomenon that is detailed and discussed on the National Center for Victims of Crime Web site (2003). Although that category is focused primarily on those who use the Internet to victimize targets both locally and across international boundaries, it also references the making of false accusations, the purpose of which is to damage reputations and affect the acceptability of the target to others in their environment. Where most cyberstalking behavior involves the deliberate targeting of some victim and tracking of same, the focus of our attention is the use of the Net for vindictive and vengeful purposes. There has been some development of litigation to address this type of problem and there are legal prohibitions across a number of states, as well as in U.S. federal law, referencing the Violence Against Women Act of 2000.

In a discussion of this area, some studies were referenced, including one of 50 identified Internet stalkers conducted by the Royal Free Hospital and University College Medical School in London. Apparently, stalking is a seriously increasing problem in the United Kingdom, with Internet stalking a not-infrequent occurrence (bullyonline.org, 2010). In this discussion, several types of cyberstalkers were detailed, one category of which was considered the most dangerous: "vengeful stalker...the most dangerous type whose mission is to get even and/or take revenge. Mostly male, he has a grudge and is going to do something about it." Other types included intimate partner, delusional,

---

* On December 4, 2010, CNN reported that the U.S. federal government had issued a memo telling all federal employees that they were not to look at the Wikileaks release of documents on either their office or personal computers, a likely exercise in futility and opportunity for the "Don't put beans up your noses" principle articulated in the folktale to operate.

erotomaniac, harasser, and troll. (The latter, in useless but "ranting" discussions, tries to create what might be termed neurotic interaction with the target.) Even here, this information, which also includes some notions about how to respond or deal, is primarily focused on what might be called the traditional stalker mode, rather than the disgruntled client, whose only purpose is to get back at a professional.

Another aspect of the Internet that is important to this area and in some ways not unrelated to the development of stalking behavior are the available special interest sites. Fathers for Equal Justice and Fathers for Equal Rights are two organizations referenced on sites. These groups emphasize the position that fathers have never been on an equal playing ground in the domestic relations courts and offer a variety of vehicles for mounting more successful custody and visitation suits on their own behalf. Another group, from the opposite side of the spectrum, is the Battered Mothers Custody Conference (2010) site. Its major focus is articulated: "To connect battered mothers with organizations working locally, nationally, and internationally to combat unjust family court practices that continue to do untold harm to battered mothers and their children." This site uncritically accepts statements from individuals across the country and elsewhere in which it is alleged that unfair court practices and alliances with men who victimize women and children have allowed cases to be decided in their favor. Mothers on these sites will allege that they have not seen their children for years and that they are entirely innocent, merely the ongoing victims of men who maltreated them during the marriage and who then took vengeance on them when they complained.

All of these kinds of sites will list or link to people including professionals who are seen as sympathetic to the position and goals of the special interest group involved. In the case of the Custody Conference, there is a categorical rejection of the involvement of guardians *ad litem* (GALs) and mental health professionals, especially those who have found any kind of validity to the notion that mothers might engage in parental alienation of their children. What can be said, based on our experience with the courts, is that indeed there are cases where injustice has occurred and evidence has not been carefully and in an unbiased fashion developed or presented, resulting in those inequities. However, we have documented the source material on special interest sites to be extremely unreliable and to include outright lies and falsehoods, some of which of course are also used in direct Internet attacks against professionals who have failed to fulfill the expectations of specific parties.

There is little that can be done by a victim of unjust Internet attacks. Responding merely maintains the visibility and operational behavior of the attacker. In general, people who are reading the accounts of those who have a very specific and biased position are already prone to believe rather than critically review what is being stated. These special interest groups tend to be unbalanced and nonobjective in their presentation and certainly do not reflect the activity of serious investigation. The public presentation of information that can be demonstrated to be false and which can also be demonstrated to affect the reputation of a target may become a basis for civil suit action. However, in far too many cases, the individual engaging in such activity does not have the wherewithal to make the filing of a suit particularly economically feasible. If the individual moves from simply expressing false ideas about the target to some kind of active stalking of the target and the use of threat behavior, the potential for activating the criminal justice system exists.

One source provided general advice on how to deal with stalkers (flayme. com, 2010). That advice was obviously not informed by any kind of empirical or, for that matter, specific legal expertise, and at the end of the recommendations, the site makes the following statement: "Much of the information is untested, based on personal experience, theory, and best guess—it is not guaranteed to help, and may not be appropriate to your own situation." Among the information offered is to do absolutely nothing in order to avoid any feedback and reinforcement and to save any and all messages that might be directed at an individual. However, the list then goes to ways in which to respond that might increase or decrease the likelihood of more negativism, none of which appear to be particularly well informed or likely to have a beneficial impact, based on what is known about human behavior.

More clinically and empirically informed sources underline the importance of early recognition of stalking potentials, citing inappropriate behavior that was characterized as "deranged transference" (more likely to be seen in a therapy context) and boundary violations (Lim & Herschler, 1998). Meloy (1992) noted that clients with "pathological narcissism," when confronted with some negative evaluation, have serious potentials for rage-based reactions. His study led to recommendations of the importance of comprehensive assessment that looks at personality disorder features as well as history involving substance abuse.

One Psychologist's Experience

An extended interview of one professional resource illustrated in many ways both the problems in this area and the necessary cautions that must be taken in order to practice effectively. It also, perhaps regrettably enough, illustrated why highly competent persons in the field may find themselves withdrawing from dealing with these kinds of cases. This trained forensic professional indicated that he had been involved in doing this kind of work in part because of a very specialized background that he held and because there were not a lot of people who were able to undertake these kinds of evaluations. His experience took place some years ago when these kinds of cases were beginning to emerge in some force. The particular case, however, that in effect was the straw that broke the camel's back involved the following set of facts.

He was asked to provide an opinion in a case that already had a significant history. The children had been in the care of the mother and she had removed them from the jurisdiction and from all contact with the father. She and the children were actually returned by law enforcement authorities. The children wound up being placed with the father because of this behavior. At the point at which the professional was engaged, the children had been in the caretaking of the father for a year's time and the mother had had supervised visitation. The children included a teenager and two elementary-school-aged siblings. All three, and perhaps most importantly the teenager, were maintaining that they wished to return and live with their mother. However, their functioning had been quite good during the time that they were with the father and there were no indications that the father had behaved inadequately with respect to his parenting duties. The allegations that were made in this case by the mother, however, were that the father had committed domestic violence against her and also against the children. Those allegations had not been sustained by any independent evaluations in the past, and there were no current indications that the father was acting in ways inconsistent with the welfare of the children.

After an evaluation, which would meet all the requirements even at this point for an appropriate child custody assessment, the professional recommended that the children continue in the primary care of their father. Subjectively, the professional felt that domestic violence reported by the mother against herself in the past could not be ruled out; however, there was no indication that that behavior had extended to the youngsters, past or present, and there was no way to independently confirm that it occurred at all. In the course of what turned out to be six days of testimony, the professional received a certified letter from the state board indicating that the mother had filed a complaint against him, stating that he had not conducted a proper investigation. The specifics of that complaint, however, were that he conspired with the local county human services agency and the judge to deprive the mother of her civil rights, which would have specific importance in what then ensued.

Also of relevance to this picture was that there was a psychologist involved in a prior phase of the case, who also recommended against the wishes of the mother. That professional was also the subject of a board complaint by the mother; after the investigation and a hearing, the board suspended the license of that professional. However, that original situation differed from the current one. The "charges" were different in that it was maintained that the psychologist had had inappropriate *ex parte* contact with a party or the court. Furthermore, it was also demonstrated in the course of the hearing that the psychologist did not know how to use the psychological tests on which he had relied. In other words, a review of that file showed that the board's action had been based on findings supportive of their conclusions. Nonetheless, it set up a history that could well make the situation of the currently active professional more difficult. He indicated that he had to, at his own expense, hire counsel and prepare for this board complaint, in part because his malpractice insurance decided that because it was a civil rights case, he was not covered. He immediately changed insurance companies but then had to litigate against the original insurance company to recover from them the costs of his defense.

In pursuing this case, the psychologist had followed good forensic procedures of making sure all the documentation was in place and that the record fully reflected all of his activities. Furthermore, his expertise for the use of any procedures that he employed was well founded and demonstrated at the hearing. A further complication existed. The psychologist noted that, unlike in the "real" courts, the board was not bound by the scope of the complaint. The board in effect combines investigative and adjudicative functions and not only could review the entire file, but could go forward in the hearing to question and take action on the basis on anything found rather than things only relevant to the complaint made. In other words, many of the rules of evidence that constrain the criminal or civil justice process do not so limit the activity of an investigating licensure board, making the situation much less controlled for the person against whom a complaint is filed. The case was dismissed and the psychologist has continued to make substantial contributions to the profession. However, he decided never again to work on the custody evaluation cases due to the high litigation potentials and has effectively sustained a decision to focus his professional efforts elsewhere.

This case clearly illustrates the legal threats and actions that can be part of the landscape for any professional dealing in these kinds of cases. It also well illustrates the importance of knowing good forensic procedure and following it, and it underlines that persons without experience in the forensic arena are well advised to avoid becoming involved in cases like this.

Practicing Defensively

Ethical Perspectives

Obviously, the appropriate ethical references for persons doing child custody evaluations are the ethics of their respective professions. In the particular case of psychologists, who perform most of these assessments, the

American Psychological Association has issued both ethical standards that are pertinent to the area and an elaborate set of ethical guidelines, which are to serve the purpose of assisting practitioners. It is well known, however, that although guidelines do not have enforceability in distinction to ethical standards, the very fact that they were issued under the auspices of the national organization gives them significant credibility for mounting lawsuits. Furthermore, many of the states have their own practice guidelines in this area and in many cases reference the APA documents.

Interestingly, although it would appear to be a settled matter that the avoidance of dual roles is almost a mandate and offers little wiggle room for the practitioner, there are some contrary views to the simple approach of not providing any services where a dual role is implicated. In the particular case of child custody evaluations, a major issue has been the psychologist functioning as a therapist, who then moves to provide expert opinion as to custody and visitation. The basis on which such an activity has resulted in negative outcomes in the legal arenas is that the job of therapist and the job of forensic assessor are inconsistent and cannot be encompassed by one person. Thus, the Greenberg and Shuman (1997) guidelines have been cited in many settings to illustrate the reasoning and support of the separation of those roles.

At the same time, Ebert (2005) has raised a question about the simple or the blanket application of rules that emphasize avoiding all or most dual relationships. In his approach, he suggested instead the concept of "substantial conflict of interest" and provided a model for evaluating levels of conflict of interest that may present in two different roles contemplated as the best basis for determining whether to engage in same. Such a judgment-based approach is not unattractive, particularly because cases are so divergent and areas of practice also present challenges: in some parts of the country, there is no availability of multiple sources of psychological expertise. Furthermore, it is always a problem when regulating human behavior to identify effective standards and strategies that can be uniformly applied. There are very few situations where no exceptionality might present that would challenge any given regulation. Ebert's (2005) notion about the undesirability of rules that do not allow any dual relationships reflects that reality. However, in our parsing of this area, a position of no exceptions is the better route to take. In the course of developing the ethical standards that deal with certain kinds of dual roles, such as might become involved in bartering, for example, the APA chose to take a more adjustable approach. Situations were to be evaluated for whether the services being provided were compromised by some kind of dual role (see APA, Ethical Principles of Psychologists and Code of Conduct 2010 Amendments, Section 3.05, Multiple Relationships). That evaluative and adjustable strategy allows recognition and an ability to operate in situations where an absolute prohibition would effectively end the capacity to deliver services. However, we are persuaded that the alliances involved in doing psychotherapy, and the necessity for people who are served to have some reasonable assurance that the confidences that are expressed and the behaviors that are observed will not become part of a subsequent evaluation involving a legal matter, require the security afforded by a separation of therapy and evaluative functions.

Evaluation and Investigation

The stance of science demands that persons who represent themselves as applying science or engaging in scientific inquiry must meet standards of reliability and validity and must seek information in a way that does not become a self-fulfilling prophecy for a previously held theory. Rather, information is to be sought in a way that allows it to either confirm or disconfirm theoretical tenets. In the same way, investigation is supposed to take place with what is essentially a scientific mindset. There should be independence of data gathering, attempts to look at facets of a situation, and an avoidance of coming to conclusions in advance of gathering the information. The problem in psychological work generally, however, is that the potential for both conscious and unconscious bias is not inconsequential. In the area under consideration, an illustration is found in Cohen and Segal-Engrelchen (2000) work in which they looked at social workers' court reports in custody cases in Israel. What they found is somewhat disturbing in that it was clear, at various levels of workmanship, that the social workers had preconceived notions of the appropriate roles for men and for women, using highly traditional stereotypes of man as breadwinner and woman as homemaker. These biases permeated the way in which they made their inquiries, the kinds of data they collected, and ultimately the kinds of recommendations that they made. It could be argued that the more rigorous scientific training that is characteristic of psychology and psychiatry may mitigate against such outcomes, but it is important to note that professionals can proceed on the assumed basis that they are independent, when in fact the basis is that they are not.

In another study, Bow, Gould, Flens, and Greenhut (2006) explored further the intricacies of law and science as they affect child custody evaluations. Referencing *Daubert* (1993) progeny and work proceeding from that point, they noted that prior surveys of test usage in custody evaluations had focused on the general acceptability concept. As time has proceeded and post-*Daubert*, however, there has been a general tendency in most of the states toward more and more explicit focus on meeting scientific requirements. Additionally, the legal requirement, as already seen in the Federal Rules of Evidence and in state evidence procedures, specifically looks at relevance to the purpose of the evaluation and certain other related criteria.

Marlowe (1995) specifically wedded scientific and legal principles to conclude the following:

1. A test must appropriately sample the relevant domain with sufficient range of item difficulty and discriminatory capacity.
2. There must be standardization of procedure and norms appropriate to the population of use.
3. Reliability is necessary.
4. The test should meet ethical standards and must have associated and published validity for liability and normative data.

The Bow et al. survey specifically looked for these more extended, *Daubert*-related, and legally important features, as well as sought information from the participants as to their reasons for employing the tests that they utilized. In general, the results of this survey suggested approval for, and use of, the MMPI-2, PAI, MCMI-III, MMPI-A, MACI, and Exner Rorschach. Interestingly, two other tests were approved as meeting *Daubert* standards for purposes of child custody evaluation: The Beck Depression Inventory—II and the Psychopathy Checklist–Revised. We would note, however, their usefulness would be limited to relatively unusual situations. One interesting finding of this study included that the Child Behavior Checklist (which might potentially have more application to matters involved in child custody work) was considered to meet the *Daubert* standard. However, there was referenced a case in which a *Daubert* challenge resulted in the negative finding that "[t]he CBC-L was not validated on a mentally retarded population and consists of few questions focusing on sexual abuse" (p. 32). This finding (see *Gier v. Educational Services Unit 16*, 1995) should give some pause to experts' procedures with our target population, that of equivocal abuse.

Some Practice Recommendations

Basics in Risk Management
Bennett et al. (2006) have provided a detailed handbook on risk management. Their basic general principles apply to all practice areas, including forensic: informed consent, documentation, and consultation. In DR work involving forensic assessment, the amplification and application of those principles are found in the *Guidelines for Forensic Practice*. Originally issued in 1991, current revisions are an in-process project but are nonetheless being referenced and considered important as sources of authority for practicing in the forensic area. The latest iteration is the 8/1/10 draft (retrieved from www.ap-ls. org/aboutpsychlaw/080110sgfpdraft.pdf). As the document indicates, guidelines are advisory, not obligatory, but any careful practitioner knows that to

proceed in some way diametrically different from what is recommended is to place oneself in a potentially difficult position should there be a grievance filed in the form of license action or malpractice suit. If some recommendation is not followed, a practitioner would do well to anticipate questions and have ready the foundation and circumstances that warranted the departure.

Informed Consent

Informed consent includes:

> …the purpose, nature, and anticipated use of the examination; who will have access to the information; associated limitations on privacy, confidentiality, and privilege including who is authorized to release or access the information contained in the forensic practitioner's records; the voluntary or involuntary nature of participation, including potential consequences of participation or non-participation, if known; and, if the cost of the service is the responsibility of the examinee, the anticipated cost. (Section 8.03, Draft 5, *Guidelines for Forensic Practice*)

Documentation

Maintaining a complete file is a known part of defensive practice. The adage is often expressed in clinical settings that if it isn't written down, it didn't happen. In forensic work, where psychologists and other mental health professionals will be testifying as to not only the facts of what they did but the meanings and implications of the work, the emphasis on completeness of records is extremely important. All interviews should be noted and reported in detail. It is not necessary to tape record every contact; however, certainly any forensic interviewing of alleged victims of abuse should be preserved. Bringing tapes and transcripts to court is usual rather than exceptional. All reports should indicate when such recording has taken place. In our practice, when we have taped interviews, a transcript is prepared and appended to the report. Other files that are part of the documentation process include the agreements to proceed signed by clients, which include informed consent elements and financial responsibility statements. In some cases, the expert may be retained to review data and prepare a report or may be retained to evaluate a client for an attorney as opposed to for the court. The duty is then to the attorney; an agreement is usually memorialized by way of letters to or from the attorney, and financial arrangements are with that individual as responsible party. A specific aspect of documentation that is particular to forensic work involves cases where appeals may be launched. It is noted in the current *Guidelines* draft ("12.07 Recordkeeping") that all records may need to be maintained until appeals are exhausted; experts are cautioned to inquire of counsel when cases are in that process.

Consultation

With respect to Bennett et al.'s (2006) third basic principle, consultation, the need and means should be obvious. Any psychologists who do not have extensive experience with custody evaluation should seek available consultation from experienced colleagues whenever cases involve allegations of abuse. Even those with extended experience know the importance and balance that come from soliciting collegial input. The high likelihood of complexities, both legal and psychological, and the part that will be played by an expert combine to create very significant exposure. However, consultation does not shift the professional responsibility to the consultant. In a formal consultation, the psychologist seeking same is the client and there may (or may not) be financial arrangements between the consultant and client. However, the definition of consulting is that it involves the provision of advice and counsel that the client is free to accept or reject. All case-based decision making is ultimately the client/consultee's and the professional liability resides with that individual.

Financial Issues

Finances can occasionally present as complex. Court orders in most custody evaluations specify that parties are jointly and equally responsible. However, when one party's attorney calls for a deposition, it is usually the case that that lawyer is responsible for the payment of that procedure (and the psychologist should ask for it in advance or at the time of the deposition on the basis of estimated time involved). Sometimes, however, a deposition may be initiated by one counsel, attended by the other counsel, but may come to involve the other counsel also engaging in extended questioning of the psychologist (there may also be some questioning by an attending GAL). Clarification of the financial responsibility sometimes has to occur at the point at which the process comes to be a shared rather than unilateral one. If there is division of opinion between the attorneys, the expert at the very least needs to document the discussion in the form of a memorandum sent to all counsel (and the GAL where one is appointed) and maintained in the file. (These [one hopes] relatively rare occurrences can lead to difficulties of fee collection which later can get disputed by parties; obtaining a court order with respect to financial responsibility or a copy of the court's decree that specifies same is desirable.)

One way to deal with some of these kinds of problems is to have an elaborate financial disclosure information in the informed consent that is signed in advance by parties. However, it is usually not possible to anticipate every possibility in this area, and there is a point at which elaboration itself becomes a threat, often presenting to the average individual as "legalese" designed to obfuscate and ultimately victimize. If the client cannot reasonably understand what is put before him or her, the only recourse is to take the form to counsel (who may find reasons to dispute the content). One model for financial information is found in the Appendices.

CASE EXAMPLE

Although pretrial deposition is not unknown in these cases, it is also true that most do not involve that step. In this referenced situation, a deposition was scheduled by counsel whose party was most displeased with the lack of support the psychologist provided for his position. Accordingly, the counsel scheduled a deposition at the office of the psychologist. The most important actions had already occurred: the client had been provided in advance of all services, an informed consent document which he signed that clearly stated, "Should testimony or deposition be required, fees must be paid in advance in half-day (three hour) increments by the party requesting the testimony or deposition. Should the fees exceed the advance payment, the party responsible will be billed for any overage, payment due within thirty (30) days of the date on the billing statement." Upon arrival, counsel indicated that a check would be provided as soon as the session was complete. Based on prior experience with this firm and apparent good relations, the psychologist agreed to go forward, a decision that would be subsequently regretted. At the end of three hours, the deposition was complete. Counsel indicated the client would be instructed to provide immediate payment. Several billing cycles later, with no response from the party or the attorney, counsel provided a check for two hours of time accompanied by the statement that it was "payment of [the referenced] invoice." That check was returned as incorrectly reflecting the amount due. Repeated billing resulted in no action; following a standard policy warning of placement of the bill with collections, it was turned over to that agency. The agency issued its standard warning that payment could be made immediately with no penalty, or collection efforts would formally ensue. No action occurred. A year and a half later, when a credit problem developed for the party, the attorney filed on behalf of the client a complaint with an ethics committee alleging that experts were not allowed to set their own fees per state law and that the continued efforts at collection were causing emotional harm to the client. The letter requested disciplinary action. (Of note, the fees were not in excess of what is standard in the area.) That letter also stated that the client had not been informed of financial responsibility and the policy regarding advance payment for deposition, an outright misrepresentation. After receiving notification from the lawyer of the complaint, and consultation with the malpractice insurance representative, the ethics committee and the insurance carrier were provided with a complete copy of the financial file including all correspondence, the signed financial responsibility document, and the copy of the returned inaccurate check and its misleading letter (the intention of which was to establish a record for accepting the lesser payment). The firm finally paid the bill in full but did not withdraw the complaint with its veiled intent for malpractice. No ethics breach was found. There has been no further action.[*]

---

[*] Agreeing to the arrangement of later payment when counsel arrived was contributory to this situation and illustrates the importance of not putting oneself in a vulnerable position. A responsible law firm would have arrived with the agreed sum, and a more careful practitioner would have insisted on deferring the deposition until the advance was paid.

The above case illustrates the importance of policy, procedure, and documentation as advance defenses in a very legally hazardous world at times.

Some Recommended Procedures

From the standpoint of dealing with legal challenges, it is well known that the wary practitioner is careful to constrain his or her practice to meet the guidelines that have been promulgated by official bodies. Thus, persons who provide custody evaluations are careful to not only rely upon the position of one side or the other, but instead to look at multiple sources of information, to utilize appropriate and relevant testing but to avoid unnecessary and irrelevant testing, and to evaluate parent/child relationships in the context of each side. Exceptions to these kinds of baseline procedures, if necessarily made, would need to be identified as such and the rationale for the departure made clear in reportage.

One example of an exception to the usual rule of seeing the child with both parents might occur in the case of a parent who refuses to comply or continue to comply with the process of the evaluation. In such an instance, the practitioner should document the refusal and further document the efforts made to overcome the refusal, before moving to make recommendations without the necessary data. Even in such a situation, where refusal itself is not unreasonably considered relevant information, it would still behoove the writer to speak somewhat conditionally when making recommendations. Thus, it might be stated that "based on the information collected, the following recommendations pertain; however, in view of the lack of compliance of Party B with aspects of this evaluation, it may be that other information could become available that might have a bearing on the recommendations which are made below."

In the course of dealing with the complexities that these cases involve, a strict reliance on formal court action would be counterproductive if the aim were one of facilitating the parties toward assuming control of their lives and the direction of resolution to their current dispute. However, the procedures of the courts not only are marks of formality but also exist to protect parties by maintaining fairness and reasonable transparency. Certain guidelines for communications between the evaluator and counsel when they occur prior to a court hearing but post the release of the report may allow management of what can be a difficult terrain. The basic principles include that one-sided *ex parte* communications in situations where there is a joint or independent court appointment should not occur. In situations where a one-sided appointment has been approved, and where in some cases no release of report is to occur except by the retaining attorney, prerelease contacts with that counsel may properly occur. The process of a one-sided appointment, and often a different expert appointed for the other side, is viewed as generally undesirable but nonetheless still occurs in many jurisdictions.* In the more common and more approved case of an independent evaluator, postrelease of report/ pretrial communications should be simultaneous if at all possible (e-mails sent to both and GAL, conference calls) or if sequential should involve notes for what is to be said and memoranda or dated file notes that reflect what was done.

Whenever there are allegations of sexual abuse, and any inquiry is made into the substance of those allegations with the child, the actual interview should be veridically preserved. Note taking is never sufficient to answer questions as to whether the inquiry has itself become part of a process that alters memory (McPherson, 1997). Furthermore, it is sometimes desirable to test the child's potential for suggestibility, which can then be demonstrated as part of the interview material if a transcript of the evaluator and child is available for analysis. Finally, in cases where equivocality appears present, it is sometimes possible to resolve the dilemma, in one direction or the other, by having the actual evidence of what the child says in the course of an investigative interview.

CASE EXAMPLES

Some years earlier, McPherson was the third evaluator in an ongoing custody situation where the allegation was that the child was sexually abused by the father. The first evaluator's opinion was that the allegation could not be dismissed but was not at a level that could be confirmed. The second evaluator, to whom the child was taken by the alleged perpetrator, gave as the opinion that the child seemed confused, but did not confirm the allegation. In the third interview, which was the only one preserved on tape, the child was told that parents usually prepare children when they are going to any kind of doctor. The child then was asked what he had been told by his mother about coming to see this psychologist. He responded to the effect that his mother told him to answer any questions and to be truthful. He was then referenced to the fact that there had been other doctors that he had talked to and that he had seen Dr. X when with his father. He agreed that that was the case. He was asked what the father had told him to prepare for seeing Dr. X. He responded to the effect that his father had told him to tell Dr. X that the event had not happened. And then he added spontaneously, "But it did." The rest of that interview provided, through careful nonsuggestive questioning, further detail, some of which was consistent with the fact that the father was a trained hypnotist and may have been doing things in his communication on the way to the prior psychologist's office that suggested some use of that type of technique with the child. The presence of that tape recording secured the safety of the child within the situation, and ultimately a system for contact with the father

---

* For example, in California, a "730 Evaluation" (2010) is specified under the California Evidence Code Section 730. Detailed procedures for selection and qualifications of evaluators, dimensions of evaluations, and reportage and testimony are fixed in court rules. Experts can be retained by each side to critique the court appointed and can submit reports of their findings, but there is no provision for experts to do simultaneous evaluations.

in public situations, supervised by the mother, was arrived at by the parties. The father never admitted harm-doing but was able to understand that his vulnerability to perception of same was now extraordinarily heightened, such that he would do well not to pursue independent time with the child until he was older, if then. This author did have the opportunity some years later of speaking to the child as an adolescent, who actually initiated to come in and stated that in fact he had been abused, and that he remembered quite vividly the sequence that had taken place. (However, and this is the essence of equivocality in these cases, a memory at this point may well be accurate, but it cannot be ruled out that the beliefs of the mother secured a memory that included some kind of distortion of what may have actually taken place.)

In another case, the mother was alleging physical abuse by the father of both herself and the child and had successfully managed to keep the child from seeing the father for some months. As part of the procedural requirements for custody evaluation, she under protest but bowing to the court's order brought the child in for a supervised in-office contact with the father. She did so, arriving with the child in tow. As soon as they were in the office, her anger and hostility toward the father was overtly manifest and she began in front of the youngster to make negative statements about the man. At the time, the father was in the playroom waiting for the visit to begin. An audiotape memorialized the events that followed. The child, age 5, came in, stood straight in a kind of important way, and in a recitation style made a statement to the effect that the father had hurt his mother and himself. Interestingly enough, he used third person and the father's first name in a way that was entirely inconsistent with his having been either victim or observer of victimization, and he further referenced a dispute about money between the parents, about which he could only have known from the mother. He completed the statement without any prompting, then looked at the examiner and said, "May I go tell mommy that I said everything that she told me to say? And then can I play with daddy?" He was allowed to do exactly that. He came back in and hurled himself into his father's arms and they played successfully for the rest of the hour. The documentation of this series of events did not rest solely upon the observation powers and notes of the clinician, but also on the presence of a tape, which clearly reflected the programming of the child and the subsequent connection between the child and the father, all of which were entirely inconsistent with the mother's assertion that the boy was in abject fear of the father. The father's visitation was reinstituted by the court.

These cases illustrate the value of the primary procedural mandate of preserving investigative interviews using videotape or at least audiotape when these kinds of allegations are made.

Another procedural issue goes to the importance of not exceeding the data or assigning meaning that is not warranted. It is not possible to use the finding on the so-called Lie Scale (L) of the MMPI-2 to identify that an individual is misrepresenting what has occurred with reference to specified matters. In fact, the L Scale cannot be used to identify those who are prone to lie from those without such a character defect; the scale, as with others, has multiple correlates (see, for example, Greene, 1999). The L scale is commonly elevated in the MMPIs that are administered in these contexts (Bathurst, Gottfried, & Gottfried, 1997; Hopkins, 1997; McPherson et al., 2006; Seigel,

1996). L and K are expected to be up in the usually defensive protocols that are produced as people try to convince the evaluator that they are stable, competent, and highly effective as parents of their children. In fact, a non-defensive MMPI-2 is a sufficiently remarkable occurrence in that it requires some analysis and appropriate commentary and may in fact reflect some emotional deficits produced either situationally or reflecting longer-term conditions (see Chapter 4, opening section, for a case example involving mis-reading of the MMPI).

From the beginning in these kinds of cases, emphasis must be placed on informing both sides that the evaluator is going to maintain a stance of neutrality, is going to be interested in any and all evidence that can be presented, and has as part of the general approach to investigation a quality of skepticism such that any and all information will be carefully scrutinized. Although these kinds of statements need to be made in all custody evaluation situations, it is of specific importance that there be no question on the part of either of the parties that the ongoing process is one in which there is an investigative mode in place rather than a more accepting stance, which can be associated with the experience of therapy.

In the case of planned videotaped procedures, whether with children or adults, obviously there has to be clear prior information provided to all concerned. In the not uncommon case of a temporary custodian who believes that certain acts have occurred, it is particularly important that that individual signify awareness and agreement that there will be a tape made of the interviews of the child, thus preventing a later statement and possibly an effort to have the tape excluded on the basis of lack of authorization.*

Communications with GALs most frequently occur throughout the life of the case and often involve a collaborative way of proceeding with the guardian providing information from home visits, for example, or other records that have been collected (McPherson, 1990). In some cases, however, it is best not to communicate with the guardian and, in fact, there may be a court order that the psychologist should proceed without any other influences being brought to bear such as might occur through guardian contact.

An important procedural issue involves obtaining and reading with great care the court's orders. Orders vary, and a custody evaluation may or

---

* It is interesting that we have never had a refusal from a parent in the course of these evaluations to the procedure of recording, but McPherson did have an instance in which a developmentally disabled child in the custody of the Children's Services was brought for interview to comply with a DR ongoing case and that department refused to allow recording even though both parents had signified approval. The child's verbalizations were not rapid and the evaluator's capacity to use Gregg shorthand allowed the production of an almost complete transcript in that case, but the management of rapport and interaction while simultaneously manually recording both questions and answers was challenging.

may not be the same from one case to the next. In some cases, courts have ordered separate parent evaluations but not a custody evaluation. In such a case there should be no statement as to custody or visitation, even though both sides may have been seen. The court's order specified that a psychological evaluation be made of each of the parties and a forensic psychological report reflecting each party's psychological status is the appropriate product. Informing clients at the outset of what type of order is being implemented and what is allowed by way of outcome is part of the initial briefing prior to a client's being evaluated.

Checklist for Defensive Practice

The following questions provide some guides for how to be prepared in cases where some identifiable degree of threat may exist. However, they are in essence focus questions that allow anticipatory management of cases that present with difficulties.

1. Is this a case where you immediately know there are higher levels of security that may become important (such as equivocal abuse allegations, history of litigation especially with lodging of complaints regarding counsel or other appointed persons, or a history of multiple attorneys)?
2. Have you carefully followed all procedures that are usual and customary in your practice? If not, have you documented the basis for any departures?
3. Have you carefully maintained your malpractice insurance and is your insurer aware that your practice includes forensic work? (Have you read your policy and know what is covered and what is not?)
4. Is there any record in the case for dyscontrolled physical acting out? Allegations of domestic violence are important but may themselves be equivocal. Behavior documented in police reports where officers have seen out of control behavior is more concerning.
5. Do you have security procedures that you can implement in your office (can doors be locked, is there a peephole, is the building secured at some point and if so do you know when)?
6. Is your personal location information readily available? (At one time, simply having an unlisted number reduced vulnerability; however, the Internet provides access to extended personal data for most people with any public visibility, including psychologists who serve the courts.)
7. Have you taken any courses in personal self-defense and environmental awareness?

8. Do you have visible relatives who could become identified targets by an individual who has lost the sense of concern for boundaries?

9. Have you any intuitive discomfort about an individual you are assessing in connection with a case? (The desirability of responding to "gut feelings" with respect is a well-known one in many front-line professions and occupations.)

10. If you have decided to have weaponry on premises or on your person, are you fully trained in the use and limitations of the implements and have you the necessary control over their availability?

Conclusion

Life is clearly not risk free. Practicing defensively guarantees that difficulties may only be minimized although not eliminated. The points made in this chapter go to the importance of conservatism when it comes to dealing with cases of this sort. That conservatism starts importantly with suspension of judgment and enhancement of skepticism along with careful collection of available data. Equivocal abuse cases finish with only those conclusions and recommendations that have been solidly supported, along with recognition of the existing open questions and implications of those questions for the welfare of children and their families. The wary clinician lives to serve another day, which itself is a most desirable outcome.

Intervention Options

6

In the course of a contested domestic relations case, the usual sequence involves a filing for divorce by one party, followed by a counterfiling on the part of the other party, on the basis of which, in many jurisdictions, they are denoted plaintiff and defendant or petitioner and respondent. In those settings where the latter terms are used, the idea is to remove the implication that comes from other civil law where there is a complaint against a party for some kind of bad acts and that party then must defend against the allegations. The use of petitioner and respondent is meant to convey only the timing of filings and to not carry the opprobrium of one person being offended against by another. From a psychological point of view, the more neutral terminology clearly reflects the reality of marriage relationships with their multiple and interactive nature.

These filings in cases of the sort that are the focus for this volume usually involve petitions on both sides for sole custody, although that is not always the case. The case next proceeds to a series of pretrials, during which time a variety of motions may be considered or ongoing disputes negotiated. Those disputes, when they center on the children, most frequently involve such matters as companionship time, handling of immediately presenting holidays, and taking extended vacation trips, as well as disputes as to the appropriate regular parenting contact schedule. Simultaneously, and often of some importance, other issues are being prelitigated, importantly including matters of finances, current and future support orders, limits of marital property, and the like. If the parties have separated at a time when one or the other has a career post that will require a move, the issue of geographic separation may also present.

The case will continue through this pretrial period, ultimately moving to the level of the court system. However, where the issues regarding the children are complex and appear to resist any kind of negotiated outcome (it is common for Domestic Relations (DR) and family courts to have in-house or referred mediation programs, the purpose of which is to resolve disputes and, one hopes, lead to mutually agreed upon case resolutions), the next phase prior to an actual custody hearing and a final parenting order not infrequently involves the appointment of an evaluator or a guardian *ad litem* (GAL). For purposes of the discussion to follow, these phases of the typical case are denoted: initial filing phase, interim pretrial phase, hearing and judgment phase, and post-decree phase.

Allegations may arise at any point, including prior to the initial filing for a divorce. The timing of the allegations can raise or lower the probability of equivocality and is a factor that should be considered in determining the degree to which the case fits within such a category. As with everything else, however, the timing of an allegation is not dispositive for its validity.

Initial Filing Phase

If as part of the filing for divorce there have been presented allegations of abuse or there is a unilateral act on the part of one of the parties to separate the children from the other party for whatever reason, the situation is going to require some immediate action by the court in order to secure the situation until it is more adequately assessed. Occasionally at the time of filing, there is an *ex parte* motion for a temporary order of custody to the filing party on the basis of danger to the children and a request that there be no contact until the court can more adequately review the evidence that may pertain. Most courts are reluctant to grant emergency *ex parte* orders, knowing their potential to be part of a strategy approach rather than necessarily reflecting the reality of a safety issue for a child or children. At the same time, most courts are reluctant, depending upon the kind of allegation that is made and the degree to which it appears founded on its face, to make a decision that would put a child in a dangerous situation, only to find later that the child has suffered or been grievously injured.

Ex parte orders are viewed with legal disfavor and represent exceptions to the due process that ensures the constitutional rights to liberty and property (Fifth and Fourteenth Amendments; Answers.com, 2010). When the court is predisposed to grant such petitions, they are generally time limited and highly specified as to procedure. Thus, the Rules of the Cuyahoga County Domestic Relations Court (2010) include number 24, which specifies the conditions under which a temporary restraining order (TRO) may be granted *ex parte*, and number 26, which creates the basis for a domestic violence civil protection order (CPO). The CPO involves requirements for certain affidavits and accompanying filings, along with filed police reports, and further specifies that an evidentiary hearing involving both parties must occur within seven days. (Continuances, however, can be granted by agreement of both parties or under certain other exceptions.)

Even in the case of international abductions covered under the Hague Convention, and the requirement for filing by the left-behind parent of an *ex parte* order in order to put into action efforts to locate and return the child or children, significant limitations pertain. Such an order is not viewed as informing the final outcome. The filing must include information as to any other prior existing orders. The order is often expressly time limited and often not enforceable in other than the state where issued (in other words, its efficacy is primarily geared to enabling the search and return activity; Department of State, United States of America, 2010).

In general, legal decisions involving cases where *ex parte* orders are at some issue have affirmed the rights and necessity for DR courts or courts with family law responsibilities to issue such temporary legal intervention in both child custody concerns and domestic violence assertions. At the same time, the importance of temporary status, of mandatory full hearings, and of specified conditions of such filings is noted and supported as well (see, as examples, *Kelm v. Hyatt*, 1995; *Smith v. Quigg*, 2006; and *Yazdani-Isfehani v. Yazdani-Isfehani*, 2006). These requirements underline the importance that is placed on any court option that in effect negates if only temporarily significant constitutional rights.

Courts faced with such unilateral filings have a clear decisional dilemma. In addition to legal concerns, there is the importance of balancing child protection interests against the damage that occurs when a child loses contact with a parent. In the context of divorce research, there are clear findings that support the desirability of children having contact time with both of their parents.[*] In general, children who have ongoing nonconflicted relationships with both of their parents better survive the experience of the divorce process that has altered the family structure and do better in the long run at later points. However, a number of other factors have been identified as contributing to that success, including economic factors, life stress, quality and not necessarily quantity of contact with fathers, gender disparities (boys do better in stepfather families than girls), and even possible underlying genetic factors. None of the factors identified in the research were substantially controlling but acted more in concert with the totality of the situations seen (Amato, 1993; Amato & Booth, 2001; Amato & Cheadle, 2005; Amato & Gilbreth, 1999; Amato & Keith, 1991). Developmental status of children can be a contributor to outcomes (Bray, 1991). Ellis (2000) provided a summary of impacts of divorce as including significant increase of emotional and behavioral problems; significant negative impact if there is parental conflict; protective impact if custodial parent is strong, emotionally healthy, and has excellent parenting skills; boys may do better in the primary custody of fathers and girls with mothers; and high-conflict situations provide the basis for extreme negative impacts. Wallerstein and Lewis' (1998) long-term

---

[*] Even in the extreme case of incarceration of a parent, research has supported the importance of ongoing contact between children and their fathers or mothers (Simmons, 2000).

studies have provided information about both the resilience of children and their vulnerabilities in the divorcing process.*

If there are allegations during this initial phase, the court may well order an abuse assessment to be carried out by an independent and experienced mental health practitioner who enters as a custody/visitation evaluator. Alternatively, there may be motions by counsel for an independent evaluation, which are granted by the court and with which both parties will be compelled to comply. Not infrequently, there has been a call for a social services investigation or contact with police investigators co-occurring with the petition to the DR court.

Interim Pretrial Phase

If there have been no allegations up to this point, but the assertions then arise, there may be any number of ways in which they are addressed. Again, an *ex parte* action may be sought by a party and may initiate the same sequence as above described. Because abuse allegations, whenever they arise, usually also involve a referral to the social services agency, it may be that the court will grant a temporary hiatus in visitation until such time as the social services department renders a report as to substantiated, unsubstantiated, or indicated. The problems with those reports in this context have been discussed elsewhere. What can be said is that if the allegations are unsubstantiated, the court will usually reinstate the prior ordered contact program. If the court becomes convinced that the allegations were deliberately falsified, a more extreme response may occur of placing the children with the person prior alleged to be abusive. However, as shown below, vulnerability in this situation extends not only to the children and to the relationship between the children and one or more parents, but also to the person who has been accused in the situation.

Hearing and Judgment Phase

If allegations arrive in the course of the trial, they undoubtedly will be brought to the forefront of that process through emergency motions and evidence presented by one side or the other. If the allegations occur post the hearing but prior to the judgment, they may occasion a necessity for another hearing. If, however, they follow the rendering of a judgment, the handling will

---

* Studies by Wallerstein (1991) and Lewis (1998) have significant limitations of lack of random sample selection, probable overweighting with emotionally impaired parents, and lack of contrast groups. Results are informative but far from conclusive.

occur by reference first to the social services department (or police investigative unit) as well as a simultaneous post-decree filing with the court, representing a substantial change of circumstances' motion, and asking for relief. (It should be noted that DR courts generally wish to achieve solutions and do not look with favor on the return of cases for new processing. For that reason, once there is an order, to obtain a reopening of the case there has to be shown some persuasive reasons why the stability already achieved should be disrupted. In effect, it is intended that it be a little harder to reopen a case than to file one initially. This legal procedure is entirely consistent with what is known about the needs of children and families, where unnecessary and disruptive to relational contacts events are more likely than not to be harmful.)

The timing of allegations becomes a variable that will be important to trained investigators who evaluate these kinds of situations. The potential for allegations can increase based on a combination of motivation due to ongoing litigation and emotionally based distortion potentials. Timing also is an issue if the court has responded to some interim matter in a way that is inconsistent with the desires of the party making the allegation. Such situations raise the potential for the allegation to represent a more deliberate type of false accusation. Finally, in the worst of these kinds of situations, and particularly where inquiry directly to the victims has resulted in some endorsement of the alleged abuse, the potential for multiple court involvements is activated. If human services reports substantiate the abuse, it may be that the prosecutor will proceed to lodge charges against the alleged offending party. If the finding is indicated, it is possible that a filing might be made in the juvenile court with an adjudication of abuse and some degree of authority then coming to be vested in that setting.

Post-Decree Phase

Intervention Options

Part of the work in dealing with these kinds of cases involves coming up with recommendations to the court that respond to the multidimensional aspects of these cases. Specifically, all research on court functioning, including what has been developed in the course of the inquiries made by these authors,

---

' As with many aspects of the law, pivotal concepts are defined, but the definitions are far from unequivocal. A change of circumstances, to warrant a change in an existing parenting order, must represent factors that are materially and substantially different from what was the case when the order was made. Examples given include a party's physical or mental condition, a remarriage, the use of a child as a pawn, removal and hiding of a child, conviction of a crime, or even age of the child if it has resulted in some specific need that cannot be met under the existing order (Dorst, 2010).

shows an emphasis on wanting to protect children. Courts and society at large generally place the protection of the young as a high, if not highest, value. In the traditional metaphor, it is the children who are to get into the lifeboat first. At a very fundamental and evolutionary level, it is the protection of the young and their potential life that furthers the aims of maintaining society and the species.

Another important if nonetheless the secondary goal, particularly of a legal system with its traditions going back to Magna Carta and even beyond that to the Book of Genesis, 18, of biblical lore referencing up to 1,000 BCE (Barton, 2001), is the protection of the innocent from being penalized when they have not committed any crime. In the case of these kinds of situations, even where only the domestic relations court is involved, the effect of having been publicly identified as an alleged perpetrator can affect vocational functioning, personal functioning, and relational functioning, and of course where there is an unresolved situation with all emphasis placed on safety of the child by means of complete separation, there is loss of a child and loss to the child of a parent. Therefore, the development of intervention options that respond to both sides of this extreme dilemma is of significant importance. A number of options exist and can be included singly and in combination.

Supervised Visitation

An intervention available to the court—which may be ordered at any point that allegations are brought to the forefront—is that of supervised visitation. A variety of models for that supervision exists and must be evaluated as to their appropriateness on a case-by-case basis. The easiest by far involves relative supervision. In that model, the alleged perpetrator of the abuse agrees to supervised visitation at the home of a family member or with a family member present in his or her home throughout the time that the visit takes place. Supervised visitation of that type can also occur in a public place. The designated supervisor would need to accept responsibility for reportage to the court in the event that there are inappropriate actions or communications occurring during the course of the visits. Obviously, where there are reportage requirements, a family member may well be placed in a position of conflicting loyalties. Supervised visitation by a family member is more successful where the alleging party expresses confidence in the arrangement. Relative supervisors, as well as any others (see below), are vulnerable to become fact witnesses in subsequent hearings related to the situation. Supervisors are well advised to keep notes of what occurs and be prepared to speak at the factual level for what they have seen and heard. Relative supervisors would not have the additional burden or expectation of becoming expert witnesses and thus would not be offering an opinion as to the meaning of behavior or its implications for the best interests of the child or children. Other more independent and professionally credentialed supervisors might, however, have an expert testimony role at some point, depending upon the situation and whether they were qualified for that role.*

Supervision that has somewhat more independence from both of the parties may be provided by persons who have other roles with respect to the child or children and no specific connections to either parent, financial or otherwise. Such supervisors might include teachers or daycare providers or other third-party caretakers. These types of supervisors are usually paid, and it is often most appropriate to require equal fiscal responsibility between the parties. In some cases, supervision has been provided through the services of a religious institution, church, or synagogue, for example, where persons on staff or among the clergy assist in this way. Sometimes that kind of supervised visitation takes place on the institution's property.

Paid Professional Supervision Services

In recent years, a number of formal supervisory services have developed. Most frequently, these offices are privately situated and they often employ social workers or social workers in training. Some are under the auspices or overall direction of a qualified mental health professional and some are directed by legal professionals. Their degree of independence is of a high order, but the cost is often prohibitive to many of the people for whom supervision is ordered. Persons working for such organizations are trained in the legal requirements of the situation in their established responsibilities, and there are contracts that represent both fiscal and procedural conditions that are signed.

One such service in the northeast Ohio area was created about two years ago by an experienced domestic relations attorney who had also served in many cases as a guardian *ad litem*. After a period of 10 years of setting up supervision in a variety of cases, and with the encouragement of a local magistrate, the attorney established a formal supervision service.† He provided a

---

* Qualifications of an expert include training, experience, and education (see "Rules of Evidence," Chapter 4). Professional supervisors are often in training for social work degrees and have some substantial experience in that field. They would meet qualifications to give an opinion about the visitation behavior they have seen and the degree to which it falls within or outside required dimensions of conduct.

† The authors are indebted to Attorney Jeffrey Fanger for volunteering to respond to our inquiries about his program and experiences. His model is particularly noteworthy for the way in which it was structured for legal and physical protection policies.

professionally crafted legal basis with contracts that specify the conditions of the service and the fiscal responsibilities. Parties must sign contracts and must maintain the agreed payment for the service to be provided. Supervisors are all individuals with backgrounds involving children, including mostly social workers or social work graduate students and some with educational degrees. All are formally trained in the role they will undertake. That role is specifically to be the eyes and ears of the visitation, or as the director also stated, "living recording devices." Arrangements have been made for supervisors to be covered by a social work related liability policy. Specific conditions may be dictated for specific cases, such as the place of visitation and the conditions of any transportation involved. Supervisors are taught that they are not law enforcement personnel or therapists. They all carry cell phones and have access to immediate legal advice for any situation that may develop regardless of time of day. Their focus involves monitoring interaction that is ongoing. One of the more difficult areas for that monitoring is the content and quality of verbal behavior. Inappropriate remarks do occur when parents are under supervision and there are limited options except that of a correction and reportage to the court. However, Fanger noted that in the vast majority of cases when there is a person present in the room—hearing, seeing, and noting that which is transpiring—the behavior is constrained in desirable directions and appropriate.

Relative Supervised Visitation

As a longer term potential way of addressing cases where there is no comfortable resolution as to the facts, relative supervision can sometimes provide the necessary security for both sides. Unfortunately, in many such cases, relatives of the alleged perpetrator are viewed by the other party as nonsecure and relatives of the latter are either not available or do not represent a comfortable alternative for the alleged perpetrator. Nonetheless, such arrangements can sometimes be established and can be made more palatable to the alleged perpetrator if they are framed in terms of his or her security as well as the child's. Such an option, however, usually is not practical for a long-term situation, except where visitation takes place at a grandparent home and grandparents are willing to assist.

Therapy for Children

When allegations are first made, it is not uncommon for children to be referred for therapy. Therapy can be part of a security system and can be recommended when it is not in place as part of resolving the case. However, there are certain important caveats, as the following legal case illustrates. In this Ohio case (*State v. Johnson*, 1996), the court roundly criticized the work that was done by a child abuse investigator whose one saving grace, from the standpoint of these writers, was that she made a tape of what she was doing.* The review of that tape by the judge allowed the following kinds of remarks in the decision rendered:

> It is apparent to this court that based upon the testimony of Dr. Campbell and upon a review of the tape of the interview, Wright interrogated the child with only one objective in mind. That objective was to obtain information that could lead only to an indictment of the defendant. Her objective was never to obtain the truth of the matters alleged. It was Dr. Campbell's professional opinion that the likelihood was "alarmingly high" that this alleged victim's testimony is not reliable because her memory has been destroyed by the nature of the interview conducted.
>
> The interview was unacceptably long and did not take appropriate breaks. The interview of this 3-year-old child lasted for over one hour in a closed room.
>
> What is notable to this court is that the child repeatedly answered all questions in the negative and denied that anything had happened. Throughout the vast majority of the interview, the child denied that anything had occurred in the car with the defendant. Approximately halfway through the interview, the child said something bad had happened, and at the end of the interview the child made a gesture and pointed to Wright. Both of these incidents are described in detail later in this opinion.
>
> Early in the interview, when given an anatomical doll and asked what "Hubie" did to her in the car, the child laid her head on the doll's shoulder. When asked repeatedly what she did in the car with Hubie, she answered, "We took a nap." When asked repeatedly if bad things were done, the child repeatedly answered, "No, no, no." When asked, "Did Hubie do something to you?" the child replied, "Nope." This interview was conducted in such a manner that it is obvious to the court that this child eventually realized that she was not going to be allowed to see her grandmother/mother or to leave the room until she told Wright what Wright wanted to hear. Early in the interview, Wright stated to the child, "We are almost done." However, the interview continued for well over three-quarters of an hour after that point in time.
>
> At various times Wright would say, "Just a few more questions and we will get your mommy." That did not happen. When asked if she played games in the car with Hubie, the child replied, "No." All through the interview, this child said, "No." More than halfway through the interview, Wright asked the child if something good or bad happened in the car. The child answered,

---

* The description made it clear that the basic rules of investigative interviewing of children were repeatedly violated including nonacceptance of negative responses; physical restraint (the child was held on the interviewer's lap at times); promises, some false; and inducements. It is not surprising that Dr. Terrence Campbell, an acknowledged expert in this field, was able to present well-grounded testimony that discredited the procedure and provided foundation for rejection by the court.

"Bad." Immediately thereafter when asked if the child could show her on the doll what "bad" had happened, the child replied, "No." The child began asking for her "Mommy." At that point, Wright left the room and promised the child that she would get her mommy and return. Instead, she came back into the room with cookies and gave the child a cookie. Dr. Campbell testified that the cookie was used to reward the child for saying that something bad had happened. Wright then stated that her mommy had gone to the bathroom and would come to the room when she was done. This did not happen. Immediately, Wright began asking if Hubie had done something bad in the car. Again, the child began answering, "No, no." At this point, Wright asked the child if Hubie was a good guy and the child said, "Yes." She also asked her if her grandmother was good or bad and the child did not answer. On more than one occasion Wright asked the child if Hubie was a good guy and the child said, "Yes." Wright asked the child if someone told her not to tell and she said, "No." The child repeatedly refused on numerous occasions to say what Hubie had made her do in the car. At this point in time the child finally said that Hubie "pooped" and "peed" in the back of the car. When asked if Hubie touched her pee-pee or if she touched Hubie's pee-pee, she repeatedly replied, "No." When asked if Hubie had his pants on the child replied, "Yes." When asked if she touched Hubie's pee-pee or if Hubie asked her to touch his pee-pee, the child replied, "No."

Finally in frustration, Wright told the child that if she answered her questions she would go get her mommy. This promise had been made to the child before. The child began running to the door, pulling on the door, switching off and on the lights, and making every effort possible to get out of the interview situation. It is apparent again to this court that this child realized that she would have to say what Wright wanted to hear in order to get out of the room and see her mommy. Again, when the lights are turned on and the child returns to Wright's lap, the child again says that Hubie did not make her put her mouth on his pee-pee. She answered that question in the negative repeatedly. When asked if anyone did that to her she said, "No."

The state wants the jury to view only the final few seconds of this tape or have Wright testify only to this part of the interview. This part of the interview begins with Wright asking the victim if she (the victim) is going to tell her (Wright) what happened in the car. The child answers "Nope." Wright next asks if the victim is going to tell her mom what happened in the car. Again the response is "Nope." Wright then asks, "Who peed in your face?" The child answers, "The doggie." Wright asks, "Did Hubie pee in your face?" The answer is, "Nope." Then Wright instructs (not asks) the child to show her (Wright), "What you did to Hubie's pee-pee." Wright then puts the doll in the child's face. The child then puts the doll's private part in her mouth and looks at Wright. Wright asks, "Who had you do that?" In answering, the child makes no verbal reply but the child takes the doll and repeatedly points to Wright with the doll indicating that Wright made her do this. Wright asks,

"Is that what you did in the car?" There is no response from the child and the interview ends.

At the adult level, there are now significant case decisions documenting that false memories can be created and believed, and that when legal actions are then taken to harm alleged former abusers, the potential exists for the tables to turn and therapists to find both licensure actions and malpractice suits successfully mounted against them (Brown, Scheflin, & Hammond, 1998). In addition, it is clear that although children generally do remember traumatic events, they are also more vulnerable to postevent information and distortion when they are very young than are adults (Kuehnle & Connell, 2009). As a result, therapist input in equivocal situations needs to be circumspect and managed with significant awareness of the fragility of the memory process. Substantial psychological research and literature has formed the basis for the scientific finding that the phenomenon of false memory exists and can be created in situations where authority of a therapist and suggestibility of a patient combine. Hypnotherapy is particularly known to enhance the suggestibility factor with the result that specific cautions, including the need to record sessions, are suggested when therapy commences in cases involving reported returned memory and there are potential legal sequelae (Brown et al., 1998).

If a child services investigator with an agenda can coerce a small child to state falsely that acts of abuse have occurred, and ultimately change the child's memory system, and if a therapist with preconceived notions of etiology can assist a patient in the creation of false memory, it is quite clear that undertaking therapy in equivocal abuse cases is a hazardous practice area. An even worse case scenario occurs when the prosecutor in a putative but insecure abuse case asks a therapist to develop information about the abuse and provide it to enhance the state's case. The therapist who becomes identified with such an investigative and legal goal is compromised and the therapy becomes an iatrogenic force that adds to the harm of a child in this type of family and legal situation.

Obviously, a child who has suffered significant abuse at the hands of a parent may (but will not necessarily) evidence traumatic reactivity; depending upon the nature and extent of what has occurred, significant longer term posttraumatic symptoms may present. Even, however, in equivocal cases, the placement of the child at the center of a very significantly heightened set of interparental tensions is not going to be psychologically healthy. Therapy for children in this situation is not an irrational or inappropriate intervention to assist them with their environmental stress. However, therapy for a child in an equivocal situation that seeks to be part of the substantiation process not only is dangerous to the child patient but also becomes a vehicle by which a form of witness tampering occurs. In the world of the criminal courts, coercion and contamination of witnesses is a serious and felonious behavior.

Therapists need to follow a list of cautions in making decisions to see children under these circumstances (see Table 6.1).

Child Therapy as a Means of Establishing Security

Therapists chosen for this work need to have experience with high-conflict domestic relations cases. The therapist also needs to be willing to have close to equal contact with both the allegating parent and the alleged perpetrating parent. Sessions need to be arranged where the children are seen in the context of each of these persons, and it is recommended that the therapy be enhanced by the use of the Secrets instruction (see Appendix E). Similarly, the Roving Reporter instruction is implemented when visitation moves to more normalized dimensions as a way to enhance the security of the alleged perpetrator against future allegations and to raise the security of the primary care parent about the safety of the child. The visitation parent makes a tape sometimes during, but definitely at the end, of the visit in which a brief discussion occurs about the visitation experience. The visitation parent is encouraged to bring up things that might have happened that didn't work out so well, such as when a punishment was levied for some misbehavior, or when some desired goal was not reached. If there was an accident or similar event, that occurrence should be explored and discussed with the child. An effort should be made to make this "interview" into an enjoyable process. Brevity is not only the soul of wit but also the best strategy when using this device. The tapes are maintained. They are available for review by the residential parent. They can be brought into court later if allegations present and they can become a record of visitation that is also a record of a child's growth and development and thereby an enjoyed possession of the child when he or she gets older.

Age of the Child

The aging process of the child, although not an imposed intervention, is a process that carries potentials for increasing security and changing the character of the overall situation. Children are growing organisms and they become more and more their own security as a function of their growth and development. A child at the age of 15 months has little or no capacity to secure any kind of safety for him- or herself. A child at the age of 7 has a significant capacity to secure his or her own safety by virtue of what is usually present in the way of verbal capacity and memory function. Up through the ages of 5 or 6, there is substantially more insecurity of memory and more vulnerability to suggestion than is the case afterwards in the normally developing

Table 6.1 Do's and Don'ts for Therapists

Do's	Don'ts
1. If there is no order that provides full custody, either temporary or permanent, to a parent who brings a child to the therapist's office, the therapist has a duty to notify the other parent and obtain permission from the other parent for the ongoing work that is proposed. If a parent has a temporary authority to act as a sole custodian, the therapist should treat, as an ethical if not legal duty, the requirement of notification to the other parent. Furthermore, in many jurisdictions, if not most, a noncustodial parent has a right of notification and access to medical, educational, and psychological treatment records. (The therapist also has a duty to make clear to the child at the level of the child's understanding, and to the custodial parent, the limits of confidentiality.)	1. As already indicated above, the therapist should not see the child and alleging parent without attempted contact on the other side of the dispute.
2. The therapist should make every effort to meet with the other parent, and preferably with the child and the other parent at some point. However, depending upon the legal status of the case, a joint meeting may or may not be feasible (restraining orders have sometimes been issued). However, the therapist who proceeds to initiate therapy with a child in a situation that is equivocal and not finally adjudicated potentially becomes a source of harm to the child, thus violating the most essential ethical canon in all areas of mental health and other health-related treatment. As already indicated, therapists can be vulnerable to license actions should they not successfully proceed with great care in this kind of situation.	2. Under no circumstances should the therapist employ any kind of hypnotherapy or other mode that emphasizes the use of suggestion.
3. Therapists should make excellent records of their sessions. The job of the therapist is to listen to the child but not to inquire and enter the role of investigator in cases where the criminal court becomes involved. The job of the therapist is to provide for the child a protected arena within which the child can reflect upon his or her feelings and come to some positive reframing of the situation in a way that allows healthy adaptation.	3. The therapist should avoid re-raising the incident and discussing same with the child. Obviously, if a child brings up issues related to the allegations, it is appropriate for the therapist to listen and to reflect with the child about how he or she feels. However, any inquiry that may be made at this point is more likely than not actually going to change the memory system of the child, especially if very young.
4. The therapist should seek, if possible, an order from the court that exempts the therapy record from the court procedure. In other words, the therapist needs to be able to offer the child a confidentiality that only has the usual exceptions of harm to self or others, as falling under the duty to report.	4. In any case where the therapist has become aligned with one side or the other in the course of the ongoing domestic relations dispute, that therapist should be automatically disqualified from any post-decree participation.

Table 6.2 Developmental Guideposts in Relation to Personal Safety

Age	Speech/Intellectual Level	Capacity to Provide for Own Safety
0–18 mos	Speech development will not support narrative reporting.	None. Cannot provide information re: experience.
18 mos–3 yrs	Can use simple sentences. Uses pronouns I and you; speech may be hard to understand.	Minimal to partial. Can answer Y/N questions. Can give limited info re: experience. Is very suggestible and may be misunderstood or misunderstand what is said.
3–6 yrs	Can talk in sentences. Speech is understandable. Understands some cause/effect sequences.	Significant but not excellent. Can reflect on experience and answer factually. Is still very suggestible and prone to yes set responding.
6–12 yrs	Verbal development and intellectual process moving toward adult levels.	Good to excellent. By age 9, is not more or less suggestible than adults.

youngster. Children who are extremely verbally precocious arrive at points of personal safety faster, and those who have severe cognitive limitations may never achieve that status. But with the range of low-average to above-average functioning, the approximate years are good benchmarks. Table 6.2 illustrates these developmental aspects.

Any therapist involved with children, either prior to the filing for a divorce or afterwards, needs to understand the importance of not becoming part of the divorcing process and not moving into some kind of nonvalid and legally compromised evaluator stance. If there is a concern about child abuse or neglect, therapists in the United States or Canada have a mandated report to make to an investigative authority. As was seen in the interviews of police officers, most investigators and probably most courts at this point understand that therapists cannot become arms of the law and do not secure the safety of children by ending the confidentiality of the therapeutic process. However, by providing support and enhancing the reality testing of children through modeling and reinforcing reality-based responding, therapists can assist children during a painful period of their lives while protecting both themselves and the process.

Reunification Therapy

This relatively new development is being ordered by domestic relations courts in cases of allegations that wind up either unsubstantiated or substantiated at a level demanding separation. In these instances, however, the children and parent have been separated for an extended period of time. It is also ordered in cases where older children have become enmeshed in the struggle and have taken a position themselves that is viewed as deriving from either alienation activity on the part of one parent or parenting lapses by the other parent. Reunification therapy may be ordered as part of the divorce decree, and sometimes the particular resource is specified. The procedure that is generally followed includes seeing all family members, separately if necessary, but more desirably together. All members of the family should be informed of the scope of the court's order and the expectations of the process. Reunification attempts best proceed by getting the family involved in designing the actual procedure by which reunification will be worked through. That procedure may involve an agreement on the part of the child to some initial brief contacts or public place contacts and ultimately a schedule whereby the child becomes more and more involved in an expected pattern of companionship time.

The goal of the reunification, although it is exactly what the title implies, does not have to be laid out in specific terms at the outset, although some court orders may do exactly that. (In some cases, intransigence on the part of a litigant requires a very specified timetable for completion of the process with the "teeth" of a potential contempt status either stated or implicit.) Where a less individually driven scenario exists—and not infrequently where the separation represents a failed dynamic between the child and parent rather than any deliberate sabotage by the other parent—an order does not need to include a potential negative outcome. In such cases, a more acceptable conclusion is likely to occur, with the family working in the therapy to clarify the goal and the progression that will lead to success. The result is a joint project in which all have some sense of ownership and much less potential to feel they are the targets of some imposed procedure.

At the point at which a final order was rendered in a divorce, McPherson was referred a family where the oldest child, a teen, had been refusing to visit based on some, to her, very negative interchanges with her father. When he slapped her for what was admittedly quite disrespectful verbalization on her part, she responded by refusing to go to weekend visits "until he apologizes." At the time, the divorce was in process. The other two younger children were expressing ambivalence about visiting, wanting her to be with them (while she adamantly refused). The father's position, based on his own upbringing, was that she deserved the response for being so out of line and he was not willing to apologize (in many ways, their refusals nicely illustrated the similarities of their respective personalities). The children were seen first, both as a group and individually; the mother was interviewed and indicated her support for getting the visitation re-established (she noted that it was beneficial to her to have some weekend time to herself and she expressed that it was good for the children to have time with their father). The father was seen; some time was spent discussing with him some of the changes that have occurred in the culture from when he was a boy and emphasizing his importance in the lives of the children, especially the teen. Some education was given about teenagers and the way they think and react. He agreed to a joint session with the children. Subsequently, two joint sessions were held that included the father, the mother, and the children (at all their requests). In the first, a plan was made for gradual resumption of visitation, starting with some public place events. At the second, the family reported progress and endorsed the continuation of the schedule they had designed. They cancelled the third session, indicating they felt things were going well. This family, although there was a schism created by the behavior of both child and adult, was essentially well functioning. The parents did not hate each other and genuinely wanted the situation to "work." The teen was a little uncomfortable with the role she was playing but could not lose face by admitting to same; the father wanted reunification but did not want to lose his sense of self-respect as to parental authority. Reunification works best where the combination of motives and goals are not so incompatible that combinations of education and gentle guidance cannot free the behavior of the participants.

Reunification therapy should be a confidential process, not unlike that of mediation, which is also a court-ordered intervention in cases of this sort. The therapist providing the service should be protected from any subsequent involvement in any court systems on the basis that this procedure is indeed an extension of psychotherapy and as such can only work if people are protected from exposure (obviously, with the usual exceptions for mandated reportage).

Mediation

Mediation is an intervention that is rather regularly being ordered by courts as a way not only to prevent litigation but also to intervene between parents who have continuing difficulties in their communications and may be postlitigation and post-decree. In equivocal abuse situations where there has been a finding that no abuse is supported, it is sometimes possible to manage a shared parenting order through a mandatory mediation process. Such a process requires that the parents meet, usually on a monthly basis for the first year, to review any difficulties they perceive in their ongoing communications and coparenting of their children and to resolve any unresolved issues. The usual procedures of mediation are involved in this process.

Although mediation has become an important part of contemporary family law courts, its history is quite ancient. Words for persons who were to function as mediators were found in ancient Greece (*Proxenetos, Einternuncius, Philantropos, Conciliator, Interpres, Internuncius, Interpolator, Interlocutor,* and even *Mediator*). These terms are found in both ancient Greece and in Roman law, particularly as codified by Justinian by the 6th century (Boulle, 2005; McCarthy, 2008; Roebuck, 2010; Roebuck & de Fumichon,

2004). Part of this ancient history connects the mediation function with the role that was seen as a function of village chieftains or special wisemen. Historians have noted many similarities to the specifics of how those ancient roles were defined and carried out (Roebuck, 2010; Roebuck & de Fumichon, 2004).

The defining characteristics of mediation as it is currently conducted across any number of dispute-driven areas, but specifically with respect to issues of child custody, include the following. The mediator must be a neutral and impartial individual whose job is to facilitate the parties toward the goal of resolution of the dispute.

Mediators do not themselves draft agreements nor do they give legal advice and, in fact, are expressly prohibited from doing so, including if they happen to be lawyers. Each party has his or her own attorney (unless *pro se*) upon whom the reliance for legal advice must be respected. Mediators, although they may at times serve therapeutic-like functions and particularly so when they are mental health professionals, nonetheless are different from family or couples counselors. There is much less emphasis on feelings and increasing insight than in the counseling process and much more on obtaining an agreement through rational discourse. There is little if any focus on the review of the past, which is frequently a part of the counseling process. In fact, many mediators, the current writers included, will specifically redirect couples in mediation from a discussion of that which cannot be changed, to that which currently exists and can be moderated if both parties can come to a concurrence. The mediation process is more structured than almost all counseling approaches, and that structure is articulated from the beginning.

The pivotal characteristic of mediation, which makes it a safe haven within which a potential for agreement is created, is its confidentiality status. Mediators may not be brought into court when mediation fails or even if it is successful. The notes and process and content of mediation may not be brought into court. However, as Boulle (2005) has indicated, confidentiality is not quite as complete as has sometimes been anticipated. Parties, of course, may reveal things that took place in the course of the mediation, although any attempts to bring those into the court process should be disallowed. The only exceptions to confidentiality are the legal constraints on professionals, notably those involved in the reportage of suspected child or elder abuse (but those reports are not tendered through the family court).

The downside of mediation is its reliance on the process of rationality that is comfortable and a part of the training of attorneys but often inconsistent with the thought patterns and dynamics of warring couples. Interestingly, those dynamics and resistance to rationally based approaches have also been found in couples where one or both were attorneys or highly trained mental health professionals, all of whom would have the intellectual background, and presumably the value system, that would incline them to use the process well. However, the personal and emotional foundation that defines both a marriage that is successful and one that fails can seriously disrupt in the most well trained the capacity to take the objective stance that the process needs for success. Another factor may involve gender differences. A study of outcomes of mediation versus litigation indicated general satisfaction of fathers with mediation over litigation but a sense of dissatisfaction of mothers. The authors hypothesized that these results may reflect some regional legal differences with mediating mothers in jurisdictions still favoring a tender years presumption winding up more likely to have "less" than would have been the case had they litigated. At the same time, negative emotional status declined after a year post resolution (Emery, Matthews, & Kitzmann, 1994). We would add that the acculturation of women and men is somewhat different and may favor men in terms of the capacity to use, and sometimes perhaps effectively manipulate, in the context of a mediation process.

Mediators have some very specific practice hazards. They are liable for damages that might occur if they in fact breach the contracts they have created as part of beginning the mediation process. If they can be shown to have abandoned their neutrality or violated the confidentiality standard with resulting damage to one or both parties, they can be subjected to malpractice suits or other legal actions.

As noted, mediation is often ordered or agreed to at an early stage of a custody dispute. Most mediators, however, will require that there be a moratorium on competitive filings during the course of the mediation process. Where the dispute is over custody, a filing by a party for sole custody usually results in the conclusion of the mediation with a report of no success. Where mediation occurs later in the life of the case in a hoped-for alternative way of case resolution, it is usual for motions to be withdrawn without prejudice. (Because refiling is a possibility, it may be that at least to a small degree that potential can hold the process mildly at hostage.)

Generally speaking, mediation has been considered not to be an appropriate process in cases where there is domestic violence. The situation of the insecure and unresolved allegation of abuse toward children is another case context in which this process, although having much to recommend it in terms of economy and potential for empowerment across the family system, may not be an appropriate vehicle. The problem in situations in which abuse may be occurring is the dynamic of power imbalance and the dynamic of needing to maintain an incorrect assertion versus maintaining a posture of innocence. These factors effectively interfere with the kind of communication that needs to develop for the mediation process to be successful.

Parent Coordinator Process[*]

A concept being more broadly applied relatively recently, but initiated in the 1990s, is that of parent coordination. It is an alternative dispute resolution (ADR) role, having some kinship with mediation, arbitration, and negotiation. However, there are some particular differences that characterize this role and some dimensions that have to be clearly understood. It was specifically developed to deal with high-conflict relitigating cases. The definition that was proposed in legislation before the Florida courts, and currently more or less generally accepted, was as follows:

> Parenting coordination is [the] process whereby an impartial third person, called a parenting coordinator, helps the parties to implement their parenting plan by facilitating the resolution of disputes between parents and/or legal guardians, providing education, making recommendations to the parties, and with prior approval of the parties and the court, making decisions within the scope of the court order of appointment.[†]

This proposed definition, which is essentially consistent with what is found throughout the literature and reflects usage patterns across the country, contains a number of provisions that are extremely important. First of all, parenting coordinators, or as they are called in some cases special masters, parenting referees, family court advisors, or even wisepersons, have a court-order-based function to assist in regard to situations with selected disputes. As the definition provides, such a process needs the "prior approval of the parties and the court" and must be limited to the scope of the order.

The objections or issues about the use of such an approach go importantly to an erosion of judicial authority. To respond to that, in general it is understood that the parent coordinator must not and does not have the authority to render any decisions that are beyond the scope of the existing decree, including but not limited to decisions about custody and visitation. These are specified areas that have been developed out of the court process. Rather, if there is a specific dispute that heretofore has led this particular subset of families to go back into court in inefficient ways, and which needs to

---

[*] The writers are indebted to Judge Mary J. Boyle of the Court of Appeals of Ohio, 8th Appellate District, for providing information from the Judicial College regarding the parent coordinator role.

[†] The Florida proposal for a specific enabling statute was passed by the legislature but vetoed by the governor in 2003. Ongoing work to establish such a provision in the Florida code continues, but to date, there has been no success due to multiple special interests and positions to which response is necessary.

be resolved for the interests of the child or children involved, a parent coordination process is recommended as a desirable alternative. Issues involved include such things as a child's involvement in some specific activity, a question of whether there can be some substitution of parenting time to facilitate a child's involvement in a family event on the other side, and the like.

An important issue, which has been raised and is part of the ongoing dispute about this role, is that of protecting children in cases of significant domestic violence. Parent coordinators properly are not appointed, or if appointed, do not continue to serve in cases where domestic violence has emerged or is ongoing. It is our opinion such matters belong with the various court systems that may be involved in a particular case and are best handled through the evidentiary procedures of those courts, including the domestic relations court, but also not infrequently the criminal courts. A more subtle issue involves how the law may work in different states. In some areas, there is a continuing jurisdiction of the domestic relations court over the management of the court's custody order. In other areas, jurisdiction is instigated by the filing of a motion. If the court's jurisdiction is inactive absent a motion, the ability to authorize a parenting coordinator to engage in decision making secondary to that court's order is probably compromised.

Finally, there are also some issues with respect to the vulnerability of practitioners. Parent coordinators may or may not have quasi-judicial immunity. One way to approach this aspect of functioning is to have that status conferred by the order and agreed to by the parents. In other words, what is envisioned as one way to meet some of the varieties of objections to this role is to specify the scope, specify the status of the parenting coordinator as to what kinds of disputes can be handled and what kinds cannot be approached, offer reasonable protection for the conscientious implementation of the tasks, and obtain agreement of the parties to utilize the process. As might be expected, there have been different opinions as to whether the court may order parenting coordination over the objection of either of the parties. The special master of California was regularly used in the face of a party's objection until *Ruisi v. Thieriot* (1997), which specified there must be both parties' agreement.

Specific guidelines and approaches to management of this role have been developed by the Association of Family and Conciliation Courts (AFCC) including the need for appropriate and high levels of background education and training, impartiality, nonservice when there is a conflict of interest, prohibition of dual roles including sequential, full clarification for participants of scope and confidentiality and approach and compensation, and a clear focus on safety factors. There are recommendations for extensive ongoing training. Not only is the role seen as one that is in and of itself complex and legally specified, but the population served is one that requires high levels of expertise and personal management. The parent coordinator function may well be used to serve many of the cases that are referenced in this volume; however, those that would reach the highest level of conflict may often not respond to any ADR process.

Parental Alienation Syndrome

On October 1, 2010, an Associated Press release described the ongoing *DSM–V* review process being conducted by the American Psychiatric Association as having a "Hot potato on its hands…whether to include parental alienation." The article goes on to indicate some quite political rather than scientific issues associated with this theory or concept. Specifically, there are those who take the position that parental alienation is the tool of people, notably fathers who are abusers of mothers and children, to evade responsibility or maintain continuing abuse. This faction further takes the position that mental health and legal professionals perpetuate the use of this concept because it is financially remunerative to do so, citing the use of costly evaluations, costly expert testimony, and then costly interventions that become attached to these cases as so-called remedies for the alleged condition. The other side, of course, takes the position that there is substantial evidence for the existence of this described phenomenon and that there is a great deal of damage that is done by not intervening in the ongoing effectiveness of the parental alienation operations, extending to multiple generations. It is further cited that evidence for this kind of situation has been found across many national settings.

These concerns have been addressed and discussed in some detail in *The International Handbook of Parental Alienation Syndrome* (Gardner, Sauber, & Lorandos, 2006). In this volume, a panel of 31 well-regarded clinicians, researchers, and legal professionals has provided perspectives on the existence of the syndrome, its implications, and the legal complications that exist in consequence of its identification. As might be expected, those perspectives vary in terms of the degree of confidence involved. There are some characterizations of how courts and the legal system work, which appear to us to be somewhat weak. For example, in one chapter it is recommended that the guardian *ad litem* can be appointed to change custody as part of overseeing a conflict involving alienation. Most courts, in fact, would be extremely reluctant to endow a guardian *ad litem* with such a judicial responsibility. The closest to that kind of power might be found in the appointment of a parent coordinator or special master (another term used in some courts, for example, California) who would have the specific duty of resolving an immediate conflict around specific delineated areas with a decision that of course could be subsequently appealed in the court system. As already indicated, a decision of law reflecting a custody change, for which there is substantial legal precedent and process, is not likely to be handed over by the court. Furthermore, a guardian, whose job is to develop information and become a witness of the court about those things that affect the best interest of the child, could not undertake even the limited role of parent coordinator.

What can be said about the parental alienation concept is that children do become alienated from a parent and the reasons for that occurrence are varied and contextual. One of the concerns by those who support the existence of a parental alienation syndrome is that by simply speaking of parental alienation, the proper diagnosis and therefore the proper interventions cannot occur. Gardner suggested it was akin to diagnosing cancer as opposed to colon cancer, with the latter specifying the intervention, and the former being essentially global and unhelpful (Gardner, 2006, p. 7).

Although such a concern is appropriate in that prior to doing any kind of treatment it is necessary to specify the known dimensions of the problem, it is still also appropriate to recognize that the reason for a child to be substantially alienated from a parent may not lie in the actions and the operations of the opposite parent. Other causes include the actions of the parent from whom the child is alienated, up to and including actual abuse sequences; the emergence of the child's own decision to perhaps inappropriately emancipate himself from the ongoing conflict by taking sides; or a desire for avoidance of a parent based on some other subjectively desirable characteristics (referencing parenting style, religious matters, and other routines, and especially likely to occur when a child is in the throes of adolescent rebellion).

However, all of that said, parental alienation as described by Gardner (and in spite of some of the criticisms that have been made of him, many of which are based on a misreading of his work) does exist in clinical case reports, case law reports, and also in several studies at this point. The existence of certain dynamically driven family configurations in high-conflict domestic relations cases does involve the systematic alienation of a child against a parent by the other parent. In considering the Gardner concept, it is helpful to review the specific diagnostic criteria that have been articulated. Gardner (2006) admitted that the diagnosis did not meet all the *Daubert* criteria; however, he argued that many *DSM* diagnoses were similarly situated from a scientific and legal perspective. He proceeded to define the diagnosis by reference to a description of behaviors ranked as to level (mild, moderate, and severe), based on the symptoms of the child rather than descriptors of parental behavior. He then went on to characterize three levels of parent behavior on the basis of which he felt court actions could be predicated. Some studies have been made using this as the model for identification of the syndrome. The studies are, for the most part, limited in scope and in some cases have some circularity involved (see, for example, Burrill, 2006).

There have been several studies with more adequate samples, such as the Kopetski, Rand, and Rand (2006) report, which interestingly enough documented a cross-pattern in which cases identified as manifesting the parental alienation syndrome included the development of sexual abuse allegations by the mothers in 79% of the identified group and neglect allegations in 76% of those situations where the fathers raised the allegations. This study, however, also points out another important issue, that parental alienation syndrome does not necessarily imply the development of allegations, equivocal or false, but apparently does contain a high liability for same. That point also has been to some degree obscured by those who are opposed to the diagnosis on the basis that it provides an "out" for abusers. The other substance often cited by such persons goes to the notion that children do not lie, a very old scientifically speaking and now completely discredited notion. At the same time, it is important to note that the majority of known sexual offenders are male and the actual incidence in the population of false allegations of sexual abuse is low.

Another important position reflected in the referenced *Handbook* included that at the worst levels of this dynamic, intervention will fail unless it involves action by the court to separate the child or children from the alienating parent. We would hold that in order to move to that drastic an intervention, the court has to be substantially impressed with the presence of this set of operations and equally, in the case of allegations, substantially impressed that the allegations are false. Unfortunately for the court and families and children, any equivocal aspects and "muddy" findings presented to the court raise the essential dilemma of the probability of error on both sides, a situation that can put the court in a significantly disadvantaged position when it comes to designing an appropriate outcome. Equally unfortunately, in the studies that have been done of interventions, it is a consistent finding that in severe cases, unless there is separation of the children from the alienator, the outcome is the loss of a parent and not infrequently the loss of subsequent generational contact between a parent, grandparent, and his or her grandchildren.

Consistent with the above, Lowenstein (2005), writing from a British perspective and speaking to high-conflict cases, provided some guidelines for ADR that would apply to parent coordinator work and reunification therapy in the context of the parent alienation dynamic. Lowenstein recommends an emphasis on a kind of empathy training in which each party is encouraged to understand the situation of the other. Furthermore, work with the child that needs to precede actual reconciliation with the other parent appeals to the child's sense of conscience and ability to understand how negative actions toward the other parent by the child cause emotional pain to the parent. There is also an emphasis on the unique quality of the parent–child dyad with most parents willing to do more for a child than any other people will do. The recommendations then go on to emphasize the importance of the custodial parent actively supporting the relationship with the other parent, but he ultimately arrives at a position of endorsing removal of the child from the custodial parent if ongoing interference and negativity to the other parent is not relinquished by that individual.

Summary

As can be seen in a review of the above materials, a number of new and not so new approaches to dealing with the extremes that these kinds of cases present in terms of family dysfunction exist for the court. The success of these kinds of interventions is variable and case dependent. Certain kinds of psychopathology, for example, often make mediation and reunification therapy particularly unlikely to be successful. Even the mediation process as it is envisioned and carried out by mental health trained mediators is still quintessentially a logical and rational dispute resolution model. As such, it is not uncommon where there is severe emotional pathology for one of the parties to have difficulty with the expectations of objectivity, evidence-based functioning, and negotiation with compliance to agreements, which are implicit in the process. Many times the process does not allow for some of the very real underlying conflicted and emotionally based responses that are more typical for the female but not absent in the male.˙

In the course of psychotherapy, the therapist expects to deal with inconsistencies, emotional reactivity, and the repetition of old scripts displaced onto new and not appropriate situations. Therapy proceeds by a combination of enhanced insight into such category errors and enhanced capacity to use alternative ways of thinking and self-management, as well as communication patterns. Court-related expectations are much more outcome based and expect the achievement of certain goals. Legal process is important but more or less scripted and overtly rule based. In human relationships, the process involves more intuitive, often circuitous, and not infrequently obscurely symbolic interactions by which goal achievement is reached. Wedding aspects of all of the available strategies and methods to reduce the tensions, change historic and counterproductive communication strategies, and gain acceptance of goals that are compromise positions is a difficult order.

˙ It is our experience that the most common pattern is that of the female having more difficulty remaining in the mode of linear logic and some objectivity than is true for the male. To some degree, there is social conditioning at work and there are also some biological aspects. However, inability to negotiate from strength and use of positive self-assertion over more emotionally based responding has certainly been found on both sides of the gender gap. Mental health experience and training can sometimes assist a mediator in these situations by increasing sensitivity to the more unconscious or preconscious mechanisms and dynamics that may get in the way of a successful interactive process.

Mental Health Issues

7

We have already seen that equivocal abuse frequently features a mother and sometimes a generational presentation with the maternal grandmother also playing a part. The breakdown of the marriage and its stressors become the cauldron within which incipient psychopathology can come to control perceiving, thinking, feeling, and the actions that follow. It is our contention that category mistakes and false belief systems can occur without necessarily involving underlying personal pathology. The studies of cults and the distortions observed in hostages make it clear that normal range functioning can still be disrupted by unique constellations of environmental factors (Dawson, 2003; De Fabrique, Van Hasselt, Vecchi, & Romano, 2007; Namnyak, Tufton, Szedely, Worboys, & Sampson, 2008; Robbins, 2002; Ungerleider & Wellisch, 1979). However, the cases that are most difficult to resolve often involve a combination of malevolent factors in both the external world and in the individual. Cases of this sort could perhaps be denoted as "perfect storm" situations.

Borderline Personality Disorder

In this section, the concept of borderline personality disorder (BPD) is described and the complications associated with assessing and treating individuals with this disorder in alleged abuse cases are considered. BPD is a problem commonly seen in women and its occurrence in men is relatively rare. Most men with these types of personality dynamics, because of their behavioral manifestations, become categorized in the sociopathic spectrum diagnostically.

Although Knight (1953) is often credited with being the first to coin the term "borderline" to describe this clinical phenomenon, the concept of borderline functioning was mentioned in 1942 by Herman Rorschach (the developer of the Rorschach Inkblot Test) who noticed that there were individuals who appeared to function adequately in their daily lives but when faced with the unstructured Rorschach stimulus cards produced rather decompensated responses. This observation was parallel to clinical reports of patients who presented for psychoanalysis presumably because they had higher levels of ego integrity and functioning but, due to the lack of structure in psychoanalysis, were unable to tolerate this procedure and actually regressed into psychotic states. This decompensation was most often manifested in the negative or psychotic transferences (the relationship that develops between the patient and the therapist in psychoanalysis comes to reflect patterns from the patient's history; Gunderson, 1984).

Psychoanalytic literature organized these patterns into the two categories of psychotic and neurotic. The psychotic group included those who had lost contact with reality and presented with hallucinations and delusional belief systems. The neurotics were thought to have higher levels of functioning (ego integrity) but had dysfunctional personality styles that caused significant adjustment problems in their lives. These latter patients relied on psychological defenses that enabled them to reduce their anxiety level, but in the long run these temporary psychological measures did not facilitate the resolution of their conflicts (Gunderson & Singer, 1975; Kernberg, 1979; Kohut & Wolf, 1978).

According to the psychoanalytic model, the patient suffering from BPD was believed to vacillate between neurotic and psychotic states. Therefore, the psychotic aspects of the disorder often interfered with the person's ability to perceive situations accurately and deal with the realities of life, and the neurotic component was responsible for causing the high levels of anxiety that characterized interpersonal and intrapsychic situations. Thus, the term borderline was used to imply that the individual afflicted with this problem was on the border of psychosis and neurosis (Gunderson, 1984).

As pervasive as this problem seemed to be in clinical settings and in spite of its prominence in the psychoanalytic literature, it was not until 1980 that BPD was formally accepted as an Axis II diagnosis (personality disorder) in the diagnostic nomenclature by the American Psychiatric Association (1980). For our purposes, it is instructive to begin with the basic definition of this disorder, as found in the *Diagnostic and Statistical Manual of Mental Disorders–IV (DSM–IV–TR)* (American Psychiatric Association, 2000). In that description, the primary characteristics include references to the long-standing nature of the maladjustment, its relational characteristics, and features of impulsivity, abandonment fears, self-concept instabilities, emotional lability, anger and rage-related problems, and the potential for episodes of psychosis. Further refinements may be found when the final version of *DSM–V* is published.

One of the main difficulties with individuals with BPD is their strong tendency to cognitively distort. Distortion can be manifested in the way they perceive their own feelings and thoughts or in the way they interpret the intentions of others in their interactions with them. Distortions are often the source of a great deal of frustration and alienation for persons with BPD. They feel misunderstood and unloved by others and often accuse others of being dishonest because they have misread their intentions or statements. Those who are in relationships with them come to view BPD individuals as untrustworthy and untruthful. The reason many of these individuals can become incredulous when confronted with these inconsistencies is because the distortions are often unconscious. From their perspective, they are reflecting accurately the world as they have experienced it.

BPD is considered to be one of the most difficult of the psychological problems to treat. The therapeutic hurdles are partially related to the chronic nature of the condition and the fact that, like other personality disorders, it is woven into the fabric of the person's psychological functioning and reflects long-standing complex internalized dynamics. The early attachment problems that are part of the associated features of this disorder in some ways become permanent features of the individual's personality. In addition, it is important to note that there is a large body of literature on comorbid conditions associated with BPD. The range includes depressive disorder, anxiety disorder, and a bipolar disorder. Paranoid thinking and interacting in hostile and unstable ways with others are among common clinical presentations. Concomitant problems of substance abuse and dependency are not uncommon. A more recent conceptualization refers to it in post-tramautic stress disorder (PTSD) terms for both diagnostic and treatment purposes (Quadrio, 2005). The addition of substance abuse problems and acting out of anger often add another layer of complexity to understanding BPD. The clinician is caught in the dilemma of assessing if the adjustment difficulties of the individual are related in a primary way to the BPD or are the negative consequences of substance abuse and addiction-related behaviors.

The complexity and intensity of the problems in patients with BPD makes them the source of a great deal of apprehension and resistance for clinicians. During graduate education in psychology, new clinicians are encouraged either to totally avoid working with patients with BPD or to have no more than one or two at a time in their caseload in order to avoid burnout. Mature clinicians also are advised to have a limited number of patients with this type of personality disorder and to seek peer supervision while treating them. These clinical experiences have resulted in the development of an overreaction toward individuals with this diagnosis, and the label itself has become rather pejorative in nature. (For example, there is a tendency to dismiss individuals who are demanding and hard to treat as being "borderline.") There is a reluctance to allocate resources for treatment of genuine BPD patients because of the traditionally held view that even with the utilization of significant efforts, there is little or no improvement in their level of functioning.

The psychoanalytic literature is replete with issues of causality that are related to early childhood development and complications that stem from interruption of bonding between the child and primary caregiver which disrupt the adequate attachment in the mother–child dyad. The seminal works of Gunderson and Singer (1975) and Masterson and Rinsley (1975) are illustrative. Gunderson and Singer (1975) identified six criteria that later on became the standard for defining BPD.

1. The presence of intense affect, generally hostile or depressive
2. Extensive history of impulse control problems
3. Adaptive socialization
4. Brief psychotic experiences manifested in loss of touch with reality and paranoid ideation
5. Bizarre and decompensated responses on the Rorschach Inkblot Test
6. Intense relationships that vacillate between superficiality and dependency

These theories generally conceptualize BPD as an affective state of depression related to a sense of abandonment which has its roots in the lack of emotional or physical availability of the maternal figure. Another aspect of causality is tied to the early experience of abuse and the way the child develops a belief system that the world is a dangerous place and should not be trusted. More current research has supported the frequent association of childhood abuse with an adult BPD diagnosis, consistent with Quadrio's (2005) PTSD conceptualization. In fact, there are those who argue that BPD in adulthood is directly and fairly invariably related to early experience of trauma, mostly caused by abuse at the hand of the child's caregivers. The early traumatic experiences are believed to disrupt different aspects of personality development that are responsible for affective and cognitive regulation and ability to cope. These developmental deficits in turn affect the ability to manage impulses and frustration tolerance in adolescence and adulthood. The ubiquitous anger that is often associated with the diagnosis of BPD develops from difficulties that are created by these destructive dynamics (Herman, Perry, & van der Kolk, 1989).

More recent theories come from the biopsychosocial model of causation. Linehan (1993a) initiated this approach which provides a comprehensive explanation of the development of the BPD. In Linehan's view, BPD is developed as a result of the interaction between an emotionally vulnerable child and an invalidating environment. Although the biological aspects that render a child emotionally vulnerable are not clearly defined, they could be related to a biochemical deficiency, such as neurotransmitter imbalance in the child's brain. Problems at this level could represent either inherited or congenital factors. Linehan defined emotional vulnerability as being highly sensitive to emotional situations, having strong and intense reactions to these situations, and having difficulty returning to a regulated baseline once the situation has passed. This inability to return to a baseline as quickly as others tends to set up the individual, who is at a constant state of high arousal, for overreaction to the next emotional stimulus. There is thus the implication that those with BPD have difficulty with modulation of emotions, preventing them from being able to inhibit inappropriate responses to emotional stimuli. Their actions then are often mood-dependent and do not seem to benefit from sufficient levels of cognitive input. They are seen as having significant deficiency in being able to calm themselves down and lower the level of physiological response to emotional situations. This inability to refocus and deal with emotionally toned situations further contributes to the negative behaviors often seen in individuals with BPD.

When a child interacts with the environment in a difficult and emotionally reactive manner, there is a greater chance that those who take care of the child may in turn react in an invalidating manner. Linehan (1993a) has suggested that the invalidating environment of the child could have been otherwise supportive if it were not for the emotional sensitivity and the overreaction of the youngster, which sends a message of failure to the caregiver who may then react to control or otherwise establish authority and refute the felt inadequacy. The invalidating environment is one that is erratic and often inappropriate to the response of the internal experiences of the child. The caregiver response to the child also comes to involve extremes, which can be manifested in overreacting or underreacting. When the vulnerable child in an invalidating environment expresses a feeling, thought, or behavior and does not receive support and validation, the frustrations that build up over time become the causal factors for many of the behavioral problems that are subsequently seen in individuals' BPD.

Another aspect of the invalidating environment is the great emphasis it puts on controlling negative emotional experiences and the behaviors associated with them. Negative feelings and their behavioral manifestations are described in negative terms that further erode the child's self-esteem and increase the level of frustration. For example, lack of motivation and energy, which are symptoms of depression, are characterized as laziness and having a bad attitude. This consistent discrepancy between a child's experiences and the environment creates a pattern of self-invalidation that results in questioning one's judgment and decision making.

Invalidating environments also significantly restrict the demands of the child and often label the child's needs in negative terms. The child is also discriminated against based on factors that he or she is unable to change. Use of punishment plays a major role in the development of BPD. In addition to its invalidating aspects of the abuse, it also causes the child to develop problems with trust and relating to others. This negative and sometimes paranoid view of the world lays the foundation for future relationship problems and difficulties with intimacy. The most devastating aspect of an invalidating environment, over the long run, is the way in which it creates emotional dysregulation by not allowing the child to develop the internal mechanisms that enable labeling of experiences and modulation of emotional expressions. The child will also have difficulty in trusting his or her own emotional responses as being valid and learning to tolerate stressful situations effectively. This inability to read environmental cues and one's own social stimulus value accurately results in inappropriate goal setting and the creation of difficulties with repeated experiences of failure that further erode self-esteem and lead to deeper self-invalidation. In effect, a cycle is created that intends toward more and more negative internal and external experience.

It is important to note that one of the most important aspects of parenting a child is to set appropriate limits and provide feedback to the child when the behaviors displayed are not effective and appropriate. In a child who does not suffer from the emotional vulnerability as described above, these interventions often result in positive outcomes and increasing ability to modulate affect and behavior appropriately. However, the same level of intervention may be perceived as invalidation in a child who is emotionally vulnerable. If the negative cycle becomes firmly established, what was criticism can escalate to become abuse.

Most theories on the development of BPD have considered emotional, physical, and sexual abuse as strong causal elements. Childhood sexual abuse has been reported in 50–75% of individuals with the diagnosis of BPD. This high prevalence of a sexually abusive background in BPD is well documented; however, it is not clear if the experience of sexual abuse is what contributes to the development of BPD or if it is that the common developmental circumstances found in BPD and sexual abuse account for the co-occurrence. Therefore, according to Linehan (1993a), this interaction between an emotionally vulnerable child and an invalidating environment is believed to result in "disorder of dysregulation" in affect, cognition, behavior, self, and interpersonal relationships.

Borderline Personality Disorder and Child Abuse

Two dynamics of BPD individuals play destructive roles in intimate relationships. One is the tendency to vacillate between idealization and devaluation of the object of affection, which can be very confusing to the person at the receiving end of this style. This dynamic also erodes the sense of trust that is required in the development of long-term security that makes relationships stable. The other aspect of BPD that is damaging to interpersonal relationships is the intense need for closeness that is followed by a sense of becoming overwhelmed when the person feels that the partner is too close. These two ways of relating by the BPD individual constantly put the integrity and stability of interpersonal relationships at risk.

Substance abuse that may initially be an attempt to self-medicate unwanted feelings can quickly become an additional problem that can further erode self-esteem and self-image and threaten the security of interpersonal bonds. Episodic binge drinking or drug use is frequently seen in individuals with BPD, and other coexisting mental health and social problems complicate accepting the abstinence required for recovery from addiction. These patterns of relating to others and problems with substance abuse and addiction create a great deal of difficulty in both interpersonal and parent–child relationships.

Newman and Stevenson (2005) provided a cohesive explanation of how becoming a parent affects the psychological functioning of mothers with BPD. They described the transition to parenthood as traumatic. The pregnancy itself could be the result of sexual acts during episodes of substance abuse and impulsivity. The BPD mother may already be in a highly chaotic relationship and her motivations to have a child may be conflicted. On the one hand she may want a child to care for or may want a child to care for her. In some cases there is a compulsion to re-enact or rework early traumatic experiences related to attachment trauma. Because of their own childhood difficulties and their unstable relationship with their parents, mothers with BPD tend to have problems with setting boundaries and behaving in balanced ways in areas of limit setting and responding to the child's needs and emotional states. When approaching parenting children in this compromised way of functioning, the interaction between the child and the mother can be rather frustrating for both of them. Out of this frustration, a sense of alienation can develop on the mother's part, and she comes to question her ability to be an effective parent. In an attempt to respond to these tensions that she senses in the child and her own frustrations, as well as the need to deny the view of herself as a "bad mother," she can become at high risk for engaging in abusive behaviors toward the child. In this way, the cycle of abuse and invalidation may continue on a generational basis fed by both genetic and environmental sources.

Mothers with BPD often have limited social resources as well. They tend to have difficulty accessing mental health treatment because of the demands of parenthood and lack of support from their family. They have often burned a lot of bridges over the years and do not have a reliable source of comfort around them. There are also occasions when those who are close to these mothers witness their interactions with their children while they are in an emotionally unstable state. As a result, there is a higher potential that others may make reports to social services agencies. Usually this kind of report results in a visit and an investigation by the county children's services social worker. The fact that someone is questioning the parenting capabilities of this insecure mother is likely to make her anxious and angry. In her mind, the mother considers herself to be caring and loving toward her child. However, under the emotional pressure of the situation, and with her general difficulty dealing with emotional arousal, she may come across as angry and disorganized to the person who is conducting the investigation. The social service person is then exposed to an angry and agitated mother who may appear to be at risk for decompensation. Based on the extent of the disorganization and the impression that the social worker may have, there are a range of outcomes that may ensue.

The child services protection agency may file abuse and neglect charges and remove the child from the mother's care and place him or her with either a family member (kinship placement) or a foster family until the investigation is completed and a reunification plan is developed for the family. These plans usually include psychological or psychiatric interventions for the family and may involve individual therapy, medication management, parent training groups, substance abuse screening and random drug testing, and possible treatment. In some cases, if there are questions of safety, visitation between the mother and the child may be limited and even supervised. Given the fact that the woman who suffers from BPD in this situation feels hurt and very angry because her position as "good enough mother" is being attacked, significant resistance to whatever program is established can occur. Furthermore, the mother may either internalize the negative feedback and become depressed and despondent or externalize it and come to feel very angry and outraged at those who have accepted these accusations.

Usually social service agencies refer these individuals for psychological evaluations and treatment. The outcomes of these procedures are often poor because they are experienced as overwhelming to a mother who is already angry and hurt by the accusations (and actively defending against them in her own mind). These mothers tend to decompensate and their functioning becomes even less effective in dealing with the stressors of their lives. There are often conflicts that develop at a personal level with the social workers, and there is an intense attempt to split between those in the system who are perceived as "good" and on her side and those who are perceived as being "bad" and against her.

Mental health professionals who are asked to treat these individuals tend to "get sucked in" by these mothers and buy into their side of the story. In an attempt to help and advocate for their patients they become the proxy fighters for their cause. They occasionally get roped into writing letters and come to court to testify in the custody hearing against the assertions of the social service agencies. These situations become more complicated as the accused mother, who now has an ally, tends to become less cooperative with the case plan recommendations because she feels that they were developed based on faulty assumptions. This brings further restrictions from the social service agencies, and the cycle of discord continues.

The strong tendency toward distortion changes the mother's view of the situation, and as time goes on she is likely to become more frustrated by the perception of injustices that have negatively affected her life and her relationships with her child(ren). As her interactions with the social service agency staff become more hostile, more negative attitudes are created toward her and a tendency toward less cooperation with her. As this pattern moves into an enhanced adversarial mode, the result is a lower chance of resolving the situation in a timely and appropriate manner. In effect, the interaction of mother and agency is now replaying the negative dynamics that have been characteristic of her relational history.

Mothers with BPD tend to engage in a dichotomous thought process and see any criticism of their parenting skills as being called a "bad mother." Therefore, instead of taking responsibility for what they have done ineffectively and perhaps inappropriately, they become highly defensive and resist any feedback offered to them that could help address their adjustment difficulties as parents. Even when they attend required parenting classes and training programs that could help them deal with their difficulties, they are highly resistant to change and perceive the ideas presented to them as being good for other parents but not applicable to them. Therefore, they do not integrate new strategies into their repertoire. For example, on one occasion when a mother who was involved with children's services in a rural county was mandated to attend specific parenting classes, she talked about how the material being taught in the groups was appropriate for mothers who had difficulty with managing their children but did not have any relevance to her life and situation because her children behaved well. She explained the children were scared of her and therefore minded. She was angry about having to attend these classes. Perhaps not surprisingly, the social worker assigned to the case had documented on several occasions that this client, when she visited her children, was not applying the skills that were taught in the group.

It is important to note that these types of distortions often are not conscious ways of avoiding responsibility or in effect lying. Rather, the inaccuracies occur because there are unconscious mechanisms that are attempts to prevent the individual from becoming overwhelmed by facing the realities of their lives. In another case, a 6-year-old girl who had been removed from her mother's home because of documented abuse, during a therapeutic visit was practicing her assertiveness skills. The young girl was asked about the activities that the mother and the daughter enjoyed together and she recalled going to the park and watching movies together. When she was asked about the type of activities she wanted to avoid, she talked about her mother hitting her with a belt when she misbehaved and asked her mother if she would stop this practice. The mother, who had a diagnosis of BPD, became very upset and called the little girl a liar and accused her of wanting to stay at the foster home instead of coming home. When the daughter tearfully protested and once again asked her mother to stop hitting her with a belt when she came to live with her, the mother incredulously indicated that she had never hit her daughter with a belt and the item that she used to punish the little girl was a "leather strap."

Another aspect of BPD that creates difficulties for mothers in cases where there is an allegation of abuse is the paranoid ideation. In cases where there are allegations of abuse and neglect, there is often plenty of fear and anxiety around the removal of children from the home and possible loss of custody. Any investigation in this type of situation is likely to be met by a great deal of resistance and apprehension on the part of the accused parent. BPD mothers are generally more vulnerable to becoming highly suspicious and they struggle with lack of trust, believing that when others have the opportunity to hurt them they will. As a result, when there are investigations of abuse or neglect, the mother suffering from BPD is likely to be hypersensitive and suspicious of the intentions of the social service agencies and the mental health professionals assigned to her case. When there is a high degree of guardedness and resistance to co-operation, most investigators become even more aggressive in their approach and look deeper and further into the situation. This dynamic is fertile ground for paranoid ideation, with clients at times even becoming aggressive toward the authorities who are investigating the situation.

Paranoid ideation is often accompanied by a tendency toward projection. Projection is an unconscious psychological operation that results in the attribution of one's own thoughts, feelings, and motives to others. The BPD person becomes accusatory toward others without bases for allegations in reality. For example, a mother who has been actively trying to keep a child from forming a positive relationship with his or her father accuses the father of undermining the child's relationship with the mother just because he bought her some school supplies or did some other positive thing for the child during one of his visits. In this situation, the mother projects her own desire to alienate the child from the father onto that parent and then misinterprets his actions in ways that are consistent with her beliefs. Projections are difficult to address because the BPD mother who makes the accusation is convinced of the negative motivation of the other person, and any denial or attempts to show her otherwise would further calcify her position and make her more defensive.

Afsarifard provided the following example. The situation involved a guardian *ad litem* (GAL) who was trying to advocate for the interests of a child in a heavily contested custody matter. The mother suffering from BPD was accusing her ex-husband of reneging on the shared parenting plan that they had drawn up during their divorce. When the GAL reviewed the material provided to him and interviewed the child, it was apparent that the mother was actually the one who was interfering with the father's visitation time and was providing excuses as to why the child could not visit with her father. When she was confronted about her behaviors that interfered with the father's visitation time, the mother became extremely angry and petitioned the court for the removal of the GAL for not being objective about the situation. When her petition was denied and she was advised by her attorney to try to work with the GAL on developing a communication protocol and for her to look into her own issues, she became very angry with her attorney. Two years later, when Afsarifard was asked by the court to re-evaluate this family, the mother had a different attorney, but the GAL was the same person. During one of the subsequent interviews with the mother, she pointed out that she had changed attorneys because she believed that he was "in cahoots with the GAL."

The difficulties in modulating emotions appropriately and being unable to utilize cognitive functions and abilities to manage the conflicts and life stressors of an individual with BPD become major impediments to recovery in treatment and are detrimental to efforts to move cases forward in the legal arena in a positive direction.

Recommendations

It is important to note that the term "borderline" is often overused and erroneously generalized to women who hold their ground and do not easily give in to the pressures that are applied to move a case along in the court or social service agency. Also, BPD, as does any other disorder, has degrees of severity and not all individuals afflicted by it have all the clinical presentations that are described by the diagnosis. Finally, just because a woman has been diagnosed with BPD in the past or during the course of a forensic or clinical evaluation does not mean that all her perceptions are inaccurate and that she is the one who is causing the problems in a given case. Their hypersensitivity may predispose them to an exaggerated response; however, exaggeration does not mean that they are lying or that the entire situation is distorted all the time. In fact, they are and have been in a usually rather dysfunctional interactive situation with their spouses, who contribute their own negative inputs.

Case Management

Certain principles can be followed that may maximize chances of success in dealing with these cases.

Comprehensive Psychological Evaluation
A comprehensive and competent evaluation is required to gain a useful diagnostic insight in any case. In evaluating a person with BPD, as with any other assessment situation, context is extremely important. For example, if a mother with BPD is having an enraged reaction to a situation where her child is being inappropriately removed from her custody, or she so perceives it, it does not mean that she is "being a borderline" but that she is reacting to her sense of loss and anger at a system that she feels has treated her unjustly, and she is coping with the loss of a child or children, an event that would promote

a severe reaction in any parent. Psychological testing including not only the MMPI-2 but also a Rorschach is frequently helpful in assessing a variety of relevant personality variables; however, in the context of custody evaluations, the same procedures should be applied to both parties. Actually, even where the behavior has led to a primary concern about the functioning of one party, the other party will be found to have significant individual problems, either reflecting traits pre-existing to mate selection or those developed subsequently in response to the ongoing interactions of the couple. A complete assessment model allows an understanding of both the individual and dyadic aspects. The use of the MCMI-III is sometimes included in these cases, but there are substantial problems around application of that test to a forensic population.

Experienced Treating Clinicians

Once a diagnosis has been established and the court or the case management group identifies the need for treatment, it is important that the required services are provided by competent clinicians and in a comprehensive manner. In general, insight-oriented and psychodynamic therapies that focus solely on validation and identification of causation are not effective in treatment of BPD individuals. Research shows that the best treatment outcomes for BPD come from therapeutic approaches that utilize a combination of acceptance (validation and support) and change strategies (skills that are required to handle problems). Skilled clinicians know that in order to be able to work effectively with individuals who struggle with BPD, they need to be firm but supportive, set and respect limits, and teach respect for these boundaries to their patients. Rules need to be clearly explained and leave little room for interpretation. Lack of clarity often results in patients making inferences regarding situations and thus creating more confusion and conflict.

Learning basic dialectical behavioral therapy (DBT; Linehan, 1993b) skills can assist individuals with BPD to be more mindful and be able to perceive situations accurately. Distress tolerance skills will provide alternative ways of managing difficult situations without major incident. Ability to regulate emotions more adaptively can result in fewer outbursts. In turn, the potential to damage their relationships with significant individuals in their lives is reduced. Finally, interpersonal effectiveness strategies can offer them tools for communicating their feelings and thoughts in order to deal with social situations appropriately.

For example, these skills can offer a mother who is going to be temporarily away from her children, because they are going on an extended visit or vacation with their father, the ability to deal with her sense of emptiness and loneliness, talk about what she wants and expects appropriately with her ex-spouse so that he is more cooperative with her demands, and be able to manage her anxiety in the moment utilizing mindfulness skills.

Parenting Coordinators With BPD Knowledge

One of the most common problems in treating patients with BPD is "getting sucked in" by their stories and distorted view of the world. Therapists who get involved in implementation of shared parenting orders or who are appointed by courts to be parenting co-ordinators need to be vigilant to keep a balance between being skeptical of what they are hearing so as to act in a fair and open-minded manner while still providing appropriate support and reinforcement. There are occasions when, based on recommendations from a custody evaluation or agreement between the parties, it is determined that the person with BPD needs to enter individual therapy.

Provision of Psychological Reports to Intervenors

It is very important that whenever possible the court and the parties involved provide the therapist with the report and the recommendations in order for the therapist to have an understanding of the issues that need to be considered in therapy. It is not unusual for a patient with BPD to present for treatment and focus the course of her work on matters that are not related to the custody and abuse investigation or determination at hand; therefore, the result may be little progress in the areas that were intended to be addressed.

CASE EXAMPLE

Pursuant to a court order, a custody evaluation was completed on a family that included parents and three minor children. Parents were in their mid-40s and had been divorced for over four years. There were allegations of abuse against the mother, who presented as being highly angry and suspicious of everyone involved. She had hired her third attorney for the present case and was having difficulties managing her feelings, even during court proceedings. She was highly volatile and was uncontrolled in the court, making statements and comments regarding the expert's testimony. For example, after the third time she shouted out, "He is lying," the magistrate was clearly annoyed. Testimony by the expert as well as that of other individuals indicated inadequacy of her parenting skills. The psychologist also noted the mother's difficulties responding to the feelings of people close to her, resulting in significant damage to several relationships in her life. She had created such tension that the children's pediatrician and school counselor had requested that she not bring the children to them and that any interaction with these professionals would require an intermediary.

At the conclusion of the case, the mother's time with the children was significantly curtailed and she was instructed to get involved in psychological and psychiatric care. The report from the custody evaluation was clear in indicating a diagnosis of BPD and specifying the need for her to receive individual psychotherapy to help her with reality orientation, substance abuse issues, and emotional regulation. A major source of frustration stemmed from trying to be a single mother raising three young children. There were allegations that she had behaved in abusive ways toward the children on different occasions. However, none of the allegations was formally substantiated. A year later, when similar allegations resurfaced and the children's father reopened the case, records were obtained from the therapist who was working with this woman. Review of the treatment plan and therapy notes revealed that none of the issues that were outlined in the custody evaluation was addressed in therapy. Instead the focus of her therapy was on how the "system" had victimized her by allowing her ex-husband (who was portrayed to the therapist as a terrible father) was given more time with the children than is usual in a standard order visitation. Records also reflected that the therapist had done a competent job in helping this woman to deal with her feelings about this situation. In that regard, everything went well. The referral was made appropriately, the patient was compliant with the treatment (showing up for appointments and doing what her therapist recommended), and the therapist did a reasonable job of working with the issue presented to her. Unfortunately, all of the issues that were intended to be addressed by the referral for therapy remained as major sources of conflict in the situation and none of them had been a focus of treatment. Although this type of distortion and hijacking of the therapeutic process and goals in custody matters and abuse allegations is not limited to individuals with BPD, their personality dynamics and their intense propensity toward distortion put BPD patients at higher risk for not addressing or even making known the real problems within themselves that need to be a focus of treatment.

It is important to note that when mental health treatment is recommended it needs to include a focus on the concerns that have been raised by the psychological evaluation. It is often helpful to provide the report to the clinicians who are going to implement the recommendations. Because these reports generally include information about other parties involved in the case, caution should be given as to how this material is handled. It may be that the material related to other individuals can be deleted to protect confidentiality without losing information valuable to the treatment process.

Narcissistic and Related Personality Patterns

Just as severe personality issues seen in BPD mothers can lead to severe conflicts in custody cases, fathers with narcissistic and antisocial personality problems can contribute to the conflicts that are often seen. In the context of cases involving high conflict over custody where significant character pathology exists, allegations of abuse become more likely.

Construct of Psychopathy

Psychologists who go into court identifying that an individual can be described as a psychopathic personality disorder can face two quite different types of challenges. A cross-examiner might raise the issue that this specific label is not found in the official nosology (the *DSM–IV–TR* at present). However, there is general recognition both within the field of psychology and among many coming from a legal perspective, particularly in the criminal law field, that the Psychopathy Checklist–Revised (PCL–R), a procedure based on the concept of psychopathic character, is one of the best predictors of violence and recidivism.*

One of the limitations of the PCL–R, however, is also a limitation of the construct of psychopathy when it is defined primarily as a subset of antisocial personality disorder and therefore references involvement in criminal activity. Significant discussion of this construct, however, has included an acknowledgment that persons who have not been involved in the criminal justice system may have the characteristics of psychopathy while at the same time operating in responsible positions in society. Coming from that perspective, and using sophisticated statistical analyses, Cooke and Michie (2001) identified three factors that defined the global concept of psychopathy: deceitful interpersonal style, deficient affective experience, and impulsive and irresponsible behavioral style. These factors are consistent with the literature on psychopathy from Cleckley (1976) forward. Using that three-factor definition significantly reduced the implication of criminal activity, with the authors acknowledging only that such was a consequence and likely correlate of a high loading on these three factors as part of the personality system. Subsequent research has confirmed the stability of this approach to defining psychopathy and has provided validation of an instrument, the Comprehensive Assessment of Psychopathic Personality (CAPP) with different populations (Cooke & Michie, 2001; Goncalves & Rebocho, 2010; Heinzen et al., 2010; Hoff, Rypdal, Mykletun, & Cooke, 2010).

Cooke and Michie's approach is not inconsistent with other explorations of the psychopathic personality. For example, Meloy (1992), taking an attachment theory and object relations approach, but also coming from the perspective of forensic work, explored the extremes of what he called violent attachments or intimate interpersonal relationships that lead to the extreme violence of murder. Furthermore, in his Chapter 8, entitled "The Female Victim of the Psychopath," he explored three case histories to illustrate the notion that when relationships occur with men of psychopathic character, the females involved also have severe personality problems that

---

* The issue in using the PCL–R under such conditions goes to the fact that it may predict on a normative basis the potential for recidivism, but it can be reasonably argued, as in the entire field of violence prediction, that applying this statistical approach to the situation of a specific individual, particularly where the outcome is of the substance of the death penalty, represents a statistically flawed and therefore ethically indefensible process. Other arguments go to the normative base and research findings that call into question prediction potentials in the prison context (see, for example, Connell, 2003; Cunningham, 2006).

are "both complementary and concordant identifications" (p. 270). Although clearly not constituting the kind of data that allow broad application and conclusions, his work in this area is consistent with other clinical experience and the general observation that marital dynamics can be understood only in the context of the interactions and interdependencies that get created. In fact, we would take the position that both consciously and unconsciously people choose each other because of both positive and negative states that are presented and wind up in situations where either positive growth occurs in the context of the marriage, or there is a perpetuation and an enhancement of psychopathology on both sides.

Narcissistic personality disorder is seen disproportionately among men. The *DSM–IV–TR* defines the construct by reference to traits of grandiosity, need for adulation and power, entitlement and beliefs of being special and unique, exploitative of others, lacking empathy, and often behaving with arrogance. The individual so designated is not the typical sociopath who commits crimes and then lies and manipulates with impunity, but rather may function in the world without criminal involvement. In the context of our concerns, Adshead (2003) proposed that there are some individuals within this category who might be better characterized as having "dangerous parenting disorder" and whose family functioning is particularly problematic. Thus, she suggested that the man might be a professional-level individual of polished manners and who in the context of a custody dispute will ostensibly be focused on the best interests of the children. However, in the context of speaking about same, he will in fact denigrate the mother and do so in ways that are hard to verify objectively. These fathers may present as self-absorbed and in other ways meet the criteria for narcissism.*

Although this father typically does not bother to undertake much responsibility for the children, he does want to present in public with as close to a perfect family as possible. When the marital situation deteriorates and there is filing for divorce, he will undertake to get custody as part of his need to win, to prove his own importance and excellence, and to punish the wife for her lack of appreciation of him. He will then begin a campaign of indulging

---

* The term derives from the mythic character who was so in love with himself that he drowned in the pool reflecting his image. The myth has a twist that is not well known: the mate of Narcissus was named Echo, and she fulfilled his need for constant reaffirmation and adulation by repeating back to him anything he said. The wisdom of this myth is seen in the relational patterns that often present in which the narcissistic man often connects with women who are Echo-like in their behavior and more likely than not of lower status in their work or elect to be homemakers. After a relationship gets past its initial romantic period, however, and the realities of child-raising result in the Echo no longer providing constant adoration and response to her husband, significant problems develop not infrequently involving his seeking reinforcement from other females. Infidelity then acts to move the marriage to a divorcing stage.

the children and working to obtain their allegiance to him and alienation from the mother. Her response to this threat to what is essentially her reason for being and her connection to the children is often to become more rigid in how she parents and even punitive, which directly feeds his strategy.

It is at this point that the children begin to raise issues regarding inappropriate conduct by the mother, which range from excessive alcohol use, unnecessary punishment, and even vague abuse allegations. In one such case, the mother was accused of "hugging the boys too much" and they stated they "were uncomfortable around her." The problems continue to proliferate as the children develop. Boys especially may pick up on negative attitudes toward the mother and refuse to alter their resistant and negative behavior. The end result can be an escalation to physical levels with resulting social services involvement. Clearly, if the mother has some significant personality psychopathology, things can move to even more difficult levels.

This section focused upon some fairly severe sorts of psychopathology, which are sometimes found in the infrequent category of the equivocal case context. The situations do not usually play out with real and severe violence of the type reflected in Meloy's (1992) work; however, somewhat lesser but clearly destructive behaviors emerge and cause ongoing damage to family systems, including both the parents, even after they have separated and divorced, and certainly to the children, as has been already demonstrated. Finally, it is not uncommon for the father to reinvolve or remarry another "Echo." In the context of her striving to please him, she will vigorously endorse his attitudes and interests, seeking to play the part of the perfect parent to the children and further creating conflict through them and even directly with the former spouse.

At times, belief systems in these types of situations become so confusing and enmeshed that even the most experienced social workers and GALs have difficulty in deciphering what is taking place. There are strong indicators and even in some cases definite evidence of excessive punishment. Supervised visitation may be imposed. The older children, especially teens, often refuse to engage at all, and if forced create such tension for the mother that she gives up trying to see them.

Once these patterns have developed and there is an ongoing or reopened custody case, professionals involved at different levels are at risk of buying into the father's view of the world and come to support his allegations. The professionals are not immune from the trap of his persuasiveness and charm. Even though having a balanced and fair approach to any evaluation is the standard of practice to which all pay homage, any seasoned practitioner can recall situations where being seduced into the dynamics that have been created has been an issue. Furthermore, when therapy is ordered to facilitate post-decree adjustment, it is not uncommon for the therapist, as part of validating patients, to reinforce the existing pathologies. It is often necessary to have a therapist working on parent–child issues who is different from the individual child therapist but who is diligent in maintaining communication between the two.

Affective Disorders

Bipolar Disorder

Bipolar disorder (BD) is one of the most misdiagnosed conditions in mental health. Its presentation involves major mood instability that includes both depressive and manic states. There is impairment in thought process with grandiosity and belief that one is able to accomplish phenomenal tasks alternating with a sense of total pessimism and incapacity. The manic or hypomanic periods can result in goal setting that is beyond the person's functional capabilities, with repeated experiences of failure that then initiate crashes into depression. During the elated mood states, the person can come to feel that he or she is invincible, with impulsive acting out including overspending, hypersexuality, and gambling. The contrasting depressive periods then manifest in prolonged sadness and decline in self-care habits and even acting out in self-harming and suicidal ways.

There is very little in the literature regarding BD and parenting issues as they relate to matters of custody. BD has a strong biological/genetic component, and the offspring of individuals with this disorder tend to have a significantly higher rate of its occurrence (Chang, Steiner, & Ketter, 2002). It is not clear, however, how much of the generational transmission of this disorder is associated with the environmental factors related to parenting style and lack of adequate parenting by individuals who are diagnosed with BD. There is some evidence that nearly 21% of children of parents with BD suffer from some form of disruptive behavior disorder (Carlson, Bromet, & Sievers, 2000).

In the context of allegations that may be raised in a contested custody matter, this issue may involve one parent reporting that the other "is bipolar" and is unable to provide safe and adequate parenting for the child or children. There may be associated reports of acting out in inappropriate ways involving physical or sexual behavior, consistent with symptoms listed for the disorder. Subsequently, a motion may be filed by the parent bringing the concerns, or even by a GAL who acts to protect the wards, to limit or terminate parenting time or request limited supervised visitation. However, when the "diagnosis" emerges primarily by a party, some careful review is necessary. If there is no prior treatment, and therefore no existing mental health records to secure the presence or absence of the illness independent of the present context, a careful assessment of mental status, behavioral status, and test responding needs to be conducted by the forensic psychologist or psychiatrist (or the appointment of same for purposes of obtaining such an evaluation). On the other hand, when there is independent evidence of this kind of condition, there is a need to contain the situation so that healthy contact between that parent and the children can be secured without putting the youngsters at risk due to deterioration in the mental condition of the parent. In a genuine bipolar condition, treatments exist that can be instituted, and over time some reasonable stability can be achieved in most cases.

In one such case, the parents who were in their mid-30s had met at a party and began seeing each other regularly. She described the early part of the relationship as intense and romantic. The relationship developed rapidly and he would indulge her with fancy gifts, spur of the moment vacations, and romantic dinners together. She described him as an outgoing person with many friends. During the third month of their relationship she became pregnant, and when she informed him of the "great news" he became very upset and strongly urged her to have an abortion. Their relationship began to deteriorate rather quickly. Following the news of his girlfriend's pregnancy, he stopped taking his medication and became symptomatic, acting out in inappropriate ways and engaging in some questionable business deals, which resulted in his arrest. He did not have a criminal history and the legal issues were resolved quickly; however, the stresses of the situation had a negative impact on him. He was hospitalized for suicidal ideation and behaviors after having been confronted with the consequences of some of his impulsive actions. He practically disappeared during her pregnancy and was contacted for the paternity test shortly after their daughter was born. He then filed a motion to visit with his daughter, and the child's mother had objected based on his emotional instability and behavioral problems. He was granted some visitation with his sister being the supervisor and no overnights until the child was 2 years old. During the course of the next two years, he returned to compliance with his medication and his mood and behaviors stabilized. He filed for more parenting time with his daughter. The child's mother objected again, pointing to the history of acting out and his diagnosis, in this case clearly supported. She made allegations referencing the ongoing situation, stating that he would become very angry in response to minor problems, such as a few minutes delay in getting their daughter ready to go with him. She reported that he had "peeled off the driveway" with his car on a couple of occasions when he was irritated. There were numerous delays and postponements in the legal process that lasted nearly one year. The court finally ordered a psychological evaluation to get input regarding the psychological functioning of both parents, including the implications for the allocation of parental rights and responsibility for the minor child.

The standard evaluation was implemented with this family. The father's mental health records were obtained and clinicians involved in his care were interviewed. Psychological tests were administered and both parents were subjected to a clinical interview that also involved assessment of their understanding of parenting issues and their approach to the child. Both parents were also observed interacting with the child, and the aunt who supervised visitation was interviewed as well. It was apparent that although the father continued to have some symptoms, he was able to relate to the child well and had bonded with her. She was comfortable around her father and interacted appropriately with him. The psychiatric records indicated that he was compliant with his medication and visited a psychiatrist every six weeks to make necessary adjustments when indicated. He had seen this therapist on a weekly basis and was cooperative with the therapeutic process. Therapeutic goals involved mood management, medication compliance, and relapse prevention. The aunt, who was present when the father would pick up the child from her mother's house, reported that there were several times when the mother was not home and brought the child more than half an hour later than scheduled. She also described situations when the mother would taunt the father, thus creating great deal of stress at the pickup.

It was concluded that the father in this case was managing his mood disorder effectively and did not pose a threat to the child's safety and well-being. It was recommended that visitation with the child expand gradually to include overnight visitation with a goal of reaching the frequency of a standard order. A 90-day period was suggested during which the child and the father were to see a therapist together on a weekly basis to address any issues that may be raised by the mother. The child was to be brought to the session by her mother, they would have their mid-week visits after their session, and the father would drop off the child at the mother's house later that evening. This measure was put into place to provide the child's mother with some assurances as well as chronicling the progression of the visits with the father. It also provided the mother with a structure that required her to be on time with her compliance being recorded by the therapist. Finally, it was also a resource where the father was able to ask questions that he may have had regarding parenting issues without being accused of not knowing how to manage the child's needs.

As indicated above, it is important to note that BD, like many other forms of mental health problems, is a treatable condition. The best predictor of success in these cases is treatment compliance. Unfortunately, when individuals who suffer from the condition begin to respond positively to treatment and feel more stable, there is a tendency to stop the medication and to develop a belief system that they never had the problem in the first place. Treatment plans that include active monitoring and motivating of the patient tend to produce more favorable results.

Major Depressive Disorder

Major depressive disorder is one of the most common mental health problems. It is often exacerbated by significant stressors in an individual's life and can be highly disabling. The *DSM–IV–TR* describes depression as the presence of a prolonged period of sadness that extends beyond two weeks, with disturbances in appetite and sleep, problems with motivation and energy, and accompanied by a negative view of the world and the future. Not infrequently, there are difficulties with self-esteem and self-image. In more severe cases, the strong sense of helplessness and hopelessness can result in suicidal ideation, intent, and behavior (American Psychiatric Association, 2000). Reported prevalence of depression is approximately 5% for a current episode and 13% for lifetime occurrence in the general population. Parental depression appears to be a major contributing factor to depression in their offspring. Lieb, Isensee, Hofler, Pfister, and Wittchen (2002) reported that children of depressed parents are three times more likely to have a lifetime episode of depression themselves.

Depression is known to affect parenting abilities. Significant research has been done in the area of maternal depression and the way it interferes with long-term adjustment of the child. However, caution needs to be taken about drawing conclusions that in a given case there is necessarily a causal relationship between maternal depression and developmental and adjustment problems in a child. Developmental and behavioral problems in children can pre-exist and be themselves the stimuli that lead to maternal depression. Also, external stressors can contribute to the development of both maternal depression and adjustment difficulties in children (Lovejoy, Graczyk, O'Hare, & Newman, 2000).

When mental health professionals are called upon to provide a custody evaluation, the report usually does not include a "Diagnostic Impression" section of the type standard for clinical evaluations. Unless there is clear evidence of a clinically relevant condition, based on other than the statements of adversaries, a formal diagnosis is not provided to the court and other referral sources that have requested the evaluation. However, diagnostic labels may come from the clinical records that are obtained or the individual who is being evaluated provides the information to the evaluator. Diagnostic labels are occasionally used as a weapon in a custody battle to discredit a parent and to limit his or her time with the children. We would take the position that a formal diagnosis of a major affective disorder, such as depression, needs to be well supported from multiple sources and is reported where it has specific relevance for the recommendations that will be made as to parenting responsibilities. It can be noted that although clinical depression occurs in both men and women, the psychological and legal literature relevant to parenting issues has mostly focused on maternal depression, and more specifically on postpartum depression and problems associated with mothering and attachment. There has been little exploration of the implications for fathering. Research that has been done allows some cautions. Even though behavioral correlates associated with depression often are not associated with aggression, depressed parents are three and a half times more likely to abuse their children physically than nondepressed parents. Also, depressed parents are prone to have problems with protecting their children from dangerous situations. They are also more likely to use physical punishment to address the behavioral problems of their children (Samra-Grewal, 1999).

In custody cases, parental depression is often raised in connection with the adequacy of parenting provided to children. The nondepressed parent often accuses the parent who suffers from depression of neglecting the needs of the children and potentially exposing them to harm. At times this can become a compelling issue that can lead to limiting parenting time for the parent who suffers from depression. When a parent is struggling with depression, he or she is likely to have lower motivation and energy to put up a fight and advocate for his or her own rights in a contested divorce. Common stressors associated with breakup of the marriage going through litigation associated with divorce can become overwhelming for a depressed parent and further compromise the adequacy of his or her parenting. In some situations the ongoing stress of litigation and perpetual conflict inherent in the case exacerbate the depressive condition and add fuel to the fire of the party who is making the accusation. In such cases, the nondepressed parent can raise allegations of abuse and neglect. The depressed parent's mental health records can be obtained as a way of documenting the severity of the depression and the extent to which that parent's coping resources are compromised.

Another context in which depression is raised in custody cases is when a parent threatens suicide and there are questions regarding the safety of the children. Suicidality can be due to the stressors of divorce or exacerbation of a pre-existing depressive condition due to severe conflict. In such cases there are often fears that the allegedly suicidal parent may harm the children as well, a not unknown scenario although far from being a likely one.

Psychological testimony as part of a custody evaluation can provide significant insight into these matters. Parental depression does not automatically lead to child abuse or neglect. Also, suicidal ideation and intent need to be evaluated carefully and both static and dynamic risk factors taken into consideration. Parents should be evaluated for their parenting skills and the care and guidance that they provide the children. Often when there is an existing depressive condition, recommendations for the treatment are made. Depression is an eminently treatable condition. Evidence-based treatment for depressive conditions is based on a combination of therapies that include cognitive behavioral psychotherapy and use of antidepressant medications.

Skill-based therapy involves opposite-action (instructions to do the opposite of what the depressed state seems to call for), positive self-talk, and healthy self-care. Compliance with such therapies can be effective in managing depressive symptoms. Antidepressant medications are highly efficient in reducing the symptoms that relate to energy, motivation, and other biological deficits that are caused by depression. The following instance may be illustrative.

> In a custody matter, during the evaluation, the father was emphatic that his ex-wife was unable to care for their two young daughters, ages 4 and 6. He reported that shortly after their first child was born, she would sleep long hours and was not attending the child. She was uncharacteristically ignoring what needed to be done around the house. She had gained extra weight during her pregnancy and did not seem to be motivated to lose it, even though in the past she had been very active and had exercised regularly. He complained that their active sex life had dwindled to minimal sexual encounters. Although she had made minor progress by taking the antidepressant medication that her physician prescribed, her condition deteriorated further after the birth of their second child. The father commented that she did not seem to care about herself or the family and he felt that their relationship more closely resembled that of roommates than of spouses. Confronting her about her inadequacies as a wife and a mother appeared to have compounded the depression. Feeling that he had no way of influencing the situation and possibly having been involved in a relationship with a coworker, he decided to file for divorce. He indicated that he worried about the children's welfare, as he believed their mother was unable to care for them and was not following through with many of the routines and basic necessities.

Psychological test results and clinical interview of the mother allowed a diagnosis of a significant depressive disorder for which she had a strong family background. She seemed to have a good understanding of the developmental needs of the children and had a healthy attachment to them. A shared parenting plan involving a standard order visitation schedule with the mother was recommended. She was referred for psychiatric evaluation for possible use of medication. It was further recommended that this matter be re-evaluated after six months. Substantial progress was made in her condition and a 50–50 schedule of visitation was implemented at that time.

In cases where there are concerns regarding suicidal ideation or behavior, hospitalization is usually a common course of action to ensure safety. Risk assessments can be conducted to help with the development of a safety plan as well as to inform aggressive treatment recommendations for the depression, utilizing medication as well as individual and group therapies.

Substance Abuse

On any given day, significant numbers of people throughout the United States use alcohol, and in some cases other substances, on what is sometimes called a recreational basis. The use of mind-altering and emotion-affecting substances is known throughout recorded history. Contemporary survey research allows certain kinds of conclusions.

Current Patterns of Abuse

The 2009 survey conducted by the Substance Abuse and Mental Health Services Administration (SAMHSA) detailed that 51.6% of Americans age 12 or older acknowledged being users of alcohol, amounting to approximately 130.6 million people. Nearly one-quarter indicated that they were engaging in binge drinking at least once a month and 6.8% acknowledged heavy drinking, defined as "five or more drinks on the same occasion on each of five or more days in the last thirty days" (Substance Abuse and Mental Health Services Administration, 2009, p. 29). Those figures illustrate that the use of alcohol is clearly a part of the culture, although it is also equally clear that a substantial cohort does not engage. However, the percentage obtained of those not using alcohol is substantially affected by using age 12 as the lower level. Other breakdowns from this survey indicated that young adults, particularly those in college, were more likely to engage in alcohol use and abuse, where the rates reached 63.9%. Similarly, the same figure pertained to full-time employed adults 18 or over. Some regional differences were identified. A slight decline in the figures on driving under the influence (DUI) can be seen in charts reflecting 2002 to the present, and the breakdown for 2009 clearly indicated that during the ages 18 to 30 the majority of DUI events occurred.

In regard to illicit drug use, there were slight declines from the period of 2002 to 2009, although significant use is documented, particularly of marijuana but also including other substances. The highest rates were found in the decade of the 1920s where marijuana use showed an increase. (An interesting peak has been noted with regard to adults aged 50 to 59, representing the maturing baby boomers, with current use rates approximately double what was seen in 2002 for that age cohort.) Another variable in use was employment status, with the unemployed showing the highest rates. There were strong associations between the abuse of alcohol and use of illicit drugs, and it was also found that young people who smoked cigarettes were more likely to be involved in illicit drug use. In general, however, the use of tobacco has declined between 2002 and 2009, and slightly more than a quarter of the population appears to use some type of tobacco product.

Although many of the overall rates of use have not showed marked changes over time in the various surveys performed, given the increase in the population in actual numbers, the population of people who are using and within which a group is potentially abusing substances has increased numerically. As a result, there is an increasing population of those who receive treatment or other forms of intervention from society.

Studies of the relationship between child abuse and neglect with substance abuse clearly show some important interactions. Overall reports of abuse and neglect have doubled from 1986 to 1997 from 1.4 million to 3 million. Substance abuse has been identified in more than 70% of those cases (U.S. Dept. of Health and Human Services [DHHS], 1999). The National Center on Addiction and Substance Abuse (CASA) at Columbia University reported that parental substance abuse results in their children being three times more likely to suffer abuse and four times more likely to be identified as being neglected (CASA, 1999).

It can be noted that abuse and neglect are also strongly associated with poverty and unemployment, and therefore the part played by substance abuse is not simple or straightforward but merely a part of a complex situation. However, these associations that lay the foundation for this area also to come to play a part in equivocal abuse cases. That part is of such sufficient importance that it is a focus of treatment and the development of guidelines from the DHHS (Howard, 2000).

It has been well supported that the impact of substance abuse is negative for marital stability and that parental drug use and abuse leads to higher risk levels of adolescent substance involvement (Cadoret, Troughton, O'Gorman, & Heywood, 1986; Cadoret, Yates, Troughton, Woodworth, & Stewart, 1995; Needle, Su, & Doherty, 1990). In the study by Needle et al., one of the more interesting conclusions involved differential effects, with males more affected than females by divorce but females more affected by the remarriage of the custodial parent in terms of raised risk levels for substance abuse. These studies illustrate the impact of parental use on children but are not exactly on point with the focus of our concerns. They do, however, underline that the use of substances, whether abuse of legitimate ones or any involvement with illegitimate ones, is one of the things that becomes a basis for ongoing litigation and allegation in divorce situations. For example, a survey of the Internet found the following kind of problem registered on divorce information sites (repeated verbatim below without corrections).

...about the Hair test we had that done---they didn't take from my root I have very long hair---anyway they cut it off like a ¼ inch from my scalp---I am assuming they did the same with him---if they could...He shaved his head like a month before court---he is slick---and I don't know---nor do I think they used body hair for him---if they did it should have come up positive---I know for a fact---he used on (dat4e) and just bought a new torch so,,he had to use after too. which would bring him into the 90 days that hair carries,,,,,,They didn't use the root for me and I suspect not on him either. I am sick over this---does a PI know how to get the type of evidence I needs? And will it you think be admissible in court? I am not trying to exclude him from the baby's life just don't want him to have sleepover visits and be alone with him for long periods of time…I want to thank you for your help---

Also there are things sold on the internet that says they can make a user pass a hair test…so he could have used that too. I think he is in active use now he is becoming very inconsistent again. I know about having my lawyer request the random tests but will the court honor it when he has a positive in their eyes? I know all I can do is ask…. Thank you again. (Retrieved Nov. 13, 2010 from http://en.allexperts.com/q/Divorce-Issues-16261/custody-visitation-substance-abuse-1.htm)

As the above paragraph indicates, the concern about substance abuse can enter when there is litigation or concern around custody visitation, and it can reflect a genuine issue with significant concerns (the use of illicit substances in front of or while caring for a child is by definition child endangerment, in addition to its being a criminal act). What is not known from this paragraph or from similar claims is whether the allegation is true or false. (The expert responding to this particular problem indicated that if the hair test is done properly, which means a root must be obtained, it will be accurate, and also confirmed that hiring a private investigator to follow and document an abuse sequence would be evidence admissible into the court in asking for supervised visitation.)

Certain developments in federal and subsequent state legislation have some impact in this arena. If the custody issue comes to involve the human services department with the removal of children, the federal and state "fast track" adoption laws may come into play. If both parents are incapable of providing for the child or children due to substance abuse related issues, the agency must, within 12–15 months, obtain permanent custody and adoption. In most cases of divorcing couples, this sequence of events is not likely to occur. However, the problem where there is a serious substance abuse issue, particularly on the part of both parties, is that there must be a case plan that includes the achievement of a stable condition of sobriety within the first 12 months of the removal of the children. In many cases, chronic substance abuse is not amenable to the time line that gets involved with the various laws that are dictating conditions relevant to both treatment and reunification (Howard, 2000).

Equivocal Allegations of Substance Abuse

As with the allegations of sexual or physical abuse, allegations of substance abuse, with implications for neglect, abuse, and endangerment, can be made in the course of divorce litigation and represent an evaluative challenge for the court and persons appointed to assist the court, such as the GAL or the custody evaluator. In almost all cases where substance abuse is alleged to be a significant factor for decisional purposes, the party alleging the abuse will indicate a basis in terms of personal experience or the children's statements when they come back from visitation. The party alleged to be substance involved invariably denies the allegation, may at times indicate that the alleging party is the one with such a problem, and may or may not acknowledge some recreational use of alcohol, although it is not uncommon for there to be such a statement. What is clear, however, is that the responses of both parties, when simple inquiry as in interviews is made, are not sufficient to come to a conclusion as to the truth of the matter. Therefore, it becomes important to consider sources of information that may reduce the uncertainty.

Investigative Options

Clearly, the possibility of using testing presents as a possibility, and it is not entirely uncommon for there to be a specification of a hair test because of its ability to reflect a period of up to 90 days prior to the time of the administration of the test. The use of other bioassay methods secures only a much shorter and more immediate time period. Table 7.1 provides an overview of major available options.

Table 7.1   Biological Assessment Options for Substance Abuse Evaluation[a]

	Potential Detection Periods		
Substance	Urine Test	Hair Test	Blood Test
Alcohol	<24 hours	<2 days	12–24 hours
Amphetamines	1–5 days	<90 days	12 hours
Methamphetamine	3–5 days	<90 days	1–3 days
Morphine	2–4 days	<90 days	1–3 days
Heroin	3–4 days	<90 days	1–2 days
Barbiturates	1 day	<90 days	1–2 days
Phenobarbital	14–21 days	<90 days	4–7 days
Benzodiazepines	7 days	<90 days	6–48 hours
Cannabis, PCP	3–7 days	<90 days	2–3 days
Cocaine	2–5 days	90 days	2–5 days

[a] These figures are approximations based on information from www.erowid.org, and Labcorp (2011). Specific tests and their qualities need to be individually and professionally evaluated in light of the purpose for which they are ordered. Tests that reflect long periods within which use has occurred should not be selected where the interest is in an immediate short-term previous period.

Psychological Testing

Psychological testing can provide some information about characteristics that are associated with alcohol or drug abuse, but those kinds of data are purely actuarial and are also associated with other issues or behaviors. In other words, an elevated MacAndrew Alcoholism Scale on the MMPI-2 is associated with problems with alcohol or other substances. The scale itself is a subtle scale and contains no items that directly ask for an endorsement or denial of substance-related issues. These items were selected because of their statistical association with the use of alcohol and drugs and, when answered in the nonscored direction, their association with nonproblems. However, subsequent research has shown that this scale can be associated with other forms of dependency issues and other addictivelike behaviors (gambling, food addictions, and even so-called sexual addiction; Peele, 1985, 1990).

There are specific psychological tests such as those shown in Table 7.2 that look at alcohol and drug abuse. Some are absolutely content valid such as the MAST. Others have somewhat more subtlety such as the SASSI. Even that latter test, however, cannot secure that these associated characteristics are invariably reflective of an alcohol or substance abuse problem. They are helpful with persons who are willing to answer them entirely honestly, but in this population, having security about honest responding is not possible.

Table 7.2   Psychological Tests Used in Assessment of Substance Abuse

Test or Technique	Reliability	Validity
Michigan Alcoholism Screening Test, and The Drug Abuse Screening Test	Data support use	Face validity Dependent upon willingness to disclose
Substance Abuse Subtle Screening Inventory	Data support use	Some face validity Some subtle scales Limited capacity to definitively identify abuse, dependency; profile based
Addiction Severity Index (Structured Interview)	Data support use	Dependent upon willingness to disclose
CAGE Questionnaire	Data support use	Dependent upon willingness to disclose; limited scope
MMPI-2	Good reliability	Clinical scales do not measure substance abuse; special scales include the MacAndrew Alcoholism Scale (subtle), Addiction Admission Scale (obvious), Addiction Potential Scale (obvious and subtle aspects) None of scales definitively identifies those with and without issues Much dependence upon willingness to disclose

As indicated in the above example, it is certainly possible to obtain more direct and unequivocal evidence from private investigators or police reports where there have been independent observations by officers of behavior under the influence. Obviously, a history of confirmed DUI charges can allow conclusions, and a history of discharge from employment due to alcohol or substance-related impairment would be equally persuasive.

In the absence of the kind of evidence that allows this issue to be concluded one way or another, there remains the consideration of the children's responses in the situation. As with direct allegations of sexual or physical abuse, children have varying responses, which may or may not allow any security about what is actually occurring. Thus, in one case where addiction was an established fact, the children acted to deny that the parent was impaired and to deny that there was any ongoing problem, in spite of events such as the shutting down of utilities due to lack of payment of bills and other observations. Conversely, children who are allied with the parents making the allegations may provide false information about the behavior of the parent they are visiting in order to support what the alleging parent is saying. Children will suggest that there has been driving with an open container or that the parent has passed out and not been available to them.

Nicotine and Alcohol—Some Further Issues

Although all problematic use of substances has implications for the short- and long-term welfare of children, there are some differences in the liabilities reflected, depending upon the substance involved. The one substance that is often ignored is nicotine. As indicated above, nicotine usage may have reduced in U.S. society, but it is far from absent. A recent YouTube Internet-based expose of an 18-month-old child who had been allowed to develop a serious nicotine habit was a source of international discussion. The impact on the development of that child's central nervous system is probably going to be profound, particularly because the youngster is shown as chain smoking in order to maintain the level of addiction that is already in place. On a much longer range basis, parental smoking also is associated with children adopting the habit as adults. When it comes to licit use of legal substances, there are serious limitations for the courts. It is not desirable for courts to take over parent lifestyle decision making and start to impose whatever may be the particular values and habits of the presiding judge. In fact, the courts usually act to establish only those parameters that return the decision making about children to their parents unless considerations that involve child endangerment or abuse become involved.

From a shorter range perspective, the documented effect of secondhand smoke has now become a basis for spurious allegations or legitimate concerns as to the welfare of youngsters. Divorce decrees have specified that there will be no smoking in cars that are used to transport to and from visitation and no smoking inside homes while the children are present. It is not totally unusual for there to be a negotiated compromise over the issue where the smoking parent agrees to not smoke at all in the house as a condition of having substantial visitation time. In some cases where a child has a specific vulnerability (for example, asthma), allegations of smoking in or around the child become allegations of significant abuse or endangerment.

In the case of alcohol, one obvious concern that is raised involves driving while under the influence but with the children, precipitating the youngsters either to involvement with the law that will be unpleasant and possibly traumatic as the driving parent is arrested or, in an even worse-case situation, to an accident in which physical harm comes to them. Another issue similar to the one discussed above with respect to nicotine involves the direct provision of alcohol to children. In Ohio, by law a parent is allowed to serve his or her child an alcoholic beverage.* The law thus respects a parent's right to include children in the rules and rituals of specific family life. In the United States and many countries, it is not entirely uncommon for children to be given some access to alcoholic substances as part of religious observances and family celebrations. The law is clear, however, that the right to allow a child's friend to partake of alcohol does not exist and in fact could become a basis for that child's parent to take legal action that could lead to criminal charges of child endangering or corruption of a minor. All of these kinds of acts can become a part of allegations that are made by parents in the course of their divorcing process and may require extended activities on the part of those who are reporting to the court around the custody issue.

However, both tobacco and alcohol, if used according to the legal rules that govern in the jurisdiction, are not criminal acts. In the case of illegitimate substance use, including both prescription and street drug abuse, the parent involved in such activities is committing a crime and the potential under such circumstances to create problems for the child or children is clear. In such cases, in addition to being in an impaired state and therefore not able to take adequate care of a child, a parent may precipitate a child's contact with criminal elements, depending upon the source of the parent's illicit drug. We have had a case in which a parent was stealing a child's prescribed medication in order to meet the parent's addictive needs. Victimization of the child was twofold in that situation. The parent was impaired as a result of the use of the drug and the child would find himself without a needed prescription when his condition required it.

---

* It is permitted for a parent, legal guardian, or legal-aged spouse to order in a public place an alcoholic drink and give same to his or her underage child or mate (Ohio Revised Code 4301.69).

Some Intervention Options

In cases where the alleged drug or alcohol abuse can be either dismissed or confirmed, certain options then follow, which are coherently based on the finding. A parent with a substance-related problem can be ordered to obtain treatment and achieve sobriety as a condition of increasing access to a child. The companionship program can be tailored appropriately, along with some requirements for demonstrated sobriety. The case of allegations that can be dismissed leads to recommendations for ongoing monitoring of the potential of the parent to make false statements and sometimes can lead to the placement of the children with the parent who made the accusations.

In the more equivocal case, the following options may be helpful to the court or parties:

1. The year of sobriety. An agreement is made between the parties in which the alleging parent agrees to normalized visitation, but the parent about whom the charges were leveled agrees to engage in a year of nonuse and an evaluation at the end of that time as to whether there may be a resumption of the use of alcohol.
2. Random testing with financial incentives. Sometimes as a part of securing the first option of the sobriety year, or in a situation where there is an agreement to variable use, the parent about whom the allegations are made agrees or is required to not use during times of companionship. There can be an option by the alleging parent to call for a biological test. The constraint, however, is placed on that call to the effect that if the alleged user passes the test, then any fee for the examination must be paid by the parent who required the test. If, however, the parent for whom the test is called either fails to take the test within 24 hours or does not pass it, then the fee for the test must be paid by him or her. In any case of a missed test, there is a failure, and the agreement specifies some reduction of visitation to a more monitored level until such time as the situation is more secured.
3. Assessment. There are problems with assessment, both biological and psychological, as indicated above. However, these problems for the most part can be overcome if the kind of testing that is ordered is appropriate to the situation.

Summary

In this section, we have provided some information about the general issue of substance abuse as it affects these kinds of situations and specifically looked at how it could become part of an equivocal allegation picture. As with any other type of allegation, the problem for the court is that real dangers present for children and absolutely secure conclusions are sometimes elusive. Clearly, this is one of the kinds of allegations that can be made in an effort to alienate children from parents or to eliminate involvement with a parent. Equally clearly, this is an allegation that can reflect a reality given the level of use that is common in society.

Conclusions

Individual psychopathology, in interaction with the enhanced and often destructive dynamics that present when high-conflict custody cases are involved, often require rather complex, multipronged interventions if the children are to be protected but also if they are to have some opportunity to benefit from the positives that exist in each parent. It has long been known that even the most severe mental health problems do not involve such pervasive behavioral impact that no potentials for being productive and relationally appropriate exist. In these cases, the histories include times when things went well and there are some bases for moving into the future in a better fashion than is seen at the time of the conflict. Identification of significant pathology, remediation and therapy to address the problems, and ongoing monitoring depending upon the nature of the situation can all play a part in achieving successful retrieval of these particular chestnuts from the fires of the ongoing conflict.

Working Model for the Forensic Evaluator

8

These cases more than most require a case-driven approach to forensic work that is to be presented to the court. In other words, a stock approach that follows a formula will only go so far in generating relevant information. It will be remembered that relevancy is one of the more important bases for any expert presentation in a court of law. All of these cases represent high conflict, serious inconsistencies and confusions, and fact pictures that defy solid conclusions as to what can be viewed with confidence as credible versus noncredible. At the same time, children's lives and futures are at stake and the courts are well aware of the pervasive risks that attend coming to final judgments.

With that in mind, our approach is one that weds a standard model of child custody evaluation with an emphasis on following the case that perhaps is more typical of classic investigation, including of the criminal type. In other words, there is a specific interest in determining the details and facts that can be supported or dismissed in situations of this sort, and the ability to do so is dependent sometimes upon the right kinds of inquiries and sometimes upon spontaneous and fortuitous events in the course of the case. Finally, when the endpoint is reached and the situation is either objectively unclear or has significant and unresolved subjective disparities, we provide some security-enhancing recommendations that may allow enough mutual confidence that a more positive post-decree period may ensue.

First Step—Conducting the Evaluation

Primary Contacts

The basic evaluation protocol in child custody constitutes the appropriate initial approach with other options subsequently included as the case develops. Each parent should be interviewed. The child or children are seen with each parent. Baseline testing is obtained from the parents that will rule in or out severe psychopathology and provide some relatively independent basis for looking at personality dynamics, usually referencing the MMPI-2. Some persons rely upon standardized questionnaires regarding the children, such as the Child Behavior Checklist. The level of scientific adequacy of such measures is not the same as that which is available for the standard psychological tests (MMPI-2 and Exner Rorschach), but there are some supportive data for the results that pertain.

Even at this level, however, there may be a need for specialized procedures that are not standard. For the most part, a general approach to the evaluation of children in these situations includes observations of children with their parents and individual interviews of the children, depending upon their age and stage of development. If, however, the case begins with allegations as part of the picture, it is almost immediate that the use of videotape or audiotape should be a part of the presentation of child interviews.* If the allegations present in the course of the case, then any reinterviews of children around the allegations should be so preserved. The importance of using nonleading questions insofar as possible and of exploring reasonable alternatives cannot be overemphasized. Appendix A provides some guides for this kind of work.

Interviews of parents are not without hazard as well, particularly when allegations have surfaced. In many cases where there are allegations of abuse, there can also be criminal charges pending or potential against an alleged perpetrator parent. Under these circumstances there are two separate processes in motion. The allocation of parental rights and responsibilities is determined in either the domestic relations or juvenile courts and the criminal case is adjudicated in the criminal court. (Abuse allegations can be made by one parent against the other or may originate from a third party, such as a pediatrician, schoolteacher, or a therapist involved in the case. Outcomes of a social services investigation may lead to criminal court action.) If the cases in the two courts are running simultaneously, careful attention should be given to the handling of the parties involved. However, it is more likely than not that custody issues will not be pursued when there is a criminal court case ongoing; the domestic relations (DR) court may wait for the outcome in the other venue.

When a present or potential future defendant in a criminal case is seen for a psychological assessment regarding the allocation of parental rights and responsibilities or visitation with the children, some inquiry into the case that has led to or may result in criminal charges is required. Although getting informed consent in all assessment situations is ethically necessary, the person being evaluated under these circumstances should be advised to consult his or her attorney prior to discussing details of the allegations brought against him or her during the evaluation. The information contained in the psychological report is subject to discovery and can be presented as evidence in the criminal matter.

In one such case, a mother who was accused of physically abusing her two sons was referred by the county children's services for an evaluation to

---

* One experienced professional interviewed for this volume indicated he records all interviews including parents and children. We have not employed that procedure but would note it has potential positives with regard to the availability of accurate information and the defense of the psychological report product.

provide recommendations regarding a reunification plan. (In the county, it was a required procedure that whenever there were allegations and the children were removed from the home that there be an assessment done and a "case plan" devised outlining the requirements for parents and the children to be reunified.) This mother was charged with several counts of felony child endangerment and her criminal case was pending. When she presented for the psychological evaluation, she was advised of the possible conflict that was inherent in the situation. If she honestly discussed the case with this evaluator, she would be indirectly providing information to the prosecutor in the criminal case against her. However, if she did not openly discuss the situation, she would be perceived as being defensive and therefore unwilling or unable to make the changes that were required for her to complete her case plan and to reunite with her children. In order to prevent jeopardizing her constitutional rights through compliance with the psychological evaluation, a compromise plan was devised. She provided the background information without getting into the details of the events that led to the criminal charges. Psychological testing was administered to gain insight into her psychological functioning and potential coping deficits in parenting skills. The report was silent on the allegations and a disclaimer was added to this effect. Recommendations regarding reunification were provided contingent upon the outcome of the criminal matter. In most of these situations it would be preferred to wait until the completion of the criminal case before embarking on the evaluation regarding the parental rights and responsibilities or visitation schedule with the parents.*

Another standard part of child custody evaluation involves the obtaining of information from independent sources, such as school personnel, school records, and police reports, especially where observations of an officer are involved as opposed to reports by the individuals, the presence of documented legal history, and medical or other relevant biological data, as it may pertain to specifics that are involved in the case. Allegations do not always reference physical or sexual abuse. As already indicated, they can center upon alcohol or drug abuse. They can also assert incompetence due to medical or mental health related issues, in which case obtaining records that predate the filing of the case may be of substantial importance (inasmuch as such records would not be potentially so colored by the current positions of the parties).

Another source of information that would be considered independent, but is often problematic, are reports of social services investigations. These investigations vary widely as to their procedures and the training and ability

---

* In situations of this sort, it is not entirely uncommon for prosecutors or caseworkers concerned about the children to feel the evaluator is being too observant of the rights of the parent. However, it is our position that the essence of ethical practice is involved in managing this situation properly.

of the worker to actually proceed from an independent investigative attitude. The reports consist very often of a file statement as to substantiated, indicated, or unsubstantiated, none of which are clearly tabbed to any data that have been collected, and there is often resistance to providing those data.* On the other hand, effective and committed social services workers in some jurisdictions will collaborate with evaluators and provide substantial input to assist in making appropriate recommendations for the welfare of children. It is important to realize, however, that there is probably going to be overlapping between the investigative approach of social services and the ongoing investigation of the evaluator, such that both may be referencing some portion of the same data pool. Because of these characteristics, social services reports are helpful and can be cited adjunctively but cannot be viewed as entirely independent in many situations in which they get presented. It is particularly important in evaluating the social services report to determine whether the investigator had contact with both sides of the dispute or only with the side making the allegations and whether the investigator actually interviewed the child using good procedure (parent not present, taping of the interview, investigative protocol including careful avoidance of unnecessary leading questions).

Other sources of information are clearly not independent and would include therapists where the service has been secured by the one side making allegations. At times, those therapists will provide "proofs" of the child's condition, often referencing a post-tramautic stress disorder, by copying and sending to both the parent of the child and to the evaluator in some instances pictures created by the child. Many therapists have little or no training in what constitutes legal proof and little or no understanding of the degree to which these kinds of creations reflect reality versus influence.† Obtaining the

---

* The human services report may provide generic definitions but does not specify the factual basis on which a particular category is checked. Thus, one county's notice included the following definitions: Unsubstantiated means "No occurrence of child abuse or neglect." Indicated means "There is (sic) circumstantial, medical, or other isolated indicators of child abuse or neglect, lacking confirmation. Due to credibility of alleged child victim's statements." Substantiated is defined as "When there is an admission of child abuse or neglect by the responsible person, an adjudication of child abuse or neglect, other forms of confirmation deemed valid by Children Services; or professional judgment that the child has been abused or neglected" (Mahoning County, Children Services, Youngstown, Ohio, 2010).

† In one particularly hard-fought case, the therapist whose training and experience involved a primary focus on intervention in cases of identified child abuse provided pictures drawn by the child and comments of the child in therapy as "proof" that abuse had occurred and indicated willingness in the divorce case to come to testify to same. In another case, a therapist had an ongoing agreement with a prosecutor to provide information from sessions that would support charges or be a basis for further indictments. In neither of these instances did the therapists feel it necessary to have any contact with the opposing side and were comfortable with presuming guilt of the alleged perpetrator.

complete records of treatment under conditions where the therapist has not been given any access to the other party and has been under the significant influence of the party bringing the allegations is an important part of investigation. Although the information is not a reliable source relative to the truth of the matters at hand, it can be descriptive of potential behaviors of the parent that would fall under the classification of parent alienation.

Ancillary Contacts

As is reflected above, certain resources are generally available and desirable as informants, including physicians and teachers and others identified as having opportunities to observe in the natural environment the children and their parents. Other kinds of contacts also occur in the course of these cases. Those contacts include attorneys for the parties and the guardian *ad litem* (GAL). In some cases, there may be an attorney for the child's asserted position; contact with that counsel might occur as well, although that source is bound by client confidentiality and therefore unable to provide significant information beyond what the preferences of the child might be. The court itself would rarely, if ever, be a source of information. The court is supposed to remain, in effect, above it all and able to exercise full independence of judgment based on the evidence brought before it. Most judges do not want to compromise that objectivity by contact with the evaluator and, in fact, judges are fairly careful about any kind of contact with the GALs who are appointed to pursue the best interests investigation that is their duty. The general rule is that no evaluator should on his or her own make contact with the court. An exception might exist where there is a need for protected records, but the best strategy for obtaining an order of the court for such data is to approach the attorneys for the parties simultaneously, asking for such an order. (In the best cases, the attorneys will jointly petition for that information, but it can be expected that in those situations where it would be clearly to the benefit of one or the other side, the attorney for that side would submit the motion. The expert, however, should approach both with the request and the reason for it, which supports transparency and neutrality.)

In any and all contacts made with sources of information, it should be clearly conveyed to the source that the evaluator is conducting an ongoing evaluation, the results shall be reported to the court and the parties, and no assurances of confidentiality pertain. Third-party contacts present certain problems in and of themselves because forensic work requires, by the guidelines of the specialty, that relevant ancillary information be obtained, but evidentiary procedures do not always permit relying upon statements of others that have not been admitted by testimony (the hearsay rules; some further discussion of this area can be found in Chapter 4 of this book). For the most part, if this kind of information is of a type generally relied upon by experts in the field, it will be admitted, although the level of confidence may be considered low by the fact finder.

Pretrial Attorney Contacts

Unlike the more formal situation of civil suit cases, communications with attorneys prior to either deposition or a court appearance do occur with some frequency in DR work. However, such contacts should not precede the release of the report except to obtain assistance in contact with a client or other needed information as to status of the case. Information regarding findings is not discussed at this juncture. After release of the report, however, contacts are not uncommon and can be productive for the case and the needs of the children. The following procedures can be suggested:

1. A conference call or meeting of both counsels with the evaluator. Other simultaneous modes such as e-mail or faxed communication may also be selected where appropriate to the purpose of the contact.
2. Sequential calls made as simultaneously as possible and following a written schedule for the inquiries being made with a follow-up memo to both attorneys that documents the contact and the information obtained from each attorney.

Contact with the GAL is another matter. In many if not most cases, the GAL is expected to have contact with the evaluator and that expectation is found in the rules (Ohio Rule of Superintendence 48 provides that such contact should occur). In fact, in the guardian's own testimony when cases go to trial, absence of such contact may be queried in order to determine whether there was some reason not to connect with the evaluator. In some cases there will be specific reasons for the guardian and the evaluator to maintain independent evaluations with no contact until the evaluator's report is released. Such circumstances are established either by court order or by a decision on the part of either GAL or evaluator. When either of the latter professionals determines noncontact to be appropriate, documentation of that stance and its rationale should be placed in the file.

Second Step—Reportage

Detailed but focused and reasonably succinct reports are recommended. Extended and overly elaborate documents often create more problems than they solve and, in far too many cases, encourage the practice of looking at the last pages rather than reading the entire document. Excellent counsel will prepare for either depositions or testimony by experts by careful reading of these documents and selected questioning based on the content therein.

We have seen reports that included up to 80 or 100 pages of single-spaced, detailed descriptions of interviews along with commentary and personality description that was more theoretically based than it was a reflection of the individuals and the specifics of test data. The number of words involved would be enough to meet the requirements for a novelette. The likely presence of highly problematic hearsay is significant without accompanying value for professional opinion purposes. The potential to reinforce the negative family dynamics is not inconsequential. When it is also considered that the costs of these reports and the often repetitive activities they reflect are frequently two to three times what is usual for even a difficult case handled with a more focused approach, a serious ethical question can be raised about the process.

Reports need to be written with an understanding that they will serve one primary and one potential purpose. The primary goal for writing the report is to convey in understandable prose the findings and recommendations of the investigation. The potential purpose in many cases, including these ambiguous ones, is to affect the parties such that resolutions might become possible.* (Unless there would be proof of serious harm and danger to a child, the endpoint of the legal process will be involvement of the youngsters with both parents. If psychological health is a goal, the hope is to enhance communication between these parents that allows the child an unconflicted set of family relationships.) Grisso (2010), based on his years of experience evaluating candidates for the specialty diploma in forensic psychology, has provided specific guides for forensic reportage that include the importance of identification and specificity with regard to procedures followed, reportage of data in one section (including information sought that was not forthcoming), and reportage of inferences and conclusions in another section; he also noted the need to stay focused on the forensic question. In this survey of the evaluations of candidate materials by American Board of Forensic Psychology examiners, he noted the 10 most frequent faults in reportage included opinions without adequate explanation, lack of clarity for the forensic purpose, problematic organization, inclusion of irrelevant data or statements, lack of consideration given to alternative hypotheses, lack of adequate data per se, mixing of data and interpretation, overreliance on

---

* Some forensic psychologists warn against the overstepping of the necessary objectivity of an evaluator and the importance of not engaging in intervention. Certainly, the evaluator cannot assume the mantle of a therapist or mediator. However, it remains true that depending upon how the report is written and how the evaluator engages in the pretrial contacts that may occur that there are system effects particularly around facilitation of conflict resolution, achievement of negotiated agreements, and the acceptance of some needed therapeutic inputs as part of the immediate future of the family.

single sources, poor use of the English language, and inappropriate application of tests.

Referral Question and Procedure

In this section, the purpose of the investigation and report is stated and should be entirely consistent with what the court ordered. All procedures need to be referenced. Dates of contacts should be included. It is also appropriate to include a statement in this section or at the initial part of the reported interviews to the effect that parties and children and any ancillary contacts have been informed about the nonconfidential nature of the procedure. (Sometimes, both children and adults will indicate an understanding of this instruction but nonetheless at some point will ask if they can communicate just one particular thing in confidence. When that request is made, and regardless of the likely content of the item, the evaluator must restate the ground rules. It is our impression that most of the time both children and adults will decide to go ahead and disclose whatever is on their minds. By keeping to the rules, there will be no surprises when the information surfaces later in the report and in testimony.)

Results

Each side should be presented clearly as to the positions taken in the course of the narrative information each has presented during the course of the interviews. In some cases, it is instructive to provide the interviews in sequence, an approach favored by McPherson, but it may be more feasible, depending upon the nature of the data collected, to condense the information from parents into one section and from children into another (along with sections reflecting independent data collection). However, what should be very clear in these kinds of cases are the perspectives that exist for each parent and the foundation on which they present that those perspectives are supported.

In the case of taped child interviews, it is recommended that transcripts be made and attached as addenda to the report. Tapes need to be preserved in many cases that move to a trial level. Those tapes may need to be duplicated and made available to counsel for both parties. It is not entirely uncommon that such tapes may be played in the courtroom as part of the process of expert witness testimony.

Discussion Section

In the evaluative report, it is important that the discussion allows some understanding of the expert's view of the information collected. The sections that reflect the data, including interviews of all parties and children and ancillary interview- and test-related information, should be presented in effect as the fact basis on which the expert worked. The discussion section should acknowledge the diversity of opinion that has been presented and also needs to point out when there is no empirical, scientific, or factual basis for substantiation of either position. The discussion then needs to consider the safety and welfare issues that have to do with the children in their current situation.

With respect to the allegations that have been made, there needs to be acknowledgment of the three possibilities:

1. That the allegations reflect a genuine truth, in which case certain hazards exist for the children.
2. That the allegations represent a belief, but are not necessarily representative of any supported truth, in which case certain different risks exist for the children, which need to be considered.
3. That there can be a malevolent attempt to win in the domestic relations court by knowingly making false allegations. In acknowledging that third option, it is not inappropriate to suggest that it is the least likely of the three possibilities insofar as is currently known on the basis of any kinds of studies that have been done (and also to acknowledge that research in this area would be difficult and has not been adequately conducted). Clearly, where one has a parent who has deliberately manufactured false allegations in order to defeat the other parent, the greatest risk to the child or children is going to lie in their loss of companionship with their other parent and in their incorporation into their own self-identity of a concept of damage.

Finally, there needs to be some recognition of the current status of the children, their attitudes and their beliefs as they have come to internalize them, and the kinds of interventions that may be indicated. All of the above then sets up the basis for the recommendations that follow.

Recommendations

In both this report section and in the testimony that will ensue unless the case resolves, there need to be specific recommendations that recognize the following areas:

1. The child's current and historical attachment, emotional, and security needs.
2. The well-supported finding that children in general do better if they have positive relationships with both of their parents, unless there are substantial reasons why the maintenance or achievement of such relationships cannot occur.

3. There should be listed strategies that specifically address the particular case and are aimed at the reduction of risk and the increase of security, not only for the children and their situation, but for the parents, both of whom, as a result of the equivocality of the case, are in a substantially difficult situation. In the classic case of the mother bringing allegations of either physical or sexual abuse against a father, the very fact of those allegations, if indeed he is innocent, still stands and potentially damages him and makes him vulnerable as being seen as an abuser for any event that might occur in the future as part of ongoing contact. For the mother, in the case where there is honest belief in the hazard to the child, there is anxiety, concern about being an adequately protective parent, and a strengthened potential for misperceiving events that are, in fact, not indicative of misbehavior.

Certain strategies may have general value for these cases:

1. *Psychotherapy for the Child.* Initiating the therapy, the use of the Secrets instruction (see Appendix E) involves a double-bind message that constrains both parents and the situation. Obviously not a fail-safe mechanism, it nonetheless carries some weight, particularly with children but also with the parents participating.
2. *Supervised Visitation.* Chapter 6 detailed the kinds of supervised visitation modes that exist. Supervision is usually a short-term recommendation, given the expense or the logistical difficulties, although in some cases the presence of an independent family member or even a new spouse can provide indefinitely the level of security that reassures the parent who believes there may be a problem.
3. *Roving Reporter.* This instruction (also found in Appendix E) allows the parent against whom allegations have been made to create a document that both has a positive purpose of ultimately being a record for the child of his or her growing up in the context of the relationship with the parent and also provides a basis on which the other parent can be reassured in the case of some statement of the child that causes worry or concern. It is emphasized that such an approach does not ensure against all harm doing, but it significantly reduces the potential for the misperception of harm doing, which itself is a source of damage to children in these situations.
4. *Reunification Therapy.* As described in detail in Chapter 6, this recommendation is made where there has been an effective separation of child or children and a parent, and that separation cannot continue to be supported on the basis of the data developed. Reunification therapy allows a third-party mental health professional to be involved in

a process with both parents and the children that can lead to a successful ongoing contact program.

5. *Alternative Dispute Resolution.* Another recommendation that can and should be made in most of these cases is for mediation or for the use of parent coordination (PC). Mediation becomes the vehicle whereby a third party can assist and can help avoid a return to the court on multiple and often minor issues when communications systems have not developed adequately between the parents to allow the management of disputes. Parent coordination, as already discussed, is specifically for those minor issues that must be handled and that call for immediate decision making. The issues involved usually are specified and the power of the PC is delineated.

Conclusion

No reportage or the procedures that are followed can protect against all the hazards in these cases for all participating: children, parents, professionals, and even the court. However, by proceeding with particular concern for a scientifically informed approach and legally sophisticated decision making, risks are minimized.

Top Cat

9

Top Cat—a fictional name for a fictional character—is a world-class pool and billiards player. In common with many persons in this category, his background is in physics. With a combination of that scientific knowledge and regular practice, he has achieved an enviable position as a man who can put away little colored balls into designated pockets using a stick and a cue ball. He works his way around a pool table, accurately calling his shots. While others watch with some admiration, the little white ball travels across the green felt, hits a colored ball, which obediently drops into the pocket, while the little white ball travels back toward its master, or sideways, depending upon what kind of English he has used. Top Cat is kind of an amazing guy and is so successful that one would almost think that the principles by which he is operating must be pretty linear in mode, functioning in predictable ways as long as rules are followed and the skill level is maintained.

There is literature, both popular and technical, on the physics of pool. Some of it is tongue in cheek, but all of it reflects certain basic principles of the velocity and impact laws that are part of fundamental physics. Nonetheless, there are hints of factors beyond what a purely Newtonian deterministic view of the world allows. For example, "In general, pocket billiard players will be well advised to apply the minimum energy needed to achieve the desired results, and to remove contamination from the billiard balls when possible. This strategy will amplify the effects of spin…" (Crown, 2004, p. 9). Crown goes on to add humorously, "…that the really bad player may elect to surreptitiously apply a lubricant to [the ball] with the effect of achieving consistent deflection and confounding the more skilled opponent" (p. 9).

In another article, Alciatore (2008), a physicist, described "non-ideal sidespin effects." These factors are known as "squirt," "throw," and "swerve." All of them are created by hitting the cue ball away from its center, which is almost always done by players to some degree. The loss of control over the resulting and varying impact of what is known as "English" is characteristic of the novice player.

Returning to our fictional Top Cat, because the variations that are created by small incursions into perfection of a sphere and of the table itself—the playing field—are minimal for the most part, his experience, as well as his understanding of the laws that govern play, serve him extremely well in his control over the outcomes of his efforts.

However, it may be that his faith in more or less classical physics is somewhat misplaced. In his preface to a National Geographic volume entitled

Forces of Change, Daniel Botkin (2006) noted that although there has been much interest and tracking of changing aspects of the natural world, the underlying presumption that has characterized environmental science has been that nature seeks some kind of balance, and the deranging of this balance has been caused by the unbridled behavior of human beings. However, he described and the book documents, a serious revolution in scientific thinking has now occurred in which it is understood that although human activity indeed has affected the planet and its functioning, the essential quality of the natural world is that of complexity and change with a concurrent demand for adaptation or death for all who dwell on the planet. Thus, he stated, "The transition that we are going through today for biological nature is analogous to the 17th and 18th century transition for the cosmos...new observations [then] of the motion of planets showed that changes...followed explicit, understandable, and beautiful rules" (p. 11). He then noted that the systems that are coming to be understood transcend the usual mathematics that were an outgrowth of Newtonian physics, concluding that "...the complexity of ecological systems may never allow such elegance and simplicity" (p. 11).

Let us return once again to Top Cat, and this time we put him in the real world instead of in his well-maintained, properly lighted, and exquisitely balanced billiards room. He will now have to play his game on a raft. His pool table sits upon the raft. The lake is calm, but there is still a certain amount of not entirely predictable current activity that rocks the raft gently. Every time our player walks from one point around the table to another, a shift in weight causes a significant tilt of the table. Just as he has mastered to some degree this shifting environment, a wind blows up from the south and roils the waters. Some wave action is created, making for much more activity of the raft and its occupant. The spray from the waves at times causes wet spots on the felt and spatters the balls. Finally, the balls themselves have mutated from being as close to perfect spheres as can be created by well-calibrated machines to having quite idiosyncratic characteristics. Some of them have a distinct weighting that makes them go to the left or to the right. Some of them have small periodically discharging motors that incline them to move unpredictably.

Top Cat has now arrived in the domestic relations courtroom. Whether he is expert, guardian, judge, litigant, or advocate, he will be unable to reliably predict all of the outcomes of the moves he makes, the thrust that he employs, the velocity that he achieves, or the impact angle that he chooses. His efforts will not only be in interaction with the known participants in play, but will also be affected by myriad factors that create the winds of change in the larger systems within which all of the characters are functioning.

This metaphor we submit is a much more realistic one for understanding what takes place in any courtroom, but especially the domestic relations venue. Despite relying upon and theorizing from the standpoint of a legal structure heavily based in reason and logic, in effect a Newtonian world concept, the reality is that unpredictability and unforeseen change are more characteristic of the ongoing situations with which all the players deal than is any notion of a clear-cut path to a desirable conclusion. In the cases and the recommendations that have been presented in this volume, we have tried to convey the importance of an adaptational view of the world rather than a notion of controlling outcomes. In some of the more recent discussions in family law, there has come to be an emphasis on the idea of solution focus, which is tailored to the individual requirements of cases and recognizes the need to operate creatively if a healthier and more comfortable outcome for children and families is to be achieved. Toward that end, we have presented methods and strategies that allow each case to be approached with some creative understanding of its uniqueness.

Equivocal Communication

Before taking our leave of the dilemmas we have raised, addressed, and considered from the standpoint of implications and possible interventions, it is appropriate to consider what scientific advances have been made in simply looking at the process of communication when ambiguity is a primary component.

Equivocal communication patterns have been studied, particularly toward the end of the last half of the 20th century; however, the attention has been focused on the ways in which language achieves ambiguity or equivocality and why communication modes of this type are used. In general, the presumption or demonstration has been that equivocal communication serves a prosocial purpose of allowing the speaker to avoid outright lying, while not endorsing some fact or position that will be negatively viewed by the listener. Thus, equivocal communication is frequently seen in politicians and other public figures or situations (Bavelas, Black, Chovil, & Mullett, 1990). Various definitions for this type of communicating have been presented, but all are essentially similar: "...is non straightforward communication" (p. 28).

It appears that little study has been made regarding the process of responding to ambiguous speech, except for findings that it is generally accepted and more acceptable than direct but negative messages (Bavelas, Black, Chovil, & Mullett, 1990). In the case of children, there are developmental factors at work. Children as young as 6 or 7 have been able to identify and respond to the kind of ambiguous speech that is necessary for a joke to "work," although they cannot usually explain the joke until they are older. Interestingly, a psychoanalytical approach to ambiguity in speech also focused on the intent of the speaker rather than the plight of the responder and took the position that unconscious factors contribute to ambiguous responding, opening the door for greater latitude in interpretation, which would implicate aspects of the responder posture (Isay, 1977).

One study that looked at children's functioning contrasted the behavior of preschool youngsters with communication disorders in a social play situation. The findings suggested that these children were socially acceptable to their nonlimited peers, but their own behavior involved less initiated social action outside the structured task and less verbal interaction in total, even though they had as good ability to engage in the structure of the play situation as did those without problems (Guralnick, Connor, Hammond, Gottinam, & Kimnish, 2010). There has been a study of the respondent's situation under fairly structured circumstances. Ambiguous speech stimuli of two different kinds were contrasted for their perceptual equivalents. What was found was that latencies in response time increased as a function of the degree of ambiguity that occurred (Repp, 1981). That experiment demonstrated the impact of cognitive load, which has been seen in other contexts as well, and can be used to identify dissimulation under certain circumstances (Lancaster & Vrij, 2010).

The above information supports, albeit indirectly for the most part, that ambiguous messages may be intentional, although they can occur unintentionally, and when they do occur they place some demand on persons responding. When the ambiguous messages serve the purpose of a prosocial or protective function, they are likely to be positively received. Very young children, however, are unlikely to be able to configure intentionally such responses and are much more concrete and therefore, at least from their perspective, accurate in what they are saying. That very concretism, however, is problematic to an adult who may have different and competing associations to words that a child may use.* Thus, very young children, in a social context involving a great deal of emotional vulnerability and distrust, are more likely to emit terms because they are new language users, that can be seen ambiguously and can therefore be the basis for erroneous responding.

---

* In one allegations case, the very young child in the midst of toilet training returned from a visit with her father to say to her mother that her Daddy had "waped me." Because the youngster incorrectly articulated the word "wiped," which was an accurate account of his helping her in the bathroom, the mother (with a personal history of abuse and a relatively negative post-decree relationship with the father) thought she heard and subsequently reported that the child had said the father "raped" her. The mother accurately indicated the child could not make "r" sounds and would substitute the "w" sound in r-words. This episode provided a clear example of the issues that are found in equivocal abuse allegations cases: there was negative expectation based on remote and more recent negative history (by the mother), accurate but poorly articulated verbal behavior with equivocal meanings embedded (by the child), and subsequent anger at some prolonged noncontact with his child (by the father). In the end, the mother remained worried about unsupervised contact that was in due time, postinvestigation and reportage, ordered by the court. The mother was literally unable to separate the meaning of rape to her as a victim and the clear lack of such a concept or vocabulary by the daughter.

Change

In Chapter 1, it was pointed out that changes in legal standards and definitions, notably involving concepts of best interests and shared parenting, have likely supported significant changes in marriage patterns that emerged, favoring increasing divorce rates and possibly also the development of nonmarried cohabitation and the development of nonstandard or newly fashioned definitions of family. The current approach to data gathering by the U.S. Census Bureau has recognized that nuclear families can no longer be defined as consisting of mothers, fathers, and children. Laws have been rewritten and are still being revised to recognize the equality of persons whose lifestyle and family system patterns are different from those found reflected in traditional terms. Supreme Court decisions, as well as more local case law, have recognized the acceptability of nonstandard parenting arrangements and prohibit discrimination on the basis of sexual preference or single status in the application of the best interests definitions. Although not a national reality, the concept of gay marriage has gained more credibility and some actuality in recent years. (When such unions fail, the difficulty for the courts is law that has designated a child or children as being in the custody of one of the two persons involved in the union, thus leaving the other person without standing to obtain custody or even companionship time. Because that original custody designation may or may not reflect the child's affectional bonding, the application of the now outmoded laws may inflict significant harm.)

In the midst of all of these influences and developments, and perhaps fed by the emergence of the information age with its enhanced speed of communication (with many options for both communication and miscommunication as the section on the Internet illustrated; see Chapter 5), the particularly difficult cases where very serious factors are ambiguously and insecurely present, tax the court system in extraordinary ways. Consider the following case example.

Albert and his mother and father's case problems began at the time of the divorce. With intervention of the guardian *ad litem* (GAL), a resolution in the form of a shared parenting was crafted in the face of some assertions by the father, denied by the mother, of domestic violence. The case re-emerged at the post-decree point when the mother returned to court in order to obtain some parenting time with her son. At the time that this phase of the case began, Albert was refusing any contact with his mother. When the mother was seen for her initial interview, she presented that the father was a chronic liar whose manipulations had secured a one-sided relationship with the boy and her complete exclusion.

The father's presentation included pictures of bruises on the child's arm, which he said were created by virtue of the mother's drunken grabbing of the boy's arm and beating him on his head. He had documents indicating the child had complained to school authorities and that social services have been involved. He also indicated that Albert would no longer agree to see the GAL because of a lack of confidence that there was support for the allegations. The evaluator was told that Albert was very worried and anxious about being seen because he didn't want to be disbelieved.

Albert had been in therapy for a serious trauma that he had suffered and he had numerous somatic symptoms, largely involving gastrointestinal reactivity but also extending to other physical systems. His history included that prior to this he had been seen by a psychiatrist for a post-tramautic stress disorder secondary to being sexually abused by an older male, an event unrelated to the marital struggles (although at times there were suggestions by the father that the mother's lack of parenting alertness was partially to blame). Albert's anxiety-based physiological symptoms have periodically resulted in hospitalization. The boy's second therapist was knowledgeable in dealing with children with somatic symptoms but had not had experience of dealing with situations where statements had to be viewed with extreme skepticism due to the sociolegal context. That therapist had explicitly as well as implicitly supported the boy's and the father's view of the past and the present. However, upon being provided with the results of the investigation as it proceeded, that therapist's ability to retreat from acting as a force to support the alienation of the boy from his mother was an important component in the outcome. That alienation, however, was not simply a function of the father's distortions about the past, but also a function of the things that had in reality transpired between the youngster and his mother.

The mother, in her presentation, indicated that she was more prone to have a well-disciplined approach and faulted her former spouse for being entirely permissive. Her own management of herself and her immediate environment, however, was well under what would be expected in a middle-class setting. She also presented with a chronic illness, which had left her partially disabled. Interestingly, she was active as a creative artist, and she contributed some works to benefit a small local theater.

The father's family history included the loss of a mother and an aunt, both of whom had sequentially provided parenting to him during his growing-up years. Consistent with his choice of Albert's mother, he, too, had a background in creative training and work. Also consistent from a psychological viewpoint was the choice of a mate who might provide caretaking. (The mother's rather abrupt decline of health and energy to work may have disrupted the dynamics on which the marriage was based.) It was his position, however, that the marriage was flawed from the beginning and that there was much domestic violence. It was not unimportant that he was a very imposing man of large stature and that the mother was of diminutive size and limited physical strength.

Albert arrived at one of his interviews with a list of remembered offenses that included bizarre and sexualized behavior on the part of relatives of his mother and ended with the assertion that the court-imposed ongoing visitation with a policeman present had involved the mother making a death threat, an event conspicuously missing from the officer's report. His presentation throughout the evaluation process reflected a combination of developed belief systems about the history of his family, some of which were clearly imbued with misinformation but for him were realities, plus the further active creation, knowingly, of stories that would serve his alliance with his father against his mother.

Home visits and school contacts developed information that certainly supported the presence of a great deal of dysfunctionality in the interactions of the parents and in the status of the son. Albert was clearly more dependent upon his father than is normally found among early teen boys. His school functioning fluctuated as did his health condition. Some of his negative stories about his experiences with his mother could be supported at least in part by reliable independent observations, but most of them were reiterations of statements that had been made over the years by the father and were still a part of his presentation.

Test results on the MMPI-2 and MCMI-III for both parents allowed some credibility to the presentation of the father. In the mother's test profiles, there were some indications of narcissistic preoccupations, inability to appreciate her impact on others, and the presence of significant anger in the context of inadequate control systems. The father's functioning on the test was much better defended, following the usual protocol of overstatement of virtue and adequacy, but the elevated Overcontrolled Hostility Scale that is often present in these cases was clearly in evidence and there were hints of significant insecurities on his part that could motivate some of his behavior vis-à-vis the mother and his encouragement of the dependency and affirmation that his son was able to provide.

Other investigative sources, including the guardian, confirmed that some of the time the father actually did the child's homework; was present daily at the school, much in excess of any other parent; and was always overinvolved in any school program in which the boy might participate.

It was possible to come to the conclusion that the allegations of parental abuse in the past were more likely than not significantly overstated; it was also true that there were incidents of inappropriate parenting that fed and maintained the view of the mother as dangerous and possibly at times abusing alcohol. It was not possible to convince either side of the unreliability of their respective views of each other, including the mother's need to see the father as deliberately and malevolently contriving to convince the boy of the need to have no relationship with her.

This evaluation involved an extended protocol with home visits occurring to both settings, contacts with extended family members and others who knew both sides of the dispute and the history, and significant collaboration with the guardian, who had been involved during the pre-decree period, as well as in this post-decree filing.

Ultimately, a set of recommendations was made that supported continuing the shared parenting, which clearly had never been managed in the way that any kind of coparenting is envisioned, but with specifications for combined mediation and counseling and a list of specific rules to be followed that would not allow some behavioral patterns to continue. Included in that list of requirements were that the father would end his overinvolvement in the boy's school life and end all discussions of his views of the past in the hearing of the youngster. It was recommended he be responsible to support that the boy now begin some regular normalized parenting time with his mother. It was further suggested that failure to follow any of the above constraints would lay a foundation for a change of custody of the youngster to the mother, and that under such circumstances an extended period might be recommended, during which the father would not have any contact with the boy followed by a gradual reintroduction using a supervised mode. A normalized mode would be achieved on the basis of success at each step. (The psychologist knew that such content would be unlikely to transfer into a post-decree parenting order as such, but the specific inclusion of mention of the potential for change of custody was actually intended as an indicator to the parties and counsels of the seriousness with which the evaluator viewed the disruption of the boy's relationship with his mother. It allowed both sides to know that testimony of the expert would support a change of custody absent any change of behavior on the part of the father.)

The end result of issuing that report was a meeting of the parties and their counsels and the development of an agreement that allowed withdrawal of the mother's motion for sole custody and a graduated system of reintroduction of the mother into the boy's life with appropriate therapeutic supports on both sides.

Summary

Law and psychology have often been characterized as incorporating intrinsically different ways of thinking, with the result that communication between professionals representing the disciplines can be less than successful. However, it would be our argument that, in effect, law as a discipline has more in common with psychology than it represents divergence. The different thinking patterns may be best seen in a therapy context where intuitive and less-crafted communication modes are in evidence rather than the patterns of verbalization expected in the courtroom setting and compliant with its procedural rules. However, in the degree to which psychologists and attorneys believe in the world as operating on a linear basis, both are probably speaking the same language by virtue of which both are equally at a disadvantage. Linear logic works in a very confined and restricted fashion to produce results. To the extent that linear systems are operative, prediction is clearly enhanced. Psychology has developed notably in its experimental applications in learning theory some very definite linearly stated laws that successfully predict outcomes or allow control of target behaviors. However, human beings, in their interactions with themselves, each other, and the world, do not behave according to linear systems, just as the processes within their bodies do not so operate, and processes throughout nature do not. From observations of growth and development in botanical contexts, from the study of subatomic behavior of interest to physicists, and even including the discussion of the broad patterns of global economics, the only adequate explanations derive from the complexity perspective. In complex dynamical systems, the rules that pertain sometimes incorporate linear operations at certain levels, but overall the operations are better understood as nonlinear and not necessarily predictable due to such factors as the level of observation, the level of intervention, the number and changing identity of the relevant variables, or the operation of the self-organizing principles that are in play.

In law, this type of complexity is actually observed and in some cases studied. For example, jury nullification is a known phenomenon that causes distress in some cases to its observers because it interferes with the expected outcome of the system. The notion in criminal justice is that the evidence will tip the balance of the scales and result in conviction or acquittal. In fact, juries are known to decide that the application of the law, according to the principles articulated to them by the judge, would not result in a fair outcome if applied in linear logical fashion. Therefore, they will either find for guilt of a lower-level offense or will outright acquit, in the face of every indicator that the opposite result should have pertained. Some who view this phenomenon say that the law should be written such that jury nullification cannot be allowed to occur because it offends against the appropriate orderly operation of the legal system. As with some other experiments where law has been used to try and constrain behavior, the ability to keep juries from doing what they come to believe is fair and right, in the face of some legal process that would dictate otherwise, is not likely to be successful.

Another example from the criminal law arena is found in the sentencing patterns that have emerged for judges in child pornography cases. A significant number of judges have determined from their own perspectives that the application of the sentencing structure anticipated for such crimes is not appropriate, and therefore these jurists have consistently undersentenced the persons brought before them in these cases (Cardona, 2009; Floyd & Sinclair, 2010). Perhaps predictably, the position of those critical of this judicial behavior was that the judges are supporting child abuse. The argument of these observers was that every time child pornography is viewed, a child is revictimized (Sangiacomo, 2010). It is interesting to contemplate the logic of that position. Strictly speaking, the child was victimized only for those times that he or she was photographed being the victim of deplorable acts. How many times the product is viewed is not a direct abuse of the child. However, commentators noted that the emergence of Internet pornography results in the victim being offended in an ongoing way by pictures that continue in existence. Others argued that by selling and buying such materials, there is support for ongoing victimization of children, but the degree of criminal responsibility might well be seen as below that of the producer of the product. Regardless of the position favored in this matter, it remains a fact that the expected outcome of cases is not the obtained result due to the exercise of varying individual judicial perspectives, themselves a function of how a defendant and an offense are viewed and what specific experiences also may have played a part.*

If the criminal law provides examples of uncertainty due to complex input, it is not surprising that family law is even more prone to unpredictability. The shapes of outcomes available to judges or created by litigants who reach agreement reflect the differences in the families involved and the issues at hand. When the evidence itself cannot be reduced to some kind of reliable and agreed-upon dimensions, but still either formally or informally plays a partially determinative part in what takes place, the outcomes are even more in doubt as is the foundation for whatever is the final determination.

As the players in this shifting field of willful spheres try to balance themselves and somehow achieve what each thinks is best, a demonstration of complexity plays out over and over in the domestic relations courtroom. We have tried to provide some directions that reduce some of the uncertainty, knowing that it is as impossible to end the unpredictability as it is impossible to reach a goal by continuously halving the distance from the point of departure. We have also tried to provide some directions for solutions that will enhance the security and safety of children and the courts whose work is to serve their interests.

---

* In what most would see as very unusual judicial behavior, a judge in Albany, New York, rejected professional risk assessments and sentenced a defendant in a child pornography case on the basis of his high potential to reoffend as being the result of "an as-of-yet undiscovered gene." This original (and we might note unfalsifiable) theory coming from the bench was unpersuasive to the U.S. Court of Appeals for the Second Circuit. Their ruling: "It would be impermissible for the court to base its decision of recidivism on an unsupported theory of genetics." The defendant was remanded for sentencing by a different judge on the basis of fairness. Clearly, unexpected behavior can present from many quarters in the ostensibly regulated atmosphere of the legal process (Weiser, 2011).

Recommended Guidelines for Interviewing Children in Cases of Alleged Sexual Abuse

JACK S. ANNON

The basic premise for these guidelines is that even young children may be able to provide reliable and accurate accounts of events that they have experienced or witnessed, provided that the interview is done appropriately, in a proper setting, and without manipulation by the evaluator. These guidelines are based upon the clinical and laboratory research cited in the references.

General

1. Conduct the interview as early as feasible after the first statement of possible abuse. Ensure that the evaluation is carried out by a well-trained individual who is experienced in child development and in evaluating children and families.
2. Avoid forming preconceived impressions of the incident. A way to accomplish this is for the evaluator to be relatively naive as to the circumstances of the abuse and to avoid learning any information that the child does not know. Otherwise, the evaluator may not be open to information that does not fit with information already obtained. Also, if the evaluator has previous information, there is usually strong pressure placed on the child for specific responses, and contradictory information may not be pursued.
3. Consider the demand characteristics of the interview setting. Avoid extremes, such as a room full of toys that gives the child the impression it is a playroom for "make believe," or a bare stark room with only adult furniture. Sit at a table, at the same level as the child.

4. If a one-way mirror is used, place it higher than the seated child. A clear view can be obtained in this manner, or a videotape can be made shooting down through such a small window. Too often, the one-way mirror is directly opposite the child's face with the result that many children get distracted and begin making faces at themselves in the mirror and do not pay attention to the interview.

5. Dress in comfortable casual clothes rather than in a law enforcement or medical uniform.

6. If there are to be observers, or the interview is to be video- or audio-taped, tell the child and ask the parent or legal guardian to sign an informed consent form prior to the actual interview.

The Interview

1. Videotape, or at least audiotape, all contacts with the child from introduction to farewell.

2. Interview the child alone. The only people in the room should be the child and the evaluator, unless there is a compelling need to do otherwise.

3. Do not introduce yourself with a title such as "detective," "officer," or "doctor." Just state your name and something to the effect that "I am a person who talks with children."

4. Establish rapport at the beginning. Here is where general and non-leading questions may be asked about home, school, friends, and games. This is an opportunity to use open-ended questions so the child may become accustomed to such questioning. This is also where a baseline of the child's verbal and nonverbal behavior is noted during different areas of questioning, for comparison later when talking about the alleged abuse.

5. Be friendly rather than authoritarian with the child.

6. Assess the child's developmental level and the concepts that the child has in various areas. Use materials such as pencil and paper, color crayons, or blocks to find out how far the child can count, how many colors the child knows, whether the child understands concepts of "in, on, under, beside, over," etc.

7. Find out if the child understands the concept of the difference between telling the truth and telling fibs or lies and whether the child knows the difference between "make believe" and "reality."

8. Let the child know that the evaluator has no information regarding the facts of the child's particular situation because the evaluator was not there. Tell the child to trust his or her own memory because the evaluator has no knowledge about the events in question.

Tell the child to say "I don't know" when the child doesn't know the answer and "I don't remember" when the child doesn't remember. Make it clear that the child's task is to say only what really happened and not to say what he or she thinks the evaluator might want to hear.

9. However, research indicates that just saying this may not be very helpful unless the child actually has an opportunity to practice it. So encourage children to admit they lack memory or knowledge about a particular event, rather than trying to guess. For example, the evaluator could ask, "Did the doctor who delivered you wear glasses or not?" or "What were the first words mommy said when she saw you after you were born?" Encourage the child to respond with "I don't know" or "I don't remember" to questions such as these and practice these interactions.

10. Let the child know that some of the questions may be confusing and give examples such as, "How many pie needles are in a ginbung?" or "Is a top a square or a rectangle?" Give the child a chance to say he or she is confused or doesn't understand. If the child does try to answer, let the child know that the evaluator could not even answer it, and it is OK to say "I don't understand."

11. Let the child know that sometimes the evaluator may ask the same question over again, and if this happens, it does not mean that the first answer was wrong; it could mean that the evaluator forgot that the question was asked before, or it could mean that the evaluator did not quite understand what was said before.

12. Give the child permission to correct the evaluator. This also gives an opportunity to see how suggestible the child is. For example, the evaluator could say "Now you told me that your brother was 4 years old" (when in reality, the child said the brother was 6 years old). See if the child will let it go or will correct the evaluator.

13. Let the child know that some questions may be easy and others may be difficult, and no one is expected to remember everything. Encourage children to admit they are confused rather than trying to guess, and reinforce them when they do correct the interviewer, when they do say that they don't know, or when they admit they are confused.

14. Check out the child's concepts pertaining to knowledge and function of body parts with outline drawings, which are commonly used. Anatomical dolls are sometimes used, but there is a consensus that dolls by themselves should never be used to make a diagnosis of sexual abuse. They can at best be used only as a comforter, ice breaker, or as an anatomical model or later as a demonstration aid.

15. Focused questions can sometimes be used here. For example, in regard to the body when the child gives the name for the penis or

vagina, ask questions such as "Who has one of these?" "What is it for?" "Have you ever seen one?" "What do men or women do with them?" "Did you ever touch one?" "Whose?" "What do you do with yours?" "Did yours ever get hurt?" "Anyone ever touched yours?" "Has anyone done anything to yours?"

16. Some general questions could also be around the concept of games: "Do you play games with your mom, your dad, your brother, your sister, your babysitter, etc.?" "What kinds of games?" "Does your family have any secrets?" "What kind of secrets?"

17. Do not encourage make believe by saying things such as "Make believe that this puppet is your dad and that this puppet is you" or "Now, let's pretend we are at home and...." Such instructions invite the child to engage in make believe and pretend situations. When this happens, children may use their imaginations and come up with all sorts of statements that have no basis in reality. The evaluator should carefully avoid using words such as "make believe" or "pretend" and should avoid modeling such behaviors in the interview.

18. Do not turn the interview into a "play" session. This can confuse the child. Also, children may see this as an opportunity to interact as they would with another child and to make things up. Although these types of behaviors may be appropriate in play therapy with the child who has been abused, in a forensic evaluation they are not appropriate and may mislead the child into giving false information.

19. Sometimes a memory aid such as a dollhouse might be used. However, in this case let the child know that the figures represent different real people, and it is his house to help him reenact events. Paper and pencil drawings can do the same thing. A child can draw the house and point out where different places are and where different things happened.

20. In focusing the child's attention in certain areas, as much as possible avoid direct, leading, or suggestive questions or statements since these reduce the length and quality of the statements made by the child.

21. Use invitational statements or questions in order to elicit a more open-ended response from the child, such as "And then what happened?" or "Would you please tell me more about that?"

22. Use verbal facilitators such as "OK, I see" and restatement of the child's previous statement, as well as nonsuggestive words of encouragement, which again are designed to keep the child talking in an open-ended way.

23. Once the child starts to talk about a specific area pertaining to possible abuse, allow the child to use free recall of whatever events are

remembered in whatever order the child wishes. Encourage the child to provide a free narrative account and do not interrupt the narrative with questions.

24. Stress the importance of telling everything that is remembered, even partial information, regardless of whether or not the child believes it is important. Let the child tell you as much as is recalled.

25. Once the child has narrated an event, gather more information by asking the child to start at the middle and go forward or backward in time.

26. When necessary, open-ended questions can be repeated a number of times. For example, when the child stops talking, say "Now tell me more about what happened when you walked into the bathroom."

27. Closed-ended questions that can be answered "yes" or "no" should not be repeated; otherwise, the child may feel that the previous answer was not accepted by the evaluator. The child may therefore believe that the first answer was not "right" and may change the answer.

28. At this point, it may be helpful to use elements from what is called the cognitive interview to help the child mentally reconstruct the environment and context that existed at the time of the given event.

29. Avoid coercion of any type or any implication of bribes or threats. Questions may be used to clarify, but it is important not to lead the child or suggest answers to the child. For example, avoid questions such as "Did you see the… ?" or "After he hit you what did you do then?" (when the child never said that he was hit, but only the mother had said that before the interview). If you must use questions, use objective ones such as "Did you see a… ?" or best "What did you see?" or multiple-choice questions such as "Was it red, white, yellow, or some other color?"

30. Use a neutral tone with no urgency.

31. Avoid repeated accusations of alleged offenses against a particular person.

32. Be patient and nonjudgmental throughout.

33. Do not ignore contradictions in the child's testimony of what was said earlier as compared to later. Follow up on apparent contradictions as open-endedly as possible.

34. Be concrete in the questions asked. For example, if a young child is asked "Did Leilani drive you away in her car?" the child may answer negatively if the actual vehicle used was a truck.

35. Check out the level of suggestibility in the child. As suggested by one researcher, the evaluator might ask "Lots of children in situations like this get aches and pains in their legs and feet; how about you?" In this case see if the child agrees, and if so, ask "Where?" If the child

does not agree, this means she is more likely to be resistant to that kind of suggestion.

36. Throughout the interview, test for alternative hypotheses. One researcher recommends questions such as "Sometimes kids make up a story and later believe that it is true, but it is only a daydream, did that happen to you?" Another question might be "Some people might think you made up the story to get out of the house, is there a possibility of that?" or "Some mothers might have told you what to say, is that what happened in your case?" or "Sometimes parents do some really mean things to their children, and the only way to get back at them is to try to hurt them and say that they did something else. Could that be the case here?"

37. Respect the child's wishes concerning whether or not to discuss a specific matter. Give the child permission to decline answering because the answer may be too difficult to discuss at the moment, and let the child know that he or she does not have to answer right now if he or she doesn't want to.

38. If the child says he or she wants to stop the interview, do so, and do not say "We will stop as soon as you tell me everything I want to know" or use other kinds of promises or rewards. Accept the request without pushing, and let the child know that you can meet again at another time and then maybe talk more about some of the different things. It is better to have two or three short videotaped open interviews than to try to obtain as much information as possible from a resistant or tired child all in one long interview.

39. Thank the child for the time spent and for the way that he or she has helped the evaluator to understand what has been happening with the child. Unless otherwise called for, end with a discussion of a neutral subject such as asking the child what he or she is going to do after the interview, etc.

Evaluation of the Interview

1. In evaluating the interview, look for external consistency. Does the child give the same account to different people, or are there serious inconsistencies in details or time sequences between different versions of the same incident?

2. Look at internal consistency. Does the child's story make sense? Do the time sequences, locations, and descriptive details change over the time of the interview when the child is asked to go back and recount different aspects of the incident?

3. Look at internal details. Is there sufficient detail? Sometimes children can give extremely accurate descriptions for these details; other times they may not be able to. Note if the child makes only a generalized accusation such as "He raped me" or "He abused me."

4. Look at the child's affect. Is the affect congruent with what the child is discussing? Do you see various emotions of depression, embarrassment, or anger? Or do you see inappropriate faint smiling or over-eager talk? Some children are numb and flat because of exhaustion or denial, or the flat affect could be the result of telling the story numerous times.

5. Notice the susceptibility to suggestion. Was the evaluator able to induce the child to change parts of the story or adopt ideas?

6. Note any reactions to challenges that the evaluator may have asked. If the evaluator asked the child if he or she made up the story, what is the child's response? Does the child get angry? Does the child deny it or go along with what the evaluator says?

7. Understand reasons why children might not tell the truth. Five areas have been researched: (1) children will lie to avoid punishment; (2) children can be induced to tell a lie in the context of a game; (3) children will lie to keep promises (children even as young as 2 years of age will omit important information about transgressions and accidents if adults ask them to do so); (4) children may lie for personal gain (in order to gain material rewards or gain acceptance in a group); and (5) children may lie in order to avoid embarrassment.

Reprinted by permission of H. Wakefield, for *Issues in Child Abuse Accusations*, a publication of the Institute for Psychological Therapies.

Affidavit Example

SANDRA McPHERSON

General Background

I am a clinical and forensic psychologist. I received my bachelor's degree from Kent State and then went on to graduate school at Case Western Reserve where I received my master's degree and then completed the requirements for my PhD degree in 1967. After that I continued with on-going training and passed my national boarding examinations in both clinical and forensic psychology.

My relevant work experience began when I worked a year as a social worker in Richland County, Ohio, before I finished my undergraduate degree. After receiving my PhD, I worked at The Child Guidance Center in Cleveland, Ohio, where I was involved in clinical and research functions. I have been on the staff of a local hospital which was originally known as Ridgecliff and later became the Laurelwood Hospital. I left Laurelwood to join an HMO in what became part of the University Hospitals system. My practice became more focused on forensic work, and I left the UH program to go into private practice in order to pursue what would be substantially a forensic psychology practice. Additionally, I joined the faculty of the Fielding Graduate University in Santa Barbara and I teach at various places around the country as part of that program.

From 1972–1977 I served as examiner and secretary for the Ohio State Board of Psychology. From 1977–1978 I served as president of the Board.

I currently serve on the examination faculty of the American Board of Forensic Psychology, which is the national boarding examination for forensic psychologists.

A complete listing of my educational degrees, my professional experience, and my publications is hereto attached.

Training and Experience Regarding the Investigation of Allegations of Child Sexual Abuse

In the late 1970s, child sexual abuse started to become a much more visible concern within the community. During the past three decades there has been a dramatic rise in the number of allegations of child sexual abuse. With that rise in volume of such allegations, psychologists became increasingly concerned about the protocols and procedures that investigators used when they interviewed alleged victims. Their concerns were fueled both by the research that predated the increased reportage of child abuse as well as by ongoing research concerning the susceptibility of children to suggestion during the interview process. In order to ensure that alleged victims of child sexual abuse are interviewed in a manner that will yield accurate and reliable information, protocols and procedures for interviewing children were developed that incorporated the research and experience of qualified professionals in the field of child psychology. Although some child advocates and investigators may not have adopted these protocols, there is a general consensus among well-trained and experienced professionals that certain basic procedures need to be implemented in order to ensure that potentials for accurate and reliable information are at the best levels possible.

A significant portion of my practice has involved the investigation of allegations of child sexual abuse. I initially learned about interviewing children as part of my internships and subsequent staff positions at The Child Guidance Center. While I was there, we had a training program at The Child Guidance Center to address the identification and therapeutic intervention needed in cases of child sexual abuse. In the mid-1980s, I attended workshop training by Dr. Fallon in the forensic interviewing of children identified as possible abuse victims, which included the use of anatomical dolls. Since then, continuing education has involved work specific to this area. I have also been involved in research in regard to procedures and protocols in interviewing children and have taught and given workshops related to same.

After the Ohio Supreme Court issued its decision in *State v. Gersin* (1996) 76 Ohio St. 3d 491, I have been permitted to testify in trials concerning accepted protocols and procedures for interviewing alleged victims of child sexual abuse.

The accepted procedures found in the protocols commonly used in sex abuse assessment are outlined and discussed hereafter. As is reflected in the following discussion of protocols, noncompliance with the essential elements standard to such investigatory work raises substantial questions relevant to the court because of known effects on the report of child witnesses.

Accepted Protocols and Procedures for the Investigation of Allegations of Child Sexual Abuse

A proper investigation mode is to have an interview with the child alone without any important (to the child) people present at the time, such as parents and relatives, because of the influence such persons carry and their potential for contaminating the child's responding. The presence of somebody who is emotionally invested in that child and who has either some belief about what has occurred or just some fears about it is likely to transmit those reactions to the child. That is one of the reasons why it may take more than one interview in isolated cases because some children find it difficult to separate.

An initial phase of all investigative interviews involves establishing rapport with the child. Obviously, one introduces oneself and one gets some kind of initial contact with the youngster who is involved. However, there must be avoidance of any undue overinvolvement or intensity. During this first part of the interview, one explains to the child why the interview is taking place, its nonconfidential nature must be communicated at the level possible given the developmental stage of the child, and the child is informed that the interviewer does not know the answers to any of the questions; only the child knows. The level of the child's vocabulary and ability to understand is also assessed. It is also important during this time to cover the importance of truth-telling and to gain some idea of the child's ability to recount accurately information from past experience.

The third accepted principle is that all child sexual abuse interviews should be recorded, preferably with video because one can then see the child's behavior. A highly significant amount of our communication is nonverbal. At the very least there needs to be an audio recording because while conducting an interview it is absolutely impossible to write down a complete record of everything the interviewer says and everything the child says in the sequence in which it occurs in veridical fashion, a fashion where the interview is completely and accurately preserved. Without such a record, it is not possible to know whether the interviewer has introduced critical data in a leading fashion, and it is not possible for the interviewer to have an accurate factual record later as an assist to the interviewer's memory. I have done research concerning the reliability of memories of interviewers in a nonrecorded interview context versus a recorded context. This research occurred about 10 years ago when concerns arose at various agencies about whether recording was important. In that research, my participants were a group of my doctoral-level psychology students, all of whom had had training as interviewers and some of whom had 20 years of experience interviewing. I showed them a videotape of an interview of a child on which they took notes.

Doing so is a substantially less demanding task than doing an interview and writing notes as it progresses, or writing notes at the end of an interview based on memory. These participants were simply required to sit down and take notes on this interview as they watched it done by somebody else. Six to nine months later, I had half of them respond to a series of factual questions on the basis of which significant conclusions or recommendations might be made after reviewing their notes. The other half responded to the same questions after reviewing the tape of the interview and as well as their notes. The end result was quite clear. Even with very simple factual questions, although those with the notes often were correct, they made more errors than those without the video. It was a nice demonstration that human memory, no matter how well trained, cannot retain the totality of an interview—even with good note taking—over an extended period of time.

Another extremely necessary characteristic of a forensic child sexual abuse interview concerns the form of questions that a child should be asked, particularly about substantive matters. A proper interview starts with open-ended questions. A caveat which must be made is that the younger the child, the more focus and direction is necessary in order to obtain information about a desired experience. Nonetheless, it is absolutely important that crucial elements of abuse must not be introduced in the questions of the interviewer. Rather, after there is a focus of the child on a particular incident, area, or time, questions, often starting with the prompt "I wonder" (what happened, who was there, what was next, etc.), are used. Any element that is provided by the interviewer is potentially a source of actual memory change for the child.

An interview in some ways can be conceptualized as an inverted triangle, which starts with the most general questioning that allows the child to provide relevant to the issue responses and then proceeds with directed inquiries that are not leading for any elements not provided initially by the child. Thus, the interview will preserve the integrity of memory. Memory is not a videotape. It does not record accurately what occurred. All memories change over time incorporating things that weren't really part of the story or which were part of another story. That aspect of human memory behavior has been well known anecdotally and starting in 1932 documented in research studies.

Throughout the interview as its focus narrows, there needs to be some reiteration of the interviewer's lack of knowledge so that the child is reminded that he or she is the source of information. Also important is to avoid any type of negative or positive reinforcement for specific statements, either denials or assertions, made by the child; either type of reinforcement if it occurs in the context of significant data points can become coercive and contaminating.

The importance of avoiding leading questions containing information that the child has not him- or herself provided is that such questions actually have the potential to create false memories about critical details. A child learns everything he or she knows from important others. If a child says the wrong thing, a parent corrects him. If a child comes to the wrong conclusions at school, the teacher corrects him. So, therefore, the child often starts from the presumption that everything people who are authorities say is true. Because of the power of adults in a child's life to define what is true and what is false, it's really important that the child understands that in this interview situation the interviewer is unlike all others and does not know.

The seminal article on the constructive nature of memory and the power of leading questions in the context of investigative interviewing was published by Ceci and Bruck in 1993. There was some very nice research called the "Mousetrap Experiment," in which over a period of weeks researchers came to a selection of children at their homes and queried "Do you remember when you got your hand caught in a mousetrap?" The first time, the children generally denied the event. But by the end of about 10 weeks of coming back and asking the same question, some but not all of the children had a whole elaborate story, not only of having the experience, but they knew where it occurred, when it occurred, who else was there, and so on. They had a complete story that they created simply from the very leading question that gave them the information that they had had this experience. They accepted the lead and then elaborated. At the same time, it can be noted that some resisted the lead, consistent with the findings that people vary as to their suggestibility. Suggestibility is both state and trait and it is also related to age and developmental status. More recent research has shown that when there is repeated questioning, which always has to occur in an investigation, if the questions remain open-ended and nonleading, the memory is not likely to be altered in significant ways.

A child who is introduced to something that did not happen and incorporates the data into his or her memory may then sincerely recount the nonevent. If a child's memory has been contaminated, the child may come into a courtroom setting and swear to tell the truth but the contamination is not removed by taking the oath. Another aspect necessary to consider in child witness/victim interviewing is the "yes set." Children tend to agree with what they think adults want. Closed questions that are followed by only yes or no answers can lead to endorsements of facts by error. There are ways, however, that questioning can proceed with verbally limited or very young children, which involve "stacking" and alternating the questions in a way that avoids creating a self-fulfilling prophecy by the interviewer.

Another aspect of the investigation of child sexual abuse has considered symptomatic status of alleged victims. However, outside of extremely unusual sexual knowledge incorporated into the child's behavioral or verbal repertoire, well beyond attempted touching or exploration of bodies, there are no pathognomic indicators of child sexual abuse. A child might demonstrate sexualized behavior because he has been exposed to pornography, for example, or because he has watched adults behaving in ways that they should not be behaving in front of him, or he may demonstrate sexualized behavior because he himself has been sexually abused. Furthermore, in today's world, significant sexual behavior can be seen on television in homes where parents have not maintained control over children's watching habits. Finally, all of the symptoms of emotional disturbance (nightmares, changes in eating and sleeping habits, problems in school, etc.) that have been reported in abused children also occur in the absence of abuse and may be due to other causes.

A particular approach that was essentially developed during the 1980s for child sexual abuse investigations involved the use of anatomically correct dolls as part of the interview. The use of interview aids in and of itself is not problematic, but both the way in which the dolls came to be employed and the interpretations that followed led to significant issues. The notion arose that sexualized behavior with the dolls would indicate unvocalized experience of abuse. That idea received no support when it was properly investigated. Children with no abuse histories often "play" with the dolls in what appears to be a sexualized set of behaviors, because the dolls with their genital details are unlike any other toys the youngsters have seen. From the standpoint of *Daubert* and other legal standards, there are no norms, no findings of validity, and no adequate standardization of either the dolls themselves as stimuli or their use. If employed as ways for a child—who has independently of any leading questions revealed an abuse sequence—to show what happened to him or her, they have some value. Over time, the use of dolls has diminished in favor of a set of standardized drawings that maintain a certain kind of objectivity and do not introduce the play aspect that dolls can carry with them into what needs to be a serious inquiry.

Protocols for the Presentation of a Child's Testimony in Court

Although the accuracy and reliability of a child's testimony in court is largely shaped by procedures that were followed when the child was interviewed during the course of the investigation, the same protocols employed during the investigation should be used when the child testifies in court. The general procedures of testimony, in which nonleading questions are used in direct examination and more focused and leading questions are employed in cross, are appropriate with necessary leniency to facilitate the child's expression and understanding. In particular, there needs to be avoidance of leading questions which incorporate facts that the child has not stated on his or her own during the investigative phase and ideally not stated during the direct testimony. Testimony for a child is a very stressful experience and therefore the potential for suggestibility increases.

(The affidavit then proceeds with an application of the foregoing principles to an analysis of case materials.)

Relevant but Not Exhaustive Resources

Bases for the principles and factual information provided above can be found in the scientific literature in the forensic psychology field. Examples would include, but not be limited to, articles such as the following:

American Academy of Child and Adolescent Psychiatry. (1997). Practice parameters for the forensic evaluation of children and adolescents who may have been physically or sexually abused. *Journal of the American Academy of Child and Adolescent Psychiatry, 36*(3), 423–442.

Browne, A., & Finkelhor, D. (1986). Impact of child sexual abuse; A review of the research. *Psychological Bulletin, 99*(1), 66–77.

Ceci, S. J., & Bruck, M. (1993). Suggestibility of the child witness: A historical review and synthesis. *Psychological Bulletin, 113*(3), 403–439.

Doris, J., Ed. (1991). *The suggestibility of children's recollections.* Washington, DC: American Psychological Association.

Lepore, S. J., & Sesco, B. (1994). Distorting children's reports and interpretations of events through suggestion. *Journal of Applied Psychology, 79*(1), 108–120.

London, K., Bruck, M., Ceci, S. J., & Shuman, D. W. (2005). Disclosure of child sexual abuse: What does the research tell us about the ways that children tell? *Psychology, Public Policy, and Law, 11*(1), 194–226.

Lorandos, D., & Campbell, T. W. (1995). Myths and realities of sexual abuse evaluation and diagnosis: A call for judicial guidelines. *IPT Journal.* www.ipt-forensics.com/journal/volume7/j7_1_1.htm.

Sattler, J. M. (1998). *Clinical and forensic interviewing of children and families: Guidelines for the mental health, education, pediatric, and child maltreatment fields.* San Diego: Jerome M. Sattler.

Semistructured Interview Guides

1. Descriptive information: education, training, prior work in ancillary roles or professional work, experience as guardian *ad litem* (GAL) (juvenile domestic relations [DR]).
2. What kinds of investigative activities do you use generally when you work as a GAL in the DR court (interviews, school contacts, social services, treating clinicians, other family)?
3. Handling of allegations that are questionable and arise in the course of a DR case:
   a. When a party raises a question of abuse (physical or sexual), what do you usually do to deal with the issue? Do you interview the parent raising the issue?
   b. Do you interview the alleged perpetrator?
   c. Would you interview an alleged perpetrating parent with his or her criminal attorney present in cases that have charges in the criminal court?
   d. Would you interview the alleged child victim regarding the alleged abuse?
   e. We know that when you suspect child abuse, you discharge your statutory obligation by calling social services. However, in a case where you have reason to believe the allegations lack substance, what kinds of things result in reaching the point where you see a duty to make a social services report or what, if anything, would you do before making that report?
   f. Are there any other things that come to your mind that a GAL would be well advised to do in situations involving questionable allegations that occur in the course of a DR case?
4. What are some general characteristics of these kinds of DR cases: high or low income levels; expensive attorneys; more than one counsel, especially for the alleging party; third-party involvement, especially family members of the complaining party; other?
5. Can you think of a case where there were allegations that could not be satisfactorily resolved from the standpoint of both parties? Without providing identifying information, could you describe the

case characteristics and indicate what the outcome was (family system involved, type of abuse, identification of category of alleged perpetrator [father, mother, other relative, etc.], stability or lack thereof of attorneys involved, any other information; ultimate case resolution; to your knowledge did the case return to the court after the original court action)?

Billing Policy: Forensic Evaluations and Statement of Financial Responsibility

- We cannot bill insurance for forensic (legal) cases. These services are not considered medically necessary and therefore are not covered by health insurance policies.
- We require a retainer for ALL forensic evaluations where the client or attorney is responsible.

  (Amount) for family/custody evaluation
  (Amount) for individual evaluation

- Government agencies, attorney consults, and civil suits are handled for financial purposes on a case-by-case basis.
- Retainer payments MUST be made IN FULL at the time of the first appointment. Final reports will not be submitted if fees are unpaid.
- Retainers are nonrefundable.
- Fees will be charged to the account as they occur. Should services be provided beyond what is covered by the retainer, payment in full is required prior to the release of the report.
- Clinician fee is (Amount) per hour.
- Psychological testing is billed at a flat fee for each test. For information regarding specific test fees, please see the office staff.
- Should testimony or deposition be required, fees must be paid in advance in half-day (three-hour) increments by the party requesting the testimony or deposition. Should the fees exceed the advance payment, the party responsible will be billed for any overage, payment due within thirty (30) days of the date on the billing statement. There is a minimum of three (3) hours for testimony payable in advance.
- Methods of payment accepted: cash, personal check, money order, bank/cashier's check. If your check is returned you will be charged $20.00.
- Individual cases will be considered for reduced fee on the basis of demonstrated need and available time; however, the office reserves the right to set a limit on how many pro bono or reduced-fee clients will be carried at any given time.

- For evaluations where the court or a government agency is responsible for the bill (criminal cases, employment evaluations, etc.) the responsible party will receive a billing statement upon completion of services.
- Notification of appointment cancellations MUST occur 24 hours in advance of the appointment. Should a client fail to properly notify the office of a cancellation, his or her account will be billed as follows:
  - 25% of the full fee for the first failed cancellation within a 12-month period
  - 50% of the full fee for additional failed cancellations within the 12-month period

___ I understand that any and all fees incurred (including evaluation and testimony, if applicable) are to be divided between the parties as follows:

_____ is to pay ____%, including a retainer of $ _____
_____ is to pay ____%, including a retainer of $ _____

Signature _____ Date _____

RELEASE OF INFORMATION—Forensic

I understand that this evaluation is for forensic purposes only. I agree that I will not be receiving treatment and that therefore services provided do not fall under the Health Insurance Portability and Accountability Act (HIPAA).

I agree that any and all materials collected during the course of the evaluation may be released to the following (please check appropriate line(s) and fill in name(s)):

_____ My Attorney: _____

_____ Opposing Counsel: _____

_____ Guardian *ad Litem*: _____

_____ Court (specify): _____

_____ Other (specify): _____

Signed _____ Date _____

Parent or Guardian _____ Date _____
(if applicable)

Witness _____ Date _____

CLIENT INFORMATION FORM
(PLEASE PRINT)

Personal Information: _____ **Date:** _____

First Name:_____ M.I.:_____

Last:_____

Date of Birth: ____/____/____ Social Security Number: _____-_____-_____

Street Address: _____

City:_____ State:_____ Zip: _____

Home Phone:_____Cell/Pager: _____

Employer:_____ Work Phone:_____ Ext:_____

Email Address: _____

Marital Status: (please circle one)

        Single   Married   Widowed   Divorced   Separated

Parent or Guardian (if a minor): _____

Phone:_____

Parent/Guardian Address: _____
(if different from above)

Emergency Contact: _____ Relationship:_____

Address:_____ Phone:_____

Family Information:

Spouse: _____ DOB:_____-_____-_____

Sig. Other: _____ DOB:_____-_____-_____

Children: Name:_____ DOB:_____ Name:_____ DOB:_____

          Name:_____ DOB:_____ Name:_____ DOB:_____

Forensic Cases:

Attorney:_____ Phone: _____

Guardian *ad Litem*: _____ Phone: _____

Court: _____

STATEMENT OF NONCONFIDENTIALITY

I understand that I am providing information to Dr. _____
as part of a custody evaluation for the _____ family and
that the content of my conversation(s) with the above-referenced psychologist can be included in a report which will be provided to the attorneys
and/or the court and therefore is not confidential.

PAYMENT AGREEMENT

I, _____, promise to pay Dr. _____

the sum of _____ for psychological services. I will make pay-

ments in the amount of _____ .

Payments will be made:

   ☐ Weekly (specify day of week) _____

   ☐ Bi-weekly (specify date/day of week) _____

   ☐ Monthly (specify date) _____

This debt will be paid in full on or before_____

I recognize this document as a legal contract and by signature below commit to this obligation. I understand that any breach of this contract will result in my account being immediately sent to a collection agency.

Signed _____ Date _____

Witness _____ Date _____

AUTHORIZATION FOR RELEASE OF INFORMATION—General

I, _____

(Name – Please Print)

DOB: _____ SSN: _____

Hereby authorize:

_____

_____

_____

_____

To release records for:

_____

_____

_____

_____

This information is to be released to:

Dr. _____

Address / Phone _____

I understand and acknowledge that the information exchanged may contain information regarding:

Evaluation, testing, diagnosis, and treatment including, but not limited to, all protected health information for substance abuse and mental health treatment and diagnosis

Any other medical records (including HIV/AIDS status)

Legal records

Educational records

I further release the above-named entities from any liability resulting from the release of this information. I understand that this authorization is valid only for a period of ninety (90) days from the date below.

Signed _____ Date _____
               (Client or Parent/Guardian)

Witness _____ Date _____

Instructions for Enhanced Security

Secrets

Both parents and child(ren) meet with therapist and together agree that the therapist is to be the trusted repository of secrets, and that the child is to share problems and concerns with this person who will help him or her and them to deal with any difficulties in the family or elsewhere. It is explicitly stated that the child will repeat any secrets or other things that anyone, especially the parents, tell him or her not to tell the therapist.

Both parents agree in front of each other, the therapist, and the child that they will not ask the child to reveal what is talked about with the therapist and that they understand that the child may have negative feelings about them to discuss with the therapist. They indicate the therapist and the child will be the ones to decide what is important to tell them.

Sometimes special instructions particular to the fears or background of the family situation are included with this session, which is presented as part of initiating a new era in family life and is part of revising the way in which the child has contact time with both of his or her parents in some scheduled fashion.

Roving Reporter

As part of visitation, there is a reporter session at the end (or some other creative device), at which time the visitation parent and the child(ren) make a tape reflecting their visit events, both positive and negative, and talk about how things went. A copy of the tape becomes the possession and transitional device for the child (two tapes can be simultaneously made or a two-deck recorder used which allows an instantaneous copy). Audio or video can be used (or both). The reporter series can become a long-term record that is something valuable for everyone as the child grows and develops.

Possession Parent Tape

It may be of assistance to make a facilitating tape to accompany the child on the visit that emphasizes the good times to be had and the ongoing love of the possession parent and contains reference to the future when the visit is over.

Consultation Example: Critique of a Child Interview

Below are excerpts from an interview submitted for procedural analysis. Commentary was provided on the basis of which there could be cross-examination regarding procedure that was followed. The child is 4 years old. Roman type indicates what was heard on the tape and the critique is presented italicized. All identifying information has been changed.

The interview procedure is contaminated from the beginning as shown below. The child is not asked what he was told about coming in, what he was told to say or do, and who told him.

D. I'm a policeman, OK.

Establishes authority status that is potentially intimidating.

Hold my badge for me…

Gives child a badge.

Giving things to a child as a way to introduce the interview is inappropriate.

This is your tooth? And so on.

I'm going to ask you some things, OK? If you need to tell me no, you say no, OK If you don't understand, tell me you don't understand. OK.

Some but not enough establishment of expectations of range of responses. Need for child to understand that the interviewer doesn't know the answer, and so on, instead.

We'll be on the same team, two policemen. OK.

Which sets the child up further to accept anything the interviewer says as right.

When I ask a question that is too big, you say it is too big. OK.

Children are literal at this age. A big question doesn't necessarily translate to above comprehension level for the child.

Can you say OK? (Child says OK).

Now there is a set to say what is expected rather than what is coming from within the child's own mental experience and the authority of the interviewer is further enhanced over the authority of the child (who in fact is the only possible possessor of truth here excepting, of course, the potential of the mother).

I've got a little boy, 3.

Child is 4.

This adds the authority of a parent, introduces a parent–child configuration.

Child indicates something about a go-cart and being with the detective's child and he responds that someday "we might do that."

Unless such a thing is planned, it should not be introduced as a potential, and of course it further contaminates the purpose of the interview and the roles that are to be played.

Continues with idea of doing this desirable activity, and ends with "Is that a deal, you'll have to do what I say?"

Now there's an implicit bribe, a form of mild coercion, and the authority of the interviewer as right and a source of knowledge is further reinforced. The child is now into a contingency situation; if he pleases, he will get to do something.

Do you know what your mom's name is? What's her name?

Child. Momma.

D. All right, Momma. Is it Carolyn? Yes?

Major problem. child's correct (for child) answer is only partially accepted, then the adult continues to pursue for the adult answer and gives it and asks the child to endorse with a "yes." The yes set is now being reinforced along with the adult as source of knowledge instead of the child.

D. Do you know what your daddy's name is?

Child. Daddy.

D. Do you know his first name? Is it William? It is? Is it William Smith? (Something is said by a woman in the room.)

(D. states child should say No or Yes depending, evidently in an effort to get it on the record.)

The sequence keeps the interviewer in place as authority and source of knowledge.

D. continues explaining about the tape player not being able to see nods.

This level of expectation can be hard for some adult witnesses in court; it is a barrier in a child interview because the child now has a new communication responsibility. It can be handled by the interviewer's repeating the question and saying the child nodded yes and checking to see if child agrees, and so on.

D. continues with instructions. He indicated that he might not know something.

Making sure the child understands the adult's lack of knowledge is a major job of establishing the interview parameters and should have been foremost rather than embedded in all the authority prompts that have occurred.

D. We're going to pretend like it's just me and you, OK.

Interviewer now introduces unreality. It isn't just him and the child, and the child knows it. From here on in, some degree of "untruth" is part of the picture. If it is OK to pretend mother and others are not there, it is probably OK to pretend almost anything. At the least, a confusion of reality and fantasy is introduced.

D. gets child to agree ("Deal!"). Then appears to promise something when "we get done."

Coercion piece.

D. You stay in your daddy's house much? No? How come…?

Child. Kisses and bites.

D. Kisses and bites. He does. Where does he kiss you?

Child. He kisses me on winky all the time.

D. You're kidding, really?

Could invalidate a true response. In this case, given the part fantasy, part reality confusions, it is anybody's guess what this means. (There has been no attempt to establish truth-telling.)

D. When you stay at your daddy's house, where do you sleep at?

Establishes that it is dark. Child talks about light on. Asked about TV. Dad turns it off.

Note that there is no change of tone or evident discomfort of child about this area.

D. When you lay down with your daddy, tell me, do you snuggle?

It's not entirely clear that child is in fact sleeping with the father, but if so, the snuggling is introduced by the interviewer/authority.

D. Show me how you snuggle. Oh, boy (positively responding to whatever the child did).

Now snuggling is established as a good thing to be doing.

D. Then what do you do with your daddy? What happens then? Kisses you?

Introduced by the interviewer.

D. Look, this doll is you.

Again an unreality. Far better to say, show me on the doll what daddy and you do, and so on, but only after child has provided some particular activity not introduced by the interviewer.

D. Show me where your daddy kisses you.

D. He does? You're kissing the doll down on, on his private parts, on his winky, right?

D. Is that right? Have to say yes or no, I can't hear you.

Child. Yes.

D. OK.

If this is not a true report (and given the conditions of initial disclosure, the source of information re: that disclosure, and the impact of this interview's flaws, the potential for false report presents as equiprobable to true report), the insistence on endorsement at this point not only contaminates the truthfulness issue, but also increases the likelihood of the witness becoming a source of a developing belief system held across a section of his family group.

D. Your daddy, does he touch your winky?

Introduced by interviewer.

Child. Yeah and he bites it.

D. Bites it? Does that hurt?

Child. No, he bites it a little.

D. Does it hurt?

Interviewer doesn't accept child's statement first time.

Child. No, then he stops.

D. What do you tell him?

Child. Stop, I go stop.

D. What does he say?

Child. He goes to…and he…just right…and he stops?

D. Does he touch your winky with his hand?

Introduced by interviewer.

D. He does?

Child. Yeah.

Child. He put my van on the winky.

D. He puts your van on the winky. Hold my badge so nobody will get it. It's like superheroes at times. So you have to hold onto it.

Now, not only fantasy, but supermen are introduced into the ongoing cognition of this child. All associated with the detective and his power and authority.

D. Now I'll say gimme five, you know what that is? (Hear a clap sound.) All right.

Inappropriate reinforcement immediately followed by statement about father touching winky and request to show how it is done.

D. It's OK. You take this pencil and show me what he does to you.

D. Touches it?

Child. He tickles it.

D. Tickles it.

D. Do you have clothes on when he does this? Look at me…Is your under-wear on? Does he put his hands under your underwear?

Presumably the child is signalling he has on clothes and/or underwear, and interviewer then introduces that there is touching under the underwear.

D. He does? (*Interviewer reinforces his own contribution.*) What does he say when he does it?

Child. (*No unusual emotion*) Saying something about scooting away.

D. He starts scooting away from it?

Child. Yeah and when he wakes up, he don't know. Something gone.

Child continued to say things, repeating something.

D: Do you and your daddy sleep by yourself?

Child. Yep.

Something is said between them that finishes with interviewer saying "just you and him?"

D. Do you know what pajamas are? Yeah? Does daddy sleep in pajamas? Or does he sleep without a shirt?

Child. No, he sleeps with muscle shirt on.

D. Muscle shirt. Oh boy, I've got a muscle shirt.

Inappropriate introduction of self.

D. Does he sleep with his pants on? No?

Child. No, but he wears some.

This sequence indicates a lack of clarity about what child is conveying.

D. Can you see your daddy's winky when he is sleeping?

We have not established that child is ever able to see dad during sleep.

D. Is he covered up?

They return to the doll(s) apparently.

D. This is your dad, where would you kiss him?

D. Where else?

Assumes there are other kissing places. Should have said, "Do you kiss him any-where else?" This type of mistake is a suggestibility error of some importance.

D. On the cheek? All over?

Child. Yeah.

Leads come from the interviewer.

Child. He, he don't go so far, he stays on the other side.

D. What does he do? You don't. Does he touch your winky with his hand?

Now we have ongoing repetition of the question.

Unclear discourse.

D. Is that your drink?

Child. Yeah.

Having food or drink as part of the interview is problematic.

D. Ask your mom if you can drink it.

Child. Can I drink it?

It will be remembered that the child was told to pretend no one was there but himself and interviewer. Mom is not only there (making that instruction a serious error as above detailed) but is now included in the interview process in the midst of discussing molestation. The form of which is generally created by the interviewer.

D. When your dad gets done, does he ever say anything?

Seriously flawed combining of presumed abuse with now added detail introduced by the interviewer.

Child. No.

Then says something about going to sleep. Says "and I don't like snoring."

D. Goes back to sleep?

Child. Yeah.

D. asks about holding something for the child, who says "yeah." They are doing something.

D. Does he ever say don't tell anybody?

Serious flaw. Entire notion is introduced by the interviewer. Could maybe ask if the child has been told not to talk about it, especially if the child had initiated the elements of disclosure without this much assistance.

Child. No.

D. You know what chopsticks are? You do?

Child. Yeah, he touches me with chopsticks.

Again, the interviewer brings in the substance for the child to incorporate. If the child has been coached or if there is a confluence of misinterpretation that has elaborated to include this detail, and it was given by the mother, this ploy will further secure it.

D. What does he do with chopsticks? Squeeze it?

Presumably the child showed some activity here, but it is not clear that we are not dealing with elaborations being created out of the interviewer's interpretations.

Child. He brings it up and puts it back down.

Interviewer and child engage in some type of close whispering about something, then end with why interviewer doesn't bring his child with him, "I have to work." Then says, "Hard to keep up with him" and "He's like you; sees his mommy sometimes and his daddy sometimes."

There are real problems with this diversion into the interviewer's family context.

Child. How is that?

D. That's my badge, it's OK.

D. When you daddy takes a picture of you, do you have any clothes on?

Where does this come from? Clearly not the child. If it is an area to be worked up, have to start with talking about picture taking. Have to distinguish baby pictures from current ones, and so on. Once again, the interviewer acts to introduce elements into the situation.

Child seems to say he is wearing a coat.

D. Does he ever take any pictures of you with your clothes off?

Ongoing contamination. Unless there are probable sexual pictures of this child attributable to the father, and this set of questions is designed to test the child's ability to accurately talk, it is clearly a problem to have brought up the area in this way.

D. Has anybody ever told you what to say?

Child. No.

D. No.

The question is too late and too vague to be useful.

D. Does your daddy, does he call his private parts his winky?

Introduced by interviewer, should ask what daddy calls this part and what mommy calls this part, and so on if at all.

D. He does?

Child. Yeah.

D. Do you ever see your daddy touching his winky?

Interviewer introduces yet another element into the picture and does not discriminate it from bathrooming or adjustment behavior.

Child. Yeah.

D. Tell me what he does.

D. Grabs it. Where at? Between his legs?

This is an example of a child's concretism. The penis is between the legs; the interviewer wants to know where the activity took place.

D. Where you see him do that? Is he in the bed, the bathroom, the kitchen, or where?

Child. Well he do's it at some times.

D. He does it at certain times. Like when?

Child. At night.

D. At night.

Child. Yeah, at night and day.

D. At night and day.

It is highly likely child is following along and trying to do what is expected at this point.

D. Tell me what you do at that house.

Child. I see monsters and that's it.

D. On TV.

Child. I see, I try to get him to come hide or may be home.

D. You do?

Child. Yeah, but he won't.

D. Want another drink?

Error.

D. You want to go to school today?

Child. Yeah.

D. You do?

D. You like preschool?

Child. Yeah.

D. Good.

Some talk in background.

D. You ever go to the…

Child. Chuck E. Cheese.

They talk about that. Child says that Arnie was there, too. Something about him being lost "and then I found him."

Something about daddy and Chuck E. Cheese.

D. Where were you at when he did it?

Clearly not in sequence that is reasonable; meaning here is problematic and has created a confluence of ideas that are contaminating and do not train for reality orientation and accurate reportage.

Child. On table he did it.

D. He did?

Child. Yeah.

Periodically, the interviewer is whispering to child, making it impossible to know exact words being used all of the time. Whispering itself is problematic; it speaks to secrets and fantasy rather than to the purpose of the ongoing transaction and sets up a false identification of interviewer and child. It also does not model for the child the need to speak up. In addition, it potentially gives the child the impression that the interview is confidential.

Returns to discussion of the touching/kissing.

D. Show me on your body. Does he kiss you here? Look at me, Kennedy. Does daddy kiss you here, here?

If the interviewer is touching either himself or the child in private areas, this is a very inappropriate way to proceed.

Child. Yes, he kisses my tongue.

D. He kisses your tongue? How's he do that? OK, does he kiss you here on the cheek? Show me where. Where else?

Child. Yeah. He do's it certain times. He keeps on doing it and doing it and doing it.

D. He does. Do you tell him to quit?

Child. Yeah.

D. What do you tell him?

Child. I tell him to do to that.

D. We're almost ready to leave.

Cell phone goes off—Error—Woman's voice says, "Yes, can you come down; OK, bye bye." The interview once again is active with more than just the boy and the detective.

Child. He touches it in the car.

D. He does?

Child. Yep.

Child. He keeps on and on and on and on.

D. How does he do that? He just reaches over and touches it?

Child. Yeah.

Child says something unclear.

D. Louise does?

(*I think child may not have said Louise, but the child is into yes set and endorses.*)

Child. Yeah.

D. He does.

Child. Yeah.

D. What does he keep touching in the car? You're pointing at your winky. Hey, let's go back to when you told your daddy to quit, tell me what you say.

Child. I say quit.

Note that child says what interviewer says; it would be interesting to determine whether this child says "quit" or "stop" as his usual way to get someone to end an activity he doesn't like.

Child. But he don't want to quit.

D. He just keeps on?

Child. Yeah.

D. Does it hurt?

Child apparently can't answer even with the lead, and now we see more repetition of this element.

D. What else does he do? Does he spank it?

Element introduced by interviewer.

Child. No, he hits it.

Child has incorporated the lead.

D. Oh, he hits it.

Child. Yeah.

D. How hard does he hit it? Like if this is your butt, show me how hard he hits it.

The transition to spanking has not been clearly articulated from that of penis touching. Interviewer then demonstrates act that interviewer has introduced.

Child then talks about being hit on arm.

They then talk about computer in office. And interviewer asks whether mother was on computer not too long ago when child got next to him.

D. Did you do something with your winky?

Introduced by interviewer.

Child. Yeah, I did it.

Repeats.

Then starts whispering and asks,

Did you put your winky on her cheek?

Child. Yeah.

Seems to be enjoying the hiding of this from mother.

D. Who taught you to do that?

Child. (Very quietly) Uh, daddy did.

But has difficulty articulating daddy, almost like he is trying to get it out and avoid it at the same time.

D. When you take a bath, you take a bath at your daddy's house?

Child. Yeah.

D. You do. Who gives you a bath?

Child. Daddy, Louise does.

D. Louise does, too.

Child. I don't take showers.

D. Does daddy take a bath with you or does he just give you a bath?

D: Does he to anything to your winky then?

Introduced by interviewer.

Child indicates he is tired.

D. Want another drink?

There are voices in the background.

D. Look have you ever seen one of these? This is very, very dangerous.

Child. Why?

D. That's what my little boy says.

Child. A gun.

D. Yes.

Child. That hurt.

There should never be a weapon in a child interview room, and its introduction adds a serious power element to situation.

D. You have a badge. You are a junior policeman and if I ever need your help I may call one day.

Then reintroduces Chuck E. Cheese, child talks about what he eats. Something about singing by the big screen. Child says not supposed to get up there. Talk includes others and something about 10 minutes and talking with the detective. Mother perhaps is on a phone? Or may be talking about answering questions. Child says touches it and touches it. Mother says you don't have to elaborate just answer his questions.

At this point, the problematic influence of the mother is made eminently clear.

D. Look at me, look at me. Does your daddy use a computer?

Child. Yeah.

Child. He finds something.

D. What's he find?

D. Do you ever see little boys on the computer?

If they want to know this, they should first search the computer. If they have and there is nothing there, then we have another instance of introducing information. The above question, incidentally, does not pinpoint child porn area.

Child. I don't see boys on the computer.

D. Do you ever see boys on your daddy's computer?

Child. No.

The ongoing attempt to get information by giving it.

D. Look, Kennedy, one more time, tell me what he does.

D. You're grabbing yourself. Look at me, look at me.

At this point, the coercion level is increasing markedly. Child is tired of the interview. It is intrusive and interviewer is persistent in getting what he wants. Anything the child says at this point and on is as likely, if not more so, to reflect an attempt to get the interview over as to respond to any reality-based memory.

D. What's he do?

Child. Certain times.

D. At certain times.

D. Your daddy. Does he do something to you with his hand?

(Child talks about taking some things. There are no disclosures.)

The above interview critique suggests multiple and potentially serious flaws that could well not only lead to false information in the interview, but also to contamination of the child's memory system. There is the combining of elements of maternal presence, authority, weaponry, and fantasy superpowers, all of which are inconsistent with forensic interviewing of alleged child victims.

References

730 Evaluation. (2010). Retrieved from http://www.730evaluation.com/7300verview. php.

Abel, G. (2011). Abel screening. Retrieved Feb. 2, 2011 from: http://abelscreening. com/motivations/index.html.

Adshead, G. (2003). Dangerous and severe parenting disorder? Personality disorder, parenting and new legal proposals. *Child Abuse Review, 12,* 227–237.

Alciatore, D. G. (2008). Pool and billiards physics principles by Coriolis and others. http://www.scribd.com/doc/16343339/Pool-and-Billiards-Physics-Principles- by-Coriolis-and-Others-Alciatore-AJP-MS22090-Revised-Pool-Physics- Article. Retrieved June 14, 2011.

Aldridge, M. J., & Wood, J. (1999). *Interviewing children: A guide for child care and forensic practitioners.* New York: John Wiley and Sons.

Allison, L. (2010). *Shared parenting after divorce.* Retrieved May 20, 2010 from http://law.suites101.com/article/cfm/shared_parenting_after_divorce.

Amato, P. R. (1988). Parental divorce and attitudes toward marriage. *Journal of Marriage and the Family, 50,* 453–461.

Amato, P. R. (1993). Children's adjustment to divorce: Theories, hypotheses and empirical support. *Journal of Marriage and the Family, 55,* 23–38.

Amato, P. R., & Booth, A. (2001). The legacy of parents' marital discord: Consequences for children's marital quality. *Journal of Personality and Social Psychology, 81,* 627–638.

Amato, P. R., & Cheadle, J. (2005). The long reach of divorce: Tracking marital dis- solution and child well-being across three generations. *Journal of Marriage and the Family, 67,* 191–206.

Amato, P. R., & Gilbreth, J. G. (1999). Nonresident fathers and children's well-being: A metaanalysis. *Journal of Marriage and the Family, 61,* 557–573.

Amato, P. R., & Keith, B. (1991). Parental divorce and the well-being of children: A meta-analysis. *Psychological Bulletin, 110,* 26–46.

American Academy of Child and Adolescent Psychiatry. (1997). Practice parame- ters for the forensic evaluation of children and adolescents who may have been physically and sexually abused. *Journal of the American Academy of Child and Adolescent Psychiatry, 36,* 423–442.

American Law Institute. (2002). *Principles of the law of family dissolutions: Analysis and recommendations.* Philadelphia: Author.

American Medical Association. (2008–2009). *Code of medical ethics: Current opinions with annotations.* Chicago: Author.

American Prosecutors Research Institute. (2003). *Identification and prosecution of child abuse.* Alexandria, VA: Author.

American Psychiatric Association. (1980). *Diagnostic and Statistical Manual of Mental Disorders* (3rd ed.) (*DSM–III*). Washington, DC: Author.

American Psychiatric Association. (2000). *Diagnostic and Statistical Manual of Mental Disorders* (4th ed.), text revision (*DSM–IV–TR*). Arlington, VA: Author.

American Psychiatric Association. (2010). *DSM–V*. Retrieved Aug. 5, 2010 from www.dsm5/Pages/Default_aspx.

American Psychological Association. (2003). *Ethical principles of psychologists and code of conduct*. Washington, DC: Author.

American Psychological Association. (Feb. 2009). Guidelines for child custody evaluations in family law proceedings. http://www.apa.org/practice/guidelines/child-custody.pdf.

American Psychological Association. (2010). Ethical Principles of Psychologists and Code of Conduct: 2010 Amendments, Section 3.05 Multiple Relationships. Retrieved June 28, 2011 from http://www.apa.org/ethics/code/index.aspx

Americans for Divorce Reform. (2010). *Divorce rates*. Retrieved May 21, 2010 from http://www.divorcereform.org/rates.html.

Anderer, S. J., & Glass, D. J. (2000). A therapeutic jurisprudence and preventive law approach to family law. In D. P. Stolle, D. B. Wexler, & B. J. Winick (Eds.), *Practicing therapeutic jurisprudence: Law as a helping profession.* (pp. 297–234). Durham, NC: Carolina Academic Press.

Annon, J. S. (1994). Recommended guidelines for interviewing children in cases of alleged sexual abuse. *IPT*. Retrieved Oct. 2, 2010 from www.ipt-forensics.com/journal/volum e6/j6_3_2.htm.

Answers.com. (2010). Retrieved Dec. 27, 2010 from http://wiki.answers.com.

Artis, J. E. (2004). Judging the best interests of the child: Judges' accounts of the tender years doctrine. *Law and Society Review, 38*(4), 769–806.

Association of Family and Conciliation Courts. (May, 2006). *Model standards of practice for child custody evaluation*. Madison, WI: Author.

Baldus, D. C., & Woodworth, G. A. (1998). Race discrimination and the death penalty: An empirical and legal overview. In J. R. Acker, R. M. Bohm, & C. S. Lanier (Eds.), *America's experiment with capital punishment: Reflections on the past, present, and future of the ultimate penal sanction* (pp. 385–415). Durham, NC: Carolina Academic Press.

Baldus, D. C., Woodworth, G. A., & Pulaski, C. A. (1990). *Equal justice and the death penalty: A legal and empirical analysis*. Boston: Northeastern University Press.

Barnett, G. D., Wakeling, H. C., & Howard, P. D. (2010). An examination of the predictive validity of the Risk Matrix 2000 in England and Wales. *Sex Abuse 22*(4), 443–470.

Bartlett , F. C. (1932). *Remembering*. New York: Cambridge University Press.

Battered Mothers Custody Conference. (2010). Battered Women, Abused Children, and Child Custody: "A National Crisis." Retrieved from www.batteredmotherscustodyconference.org/

Barton, J. (Ed.). (2001). *Oxford Bible commentary*. New York: Oxford University Press.

Bathurst, K., Gottfried, A. W., & Gottfried, A. E. (1997). Normative data for the MMPI-2 in child custody litigation. *Psychological Assessment, 9,* 205–211.

Bavelas, J. B., Black, A., Chovil, N., & Mullett, J. (1990). *Equivocal communication*. Newbury Park, CA: Sage.

Bennett, B., Bricklin, P., Harris, E., Knapp, S., VandeCreek, L., & Younggren, J. (2006). *Assessing and managing risk in psychological practice: An individualized approach*. Rockville, MD: The Trust.

Bernet, W. (2008). Parental alienation disorder and *DSM-V*. *American Journal of Family Therapy, 36*(5), 349–366.

Berry v. State. 10 Ga. 511 (1851).

Bogoroch, R. M., & Goldstein, L. (2010). *Reflections on the role of the expert witness.* Retrieved July 10, 2010 from www.bugoroch.com/articles/expert.pdf.

Botkin, D. B. (2006). Preface 1. The nature of change. In *Forces of Change*. Washington, DC: National Geographic Society.

Boulle, L. (2005). *Mediation: Principles, processes, practice* (2nd ed.), Chatswood, New South Wales, Australia: LexisNexis Butterworths.

Bow, J. N., Gottlieb, M. C., Siegel, J. C., & Noble, G. S. (2010). Licensing board complaints in child custody practice. *Journal of Forensic Psychology Practice, 10*, 403–418.

Bow, J. N., Gould, J. W., Flens, J. R., & Greenhut, D. (2006). Testing in child custody evaluations—Selection, usage, and *Daubert* admissibility: A survey of psychologists. *Journal of Forensic Psychology Practice, 6*(2), 17–38.

Bow, J. N., & Martindale, D. A. (2009). Developing and managing a child custody practice. *Journal of Forensic Psychology Practice, 9*(2), 127–137.

Bray, J. H. (1991). Psychological factors affecting custodial and visitation arrangements. *Behavioral Science and the Law, 9*, 419–437.

Brayden, R. M., Altemeier, W. A., Tucker, D. D., Dietrich, M. S., & Vietz, P. (1992). Antecedents of child neglect in the first two years of life. *Journal of Pediatrics, 120*(3), 426–429.

Broca, P. (1863). Localization des fonctions cérébrales—Siège du langage articulé. *Bulletins de la Société d'Anthropologie, 4*, 200–204.

Brown v. State. 736 P.2d 1110 (Wyo. 1987).

Brown, D., Scheflin, A. W., & Hammond, D. C. (1998). *Memory, trauma treatment, and the law.* New York: W. W. Norton.

Budd, K. S., Holdsworth, M. J. A., & HoganBruen, K. D. (2006). Antecedents and concomitants of parenting stress in adolescent mothers in foster care. *Child Abuse & Neglect, 30*(5), 557–574.

Bullyonline.org. (2010). http://www.bullyonline.org. Accessed July 6, 2011.

Burrill, J. (2006). Descriptor statistics of the mild, moderate and severe characteristics of parental alienation syndrome. In R. A. Gardner, S. R. Sauber, & D. Lorando (Eds.), *International handbook of parental alienation syndrome: Conceptual and legal considerations* (pp. 49–55). Springfield, IL: Charles C. Thomas.

Bütz, M. B. (1997). *Chaos and complexity: Implications for psychological theory and practice.* Washington, DC: Taylor & Francis.

Cadoret, R. J., Troughton, E., O'Gorman, T. W., & Heywood, E. (1986). An adoption study of genetic and environmental factors in drug abuse. *Archives of General Psychiatry, 43*(12), 1131–1136.

Cadoret, R. J., Yates, W. R., Troughton, E. , Woodworth, G., & Stewart, M. A. (1995). Genetic-environmental interaction in the genesis of aggressivity and conduct disorders. *Archives of General Psychiatry, 52*(11), 916–924.

California Family Code, Section 3118. California Rules of Court, Rule 5.220

Canadian Psychological Association. (2000). *Code* (3rd ed.). Ottawa: Author.

Cardona, F. (2009). Federal judges argue for reduced sentences for child-porn convicts. *Denver Post.* Retrieved Feb. 11, 2011 from http:www.denverpost.com/ci_13887009.

Carlson, G. A., Bromet, E. J., & Sievers, S. (2000). Phenomenology and outcome of subjects with early and adult onset psychotic mania. *American Journal of Psychiatry, 157,* 213–219.

Center on Addiction and Substance Abuse (CASA). (1999). *National Survey of American Attitudes on Substance Abuse, V: Teens and Their Parents.* National Center on Addiction and Substance Abuse at Columbia University.

Center on Addiction and Substance Abuse (CASA). (1999). *No safe havens: Children of substance-abusing parents.* National Center on Addiction and Substance Abuse, Columbia University.

Chambers, D. (1984). Rethinking the substantive rules for custody disputes in divorce. *Michigan Law Review, 83*(3), 447–469.

Charleston County D.S.S. v. Father, Stepmother, and Mother. 454 S.E.2d 307 (SC 1995).

Cheng, C. (2010). The end of expert practice as usual: Proposed changes to Federal Rule 26. *Expert Witnesses, 2010 Annual Review, 1,* 4–5.

Chesler, P. (1987). *Mothers on trial: The battle for children and custody.* Seattle: Seal Press.

Cleckley, H. (1976). *The mask of sanity* (5th ed.). St. Louis, MO: Mosby.

Coggins, M. H., Steadman, H. J., & Veysey, B. M. (1996). Mental health clinicians' attitudes about reporting threats against the president. *Psychiatric Services, 47,* 832–836.

Cohen, D., & Segal-Engrelchen, D. (2000). Suzi and Mr. S.: Gender role stereotyping in social workers' court reports in custody and access cases. *Smith College Studies in Social Work, 70*(3), 475–500.

Connell, M. A. (2003). A psychobiographical approach to the evaluation for sentence mitigation. *Journal of Psychiatry and Law, 31,* 319–354.

Conte, H. R., & Karasu, T. B. (1990). Malpractice in psychotherapy: A review. *American Journal of Psychiatry, 44*(2), 232–246.

Cooke, D. J., & Michie, C. (2001). Refining the construct of psychopathy: Towards a hierarchial model. *Psychological Assessment 13*(2), 171–188.

Cooper, D. (2010). Psychology, risk and safety. Retrieved Jan. 4, 2010 from http://bsmsinc.com/afrticles/bsms13.pdf.

Crosby-Currie, C. A. (1996). Children's involvement in contested custody cases: Practices and experiences of legal and mental health professionals. *Law and Human Behavior, 20,* 289–311.

Crown, S. C. (2004). Modeling the effects of velocity, spin, frictional coefficient, and impact angle on deflection angle in near-elastic collisions of phenolic resin spheres. Cornell University Library. Retrieved Dec. 27, 2010 from http://arxiv.org/ftp/physics/papers/0402008.pdf.

Cunningham, M. (2006). Special issues in capital sentencing. In M. A. Conroy, P. M. Lyons Jr., & P. P. Kwartner (Eds.) *Forensic mental health services in Texas* [Special issue, electronic version]. *Applied Psychology in Criminal Justice, 2,* 205–236.

Cuyahoga County Domestic Relations Court (2010) Rules. Retrieved from http://domestic.cuyahogacounty.us/en-US/court-rules.aspx

Daubert v. Merrell Dow Pharmaceuticals. 509 US 579 (1993).

Dawson, L. L. (2003). *Cults and new religious movements: A reader.* Malden, MA: Blackwell.

De Fabrique, N., Van Hasselt, V. B., Vecchi, G. M., & Romano, S. J. (2007). Common variables associated with the development of Stockholm Syndrome: Some case examples. *Victims and Offenders, 2,* 1–8.

De Fabrique, N., Romano, S. J., Vecchi, G. M., & van Hasselt, V. B. (2007). Understanding Stockholm Syndrome. *FBI Law Enforcement Bulletin 76*(7), 10–15.

Department of State, United States of America. (2010). Retrieved Dec. 27, 2010 from http://travel.state.gov/abduction/abduction_580.html.

Dilworth, J. (2005). The reflexive theory of perception. *Behavior and Philosophy, 33,* 17–40.

Dobson, K. (Ed.). (2010). *Handbook of cognitive-behavioral therapies* (3rd ed.). New York: Guilford Press.

Dolan, D. M., & Doyle, M. (2000). Violence risk prediction. *British Journal of Psychiatry, 177,* 303–311.

Dorst, G. L. (2010). Defining "substantial change in circumstances." Retrieved Dec. 19, 2010 from http://www.deltabravo.net/custody/cirmstance.php.

Ebert, B. W. (2005). Dual relationship prohibition: A concept whose time never should have come. *Applied and Preventive Psychology, 6*(3), 137–156.

Ellis, E. (2000). *Divorce wars: Interventions with families in conflict.* Washington, DC: American Psychological Association.

Emery, R. E., Matthews, S. G., & Kitzmann, K. M. (1994). Child custody mediation and litigation: Parents' satisfaction and functioning one year after settlement. *Journal of Consulting and Clinical Psychology, 62*(1), 124–129.

Ewing, C. P. (2006). Testing tool in question: A court's exclusion of a sex offender measurement could prompt a harsher stance on the admissibility of similar assessment tools. In Judicial Notebook, *The Monitor, 37*(1), 61.

Faller, K. C. (2007). *Interviewing children about sexual abuse: Controversies and best practice.* New York: Oxford University Press.

Federal Rules of Evidence. (2009). http://www.utd.uscourts.gov/forms/evid2009.pdf

Fineman, M. A. (1991). *The rhetoric and reality of divorce reform.* Chicago: University of Chicago Press.

Fineman, M. A. (1995). *The neutered mother, the sexual family, and other twentieth century tragedies.* London: Routledge Press.

Flayme.com (2010). Retrieved Dec. 1, 2010 from http://www/flayme.com/stalker.

Floyd, J., & Sinclair, B. (Jan. 20, 2010). Child pornography: Judicial chaos leads to horrific sentencing disparities. Retrieved Feb. 11, 2011 from http://www.johnfloyd.com/comments/january10/federal-sentencing-child-pornography.htm.

Fonagy, P., & Target, M. (1997). Attachment and reflective function: Their role in self-organization. *Development and Psychopathology, 9,* 679–700.

Fonagy, P., Target, M., Gergely, G., Allen, J., & Bateman, A. (2003). The developmental roots of borderline personality disorder in early attachment relationships: A theory and some evidence. *Psychoanalytic Inquiry, 23,* 412–459.

Frankfurter, D. (2006). *Evil incarnate: Rumors of demonic conspiracy and satanic abuse in history.* Princeton, NJ: Princeton University Press.

Fridman, D. S., & Janoe, J. S. (2011). State of judicial gatekeeping in Ohio. *The Judicial Gatekeeping Project.* Retrieved Feb. 2, 2011 from http://cyber.law.harvard.edu/daubert/national.htm.

Friston, M. (August 4, 2005). Roles and responsibilities of medical expert witnesses. *British Medical Journal.* Retrieved Dec. 25, 2010 from http://www/bmj.com/content/331/7512/305.full.

Frye v. United States. 293 F.1013 (1923).

Fulero, S. M., & Wrightsman, L. S. (2009). *Forensic psychology* (3rd ed.). Belmont, CA: Wordsworth.

Gardner, H. (1985). *The mind's new science: A history of the cognitive revolution.* New York: Basic Books.

Gardner, R. A. (1987). *The parental alienation syndrome and the differentiation between fabricated and genuine child sexual abuse.* Cresskill, NJ: Creative Therapeutics.

Gardner, R. A. (1991). *Sex abuse hysteria: Salem witch trials revisited.* Cresskill, NJ: Creative Therapeutics.

Gardner, R. A. (2006). Introduction. In R. A. Gardner, S. R. Sauber, & D. Lorandos (Eds.), *The international handbook of parental alienation syndrome: Conceptual and legal considerations.* Springfield, IL: Charles C. Thomas.

Gardner, R. A., Sauber, S. R., & Lorandos, D. (Eds.). (2006). *The international handbook of parental alienation syndrome: Conceptual and legal considerations* (pp. 5–11). Springfield, IL: Charles C. Thomas.

Ghasemi, M. (2005). Impact of domestic violence on the psychological wellbeing of children in Iran. *Journal of Family Studies.* Retrieved Jan. 2, 2010 from http://jfs.c-contentmanagement.com/archives/vol/15/issue/3/article/312291/impact-of-domestic-violence-on-the-psychological-wellbeing-of-children-in-Iran.

Gier v. Educational Services Unit 16. (1995).

Glancy, G., & Bradford, J. M. W. (2007). The admissibility of expert evidence in Canada. *Journal of the American Academy of Psychiatry and the Law, 35*(3), 350–356.

Goerner, S. (1994). *Chaos and the evolving ecological universe.* Langhorne, PA: Gordon and Breach Science.

Goldstein, J., Freud, A., & Solnit, A. J. (1979). *Before the best interests of the child.* New York: Free Press.

Gomez, H. J. (May 14, 2010). County OKs $60,000 study of race bias in justice system. *The Plain Dealer.* B1.

Goncalves, R. A., & Rebocho, M. F. (2010). The Portuguese version of the CAPP: An exploratory study with a sample of offenders. Paper presented at the 20th Conference of the European Association of Psychology and Law, Gothenburg, Sweden.

Goodwin, J. (Aug. 20, 2010). Malpractice suits drop when doctors admit mistakes, apologize. *USA Today.* Retrieved Dec. 24, 2010 from http://www.usatoday.com/yourlife/health/healthcare/doctorsnurses/2010-08-20-medical-errors-malpractice_N.htm.

Graham-Bermann, S. A., & Seng, J. S. (2005). Violence exposure and traumatic stress symptoms as additional predictors of health problems in high risk children. *Journal of Pediatrics, 146*(3), 349–354.

Gray, M. (2000). *Drug crazy: How we got into this mess and how we can get out.* New York: Random House.

Greenberg, S., & Shuman, D. W. (1997). Irreconcilable conflict between therapeutic and forensic roles. *Professional Psychology: Research and Practice, 28,* 50–57.

Greenberg, S. A., Shuman, D. W., Feldman, S. R., Middleton, C., & Ewing, C. P. (2007). Lessons for forensic practice drawn from the law of malpractice. In Goldstein, A. M. (Ed.), *Forensic psychology: Emerging topics and expanding roles*. Hoboken, NJ: John Wiley and Sons.

Greene, R. L. (1999). *The MMPI-2/MMPI: An interpretive manual* (2nd ed.). Needham Heights, MA: Allyn and Bacon.

Grisso, T. (1998). *Instruments for understanding and appreciating Miranda rights*. Sarasota, FL: Professional Resource Press.

Grisso, T. (2010). Guidance for improving forensic reports: A review of common errors. *Open Access Journal of Forensic Psychology, 2*, 102–115. Retrieved from http://www.forensicpsychologyunbound.ws.

Gudjonsson, G. H. (2003). *The psychology of interrogations and confessions: A handbook*. Hoboken, NJ: John Wiley and Sons.

Guidelines for Forensic Practice. (1991, revision in process), 8/1/10 draft (retrieved from www.ap-ls.org/aboutpsychlaw/080110sgfpdraft.pdf)

Gunderson, J. G. (1984). *Borderline personality disorder*. Washington, DC: American Psychiatric Press.

Gunderson, J. G., & Singer, M. P. (1975). Defining borderline patients: An overview. *American Journal of Psychiatry, 132*, 1–10.

Guralnick, M. J., Connor, R. T., Hammond, M. A., Gottinam, J. M., & Kimnish, K. (2010). Peer relations of preschool children with communication disorders. Retrieved July 4, 2010 from http://depts.washington.edu/child/guralnick/pdfs/peer_relations_preschool_CD_4_96.pdf.

Heilbrun, K., DeMatteo, D., Marczyk, G., & Goldstein, A. (2008). Standards of practice and care in forensic mental health assessment: Legal, professional, and principles-based considerations. *Psychology, Public Policy, and Law, 14*(1), 1–26.

Heinzen, H., Stoll, E., Köhler, D., Hucvhzermeier, C., Tiklasky, I., & Herbst, D. (2010). Validation of the Comprehensive Assessment of Psychopathic Personality (CAPP) German version—Preliminary results. Paper presented at the 20th Conference of the European Association of Psychology and Law, Gothenburg, Sweden.

Heisenberg, W. (1927). Uber den anschaulichen inhalt der quantentheoretischen kinematik und mechanik. *Zeitchrift für Physik, 43*(3–4), 172–198.

Herman, J., Perry, C., & van der Kolk, B. (1989). Childhood trauma in borderline personality disorder. *American Journal of Psychiatry, 146*, 490–495.

Hoff, H. A., Rypdal, K., Mykletun, A., & Cooke, D. J. (2010). A prototypicality validation of the Comprehensive Assessment of Psychopathic Personality (CAPP) Model. *Journal of Personality Disorders, 22*(6), 639–644.

Hopkins, L. (Dec., 1997). *The role of the K Scale as a validity measure in court ordered child custody MMPI's*. Dissertation, The Fielding Graduate University, Santa Barbara, CA.

Howard, J. (2000). Substance abuse treatment for persons with child abuse and neglect issues. *Treatment Improvement Protocol Series 36*. U. S. Department of Health and Human Services.

Hsu, J. (2010a). Brooklyn lawyer to enter brain scan as court evidence for client's veracity. *POPSCI*, 05.05.2010.

Hsu, J. (2010b). Brain scan dismissed by Brooklyn judge as court evidence. *POPSCI*, 05.07.2010.

Hurley, D. (Apr. 19, 2005). Divorce rates: It's not as high as you think. *New York Times*. Retrieved May 25, 2010 from http://query.nytimes.com/gst/fullpage.html?res= 9805E2DE1F3EF93AA25757COA9639C8B63.

"Ikarian Reefer, The" 2 Lloyds Rep. 68 (Comm. Ct. Q. B. Div.) (1993).

Inbau, F. E., Reid, J. E., Buckley, J. P., & Jayne, B. C. (2001). *Criminal interrogation and confessions* (4th ed.). Gaithersberg, MD: Aspen.

Isay, R. A. (1977). Ambiguity in speech. *Journal of the American Psychoanalytic Association, 25*, 427–452.

Issues related to bullying. (2010). Retrieved Dec. 1, 2010 from http://www.bullyon-line.org/related/stalking.htm.

Jameson, B. J., Ehrenberg, M. F., & Hunter, M. A. (1997). Psychologists' ratings of the Best-Interests-of-the-Child custody and access criterion: A family systems assessment model. *Professional Psychology, Research and Practice, 28*(3), 253–262.

Johnston, J. R., Kline, M., & Tschann, J. M. (1989). Ongoing postdivorce conflict: Effects on children of joint custody and frequent access. *American Journal of Orthopsychiatry, 59*(4), 576–592.

Judicial Council Watcher. (Oct. 26, 2010). Quasi-judicial immunity for fraud upon the court? The Stephen Doyne debacle. Retrieved Dec. 24, 2010 from http://judicialcouncilwatcher.wordpress.com/2010/10/26quasi-judicial-immunity-for-fraud-upon-the-court-the-stephen-doyne-debacle/.

Jurs, A. W. (2008). *Daubert*, probabilities and possibilities, and the Ohio solution: A sensible approach to relevance under Rule 702 in civil and criminal applications. *Akron Law Review, 41*, 609–649.

Kashani, J. H., & Allan, W. D. (1998). *The impact of family violence on children and adolescents.* Thousand Oaks, CA: Sage.

Kaufman, M. S. (Nov. 1, 2006). *Status of Daubert in state courts.* Retrived Jan. 20, 2011 from http://www.atlanticlegal.org/daubertreport.pdf.

Keen, S. (1986). *Images of the enemy: Reflections of the hostile imagination.* New York: Harper and Row.

Kelly, J. B. (2010a). *Some options for child custody parenting plans (for children of school age).* Retrieved May 21, 2010) from http://www.coloradodivorcemedia-tion.com?family?Child-Custody-Parenting-Plans-Options.pdf.

Kelly, J. B. (2010b). *The determination of child custody in the USA.* Retrieved May 21, 2010 from http://www.standord.edu/group/psylawseminar/Child%20 Custody%20USA%20(Page%2301%20of%205).

Kelm v. Hyatt. United States Court of Appeals, 6th Cir. No. 93-3141 (January, 1995).

Kensinger, E. A. (2010). Neuroimaging the formation of and retrieval of emotional memories. In press: *Brain Mapping: New Research.* Hauppauge, NY: Nova Science. Retrieved Dec. 20, 2010 from https://www2.bc.edu/~kensinel/Kensinger_Nova_BM.pdf.

Kermani, E. J. (1982). Court rulings on psychotherapists. *American Journal of Psychotherapy, 36*(2), 248–255.

Kernberg, O. (1979). Some implications of object relations theory and technique. *Journal of the American Psychoanalytic Association, 27*, 207–240.

Kline, M., Tschann, J. M., Johnston, J. R., & Wallerstein, J. S. (1989). Children's adjustment in joint and sole physical custody families. *Developmental Psychology, 25*(3), 430–438.

Knight, R. (1953). Borderline states. *Bulletin of the Menninger Clinic, 17,* 1–12.

Kohut, H., & Wolf, E. S. (1978). Disorders of the self and their treatment: An outline. *The International Journal of Psychoanalysis, 59,* 413–525.

Kolb, B., & Wishaw, I. Q. (2009). *Fundamentals of human neuropsychology* (5th ed.). New York: Worth.

Kopetski, L. M., Rand, D. C., & Rand, R. (2006). Incidence, gender, and false allegations of child abuse: Data on 84 parental alienation syndrome cases. In R. A. Gardner, S. R. Sauber, & D. Lorandos (Eds.), *The international handbook of parental alienation syndrome: Conceptual and legal considerations* (pp. 65–90). Springfield, IL: Charles C. Thomas.

Kosslyn, S. M., & Koenig, D. (1992). *Wet mind: The new cognitive neuroscience.* New York: Free Press.

Kuehnle, K., & Connell, M. (Eds.) (2009). *The evaluation of child sexual abuse allegations: A comprehensive guide to assessment and testimony.* Danvers, MA: John Wiley and Sons.

Labcorp. (2011). *Drugs of abuse reference guide.* Retrieved July 6, 2011 from www.labcorpsolutions.com/images/Drugs_of_abuse_Reference_Guide_Flyer_3166.pdf.

Laboratory for Scientific Interrogation. Retrieved Jan. 20, 2011 from http://www.isiscan.com.

Lancaster, G., & Vrij, A. (2010). The effect of secondary-task-induced cognitive load on liars' and truth tellers' eye glance frequency during an interview. Paper presented at the 20th Conference of the European Association of Psychology and Law, Gothenburg, Sweden.

Lanier, P., Jonson-Reid, M., Stahlschmidt, M. J., Drake, B., & Constantino, J. (2009). Child maltreatment and pediatric health outcomes: A longitudinal study of low-income children. *Journal of Pediatric Psychology,* jsp086v1. Retrieved Jan. 2, 2009 from http://jpepsy.oxfordjournals.org/cgi/content/abstract/jsp086v1.

Larrison v. United States. 24 F.2d 82, 87-88 (7th Cir. 1928).

Lieb, R., Isensee, B., Hofler, M., Pfister, H., & Wittchen, H. (2002). Parental major depression and the risk of depression and other mental disorders in offspring. *Archives of General Psychiatry, 59,* 365–374.

Lim, J. R., & Herschler, J. A. (1998). The stalking of clinicians by their patients. In J. R. Meloy (Ed.), *The psychology of stalking: Clinical and forensic perspectives* (pp. 163–173). San Diego: Academic Press.

Linehan, M. M. (1993a). *Cognitive-behavioral treatment of borderline personality disorder.* New York: Guilford Press.

Linehan, M. M. (1993b). *Skills training manual for treating borderline personality disorder.* New York: Guilford Press.

Linehan, M. M., Armstrong, H. E., Suarez, A., Allmain, D., & Heard, H. L. (1991). Cognitive behavioral treatment of chronically parasuicidal borderline individuals. *Archives of General Psychiatry, 458,* 1060–1064.

London, K., Bruck, M., Ceci, S. J., & Shuman, D. W. (2005). What does the research tell us about the ways that children tell? *Psychology, Public Policy, and Law, 11*(1), 194–226.

London, K., Bruck, M., Wright, D. B. T., & Ceci, S. J. (2008). Review of the contemporary literature on how children report sexual abuse to others: Findings, methodological issues, and implications for forensic interviews. *Memory, 16,* 29–47.

Lorain County Domestic Relations Court. (2011) Local Rules. (Author).

Lovejoy, M. C., Graczyk, P. A., O'Hare, E., & Newman, G. (2000). Maternal depression and parenting behavior: A meta-analytic review. *Clinical Psychology Review, 20*(5), 561–592.

Lowenstein, L. F. (2005). What can be done to reduce the implacable hostility leading to parental alienation in parents? Retrieved Feb. 2, 2011 from http://www.parental-alienation.info/.

Lowenstein, L. F. (2008). Implacable hostility leading to parental alienation. *Justice of the Peace, 172*(12), 185–187.

MacLean Family Law Group. (2010). *Custody*. Retrieved May 21, 2010 from www.bcfamilylaw.ca/family-law/custody-and-access.

Marlowe, D. B. (1995). A hybrid decision framework for evaluating psychometric evidence. *Behavioral Sciences and the Law, 13*, 207–228.

Marriage and conjugal life in Canada. Retrieved May 21, 2010 from www.divorcerate.org/divorce-rates-in-canada.html.

Mart, E. (Summer, 2009). Overnight visitation for infants and toddlers: Implications for parenting plans. *Vermont Bar Journal,* (Summer) 1–5.

Massachusetts Trial Court Law Libraries (2010). Massachusetts Rules of Domestic Relations Procedure. Retrieved Nov. 20, 2010 from http://www.lawlib.state.ma.us/source/mass/rules/dom/index.html.

Masterson, J. F., & Rinsley, D. B. (1975). The borderline syndrome: The role of the mother in the genesis and psychic structure of the borderline personality. *International Journal of Psychoanalysis, 56*, 137–141.

McCarthy, G. (2008). History and practice of mediation: A long-range view of common interests and restoration of relationships. *Suite101.com*. Retrieved Dec. 27, 2010 from http://www.suite101.com/content/history-and-practice-of-mediation-a57875.

McIvor, R. J., Potter, L., & Davies, L. (2008). Stalking behavior by patient towards psychiatrists in a large mental health organization. *International Journal of Social Psychiatry, 54*(4), 350–357.

McPherson, S. (1990, September). Some areas of interface between psychology and the guardian-*ad-litem* programs in juvenile and domestic relations settings. Second European Conference on Law and Psychology. Nuremberg, Germany.

McPherson, S. (1997, September). An investigation into the necessity of interview preservation for purposes of accuracy in testimony. Paper presented at the 20th Conference of the European Association of Psychology and Law. Stockholm, Sweden.

McPherson, S., Bailey, G. R., Conklin, D., Honeychurch, A., Miller, J., Passaro, T., & Shara, R. (2006). Overcontrolled hostility on the MMPI-2: A domestic relations consideration. In S. Giles and M. Santarcangelo (Eds.), *Psychological aspects of legal processes*. London: IA-IP.

McPherson, S., & Donnelly, J. (2005, July). Enemy images, archetypes, and propaganda potentials. Paper presented at the International Association of Law and Mental Health meeting, Paris, France.

McPherson, S. B., Yudko, E., Murray-Bridges, L., Rodriguez, P., & Lindo-Moulds, P. (2009). History of drug control. In S. B. McPherson, H. V. Hall, & E. Yudko (Eds.), *Methamphetamine use: Clinical and forensic aspects* (pp. 3–22). Boca Raton, FL: CRC Press.

Meloy, R. (1992). *Violent attachments.* Northvale, NJ: Aronson.

Melton, G. B., Petrila, J., Poythress, N. G., & Slobogin, C. (1997). *Psychological evaluations for the courts: A handbook for mental health professionals and lawyers* (2nd ed.). New York: Guilford Press.

Memon, A., Vrij, A., & Bull, R. (2003). *Psychology and law: Truthfulness, accuracy and credibility.* (ebook). New York: John Wiley and Sons. Michigan Compiled Laws, Section 722.23.

Milbank, D. (January 5, 1996). No-fault divorce law is assailed in Michigan and debate heats up. *Wall Street Journal.* A1, A6.

Milgram, S. (1974). *Obedience to authority.* New York: Harper and Row.

Milne, R., & Bull, R. (1999). *Investigative interviewing: Psychology and practice.* New York: John Wiley and Sons.

Mnookin, R. H. (1975). Review: Beyond the best interests of the child. *Journal of the American Academy of Child Psychiatry, 1*(3), 226.

Monahan, J. (1993). Limiting therapist exposure to *Tarasoff* liability. *American Psychologist, 48*(3), 242–250.

Morrison, J., & Morrison, T. (2001). Psychiatrists disciplined by a state medical board. *American Journal of Psychiatry, 158,* 474–478.

Mumford, L. T. (2007). The peacemaker test: Designing legal rights to reduce legal warfare. *Harvard Negotiation Law Review, 12,* 377–382.

Mumford, L. T. (2010). The peacemaker test: Application and comparison. *Mississippi Law Journal, 80*(2), 639–680.

Namnyak, M., Tufton, N., Szedely, R., Worboys, S., & Sampson, E. L. (2008). "Stockholm Syndrome": Psychiatric diagnosis or urban myth. *Acta Psychiatrica Scandinavia 117*(1), 4–11.

National Center for Victims of Crime. (2003). Cyberstalking. Accessed Aug. 12, 2011 from http://www.ncvc.org/ncvc/main.aspx?dbName=DocumentViewer&DocumentID=32458

National Healthy Marriage Resource Center. (May 5, 2010). *Attitudes toward marriage.* Retrieved May 15, 2010 from www.healthymarriageinfo.org/dow/marriageattitude.pdf.

Needle, R. H., Su, S., & Doherty, W. J. (1990). Divorce, remarriage and adolescent substance use: A prospective longitudinal study. *Journal of Marriage and the Family, 52,* 157–169.

Newman, L., & Stevenson, C. (2005). Parenting and borderline personality disorder: Ghosts in the nursery. *Clinical Child Psychology and Psychiatry, 10*(3), 385–394.

Opie v. State. 422 P.2d 84 (Wyo. 1967).

Peele, S. (1990). Personality and alcoholism: Establishing the link. In D. A. Ward (Ed.), *Alcoholism: Introduction to theory and treatment* (3rd ed., pp. 147–156). Dubuque, IA: Kendall Hunt.

Peele, S. (1985). *The meaning of addiction: Compulsive experience and its interpretation.* Lexington, MA: Lexington Books.

Perry, N. W., & Wrightsman, L. S. (1991). *The child witness: Legal issues and dilemmas.* Thousand Oaks, CA: Sage.

Pew Research Center. (July 1, 2010). *As marriage and parenthood drift apart, public is concerned about social impact.* Retrieved May 21, 2010 from http://pewresearch.org/pubs/526/marriage-parenthood.

Pew Research Center. (Nov. 18, 2010). *The decline of marriage and rise of new families.* Retrieved Nov. 20, 2010 from http://pewresearch.org/pubs/1802/decline-marriage-rise-new-families.

Phelps, E. A., & Sharot, T. (2008). How (and why) emotion enhances the subjective sense of recollection. *Current Directions in Psychological Science, 17,* 147–152.

Piper, A., Lillevik, L., & Kritzer, R. (2008). What's wrong with believing in repression?: A review of legal professionals. *Psychology, Public Policy, and Law, 14*(3), 223–242.

Plain Dealer, The (2009, Dec. 9). The racial bias in Cuyahoga County's justice system must end. Editorial. Retrieved Jan. 2, 2009 from http://www.Cleveland/com/opinion/index.ssf/2009/12/the_racial_bias_in_cuyahoga_co.html.

Pogash, L. (Nov. 23, 2003). Myth of the "Twinkie defense." Retrieved Oct. 3, 2010 from http://www.sfgate.com/cgi-bin/article.cgi?f=/c/a/2003/11/23/INGRE343501.DTL&ao=2.

Polikoff, N. (1983). Gender and child custody determinations. In I. Diamond (Ed.), *Families, politics and public policy: A feminist dialogue on women and the state* (pp. 183–202). New York: Longman.

Pope, K. (2010). *Therapy, ethics, malpractice, forensics, critical thinking (and a few other topics).* Retrieved Dec. 25, 2010 from http://kspope.com/.

Pope, K. S., & Vasquez, M. J. (2007). *Ethics in psychotherapy and counseling: A practical guide* (3rd ed.). Hoboken, NJ: Jossey-Bass.

Pruett, M. K., Ebling, R., & Insabella, G. (2004). Critical aspects of parenting plans for young children: Interjecting data into the debate about overnights. *Family Court Review, 42*(1), 39–59.

Quadrio, C. (2005). Axnis One/Axis Two: A disordered borderline. *Australian & New Zealand Journal of Psychiatry, 39,* 141–156.

R. v. J. (J.-L., 1999). (Canada).

R. v. Mohan. 2 S.C.R. 9 (1994). (Canada).

Raskin, D. C. (Ed.) (1989). *Psychological methods in criminal investigation and evidence.* New York: Springer-Verlag.

Ready v. Commonwealth. 824 N.E. 2d 474 (2005).

Reinecke, M. A., Dattilo, F. M., & Freeman, A. (Eds.). (2003). *Cognitive therapy with children and adolescents: A casebook for clinical practice.* New York: Guilford Press.

Repp, B. H. (1981). Perceptual equivalence of two kinds of ambiguous speech stimuli. *Bulletin of the Psychonomic Society, 18*(1), 12–14.

Richardson, M. P., Strange, B., & Dolan, R. J. (2004). Encoding of emotional memories depends on the amygdala and hippocampus and their interactions. *Natural Neuroscience, 7,* 278–285.

Robbins, T. (2002). Combating "cults" and "brainwashing" in the United States and Western Europe: A comment on Richardson and Introvigne's report. *Journal for the Scientific Study of Religion, 40*(2), 169–176.

Roebuck, D. (2010). *Early English arbitration.* Oxford, UK: Holo Books, Arbitration Press.

Roebuck, D., & de Fumichon, B. (2004). *Roman arbitration.* Oxford, UK: Holo Books, Arbitration Press.

Rogers, R., Tillbrook, C. E., & Sewell, K. W. (2004). *ECST-R: Evaluation of Competency to Stand Trial–Revised: Professional manual.* Lutz, FL: Psychological Assessment Resources.

Roisman, G. I., Padron, E., Sroufe, L. A., & Egeland, B. (2002a). Attachment from infancy to early adulthood in a high-risk sample: Continuity, discontinuity, and their correlates. *Child Development, 73*(4), 695–702.

Roisman, G. I., Padron, E., Sroufe, L. A., & Egeland, B. (2002b). Earned-secure attachment status in retrospect and prospect. *Child Development, 73*(4), 1204–1219.

Ruisi v. Thieriot. 53 Cal. App. 4th 1197 (1997).

Rumelhart, D. E., Hinton, G. E., & McClelland, J. L. (1986). A general framework for parallel distributed processing, Chapter 2. In D. E. Rumelhart, J. L. McClelland, & the PDP Research Group (Eds.), *Parallel distributed processing: Explorations in the microstructure of cognition, Volume I: Foundations* (pp. 45–47). Cambridge, MA: MIT.

Samra-Grewal, J. (1999). Custody and access evaluations: Issues for mental health professionals conducting assessments with mentally disordered or mentally retarded parents. *Expert Evidence, 7*, 85–111.

Sangiacomo, M. (2010, May 22). Man sentenced to 8 years in child porn case. *The Plain Dealer.* Retrieved Feb. 4, 2011 from http://blog.cleveland.com/metro/2010/05/man_sentenced_to_8_ years_in_ch.html.

Sattler, J. M. (1998). *Clinical and forensic interviewing of children and families: Guidelines for the mental health, education, pediatric, and child maltreatment fields.* San Diego: Jerome M. Sattler.

Schafer, J. R. (2007). *Grammatical differences between truthful and deceptive written narratives.* Unpublished manuscript. Fielding Graduate University.

Schafer, J. R. (2010). *Psychological narrative analysis: A professional method to detect deception in written and oral communications.* Springfield, IL: Charles C. Thomas.

Seigel, J. (1996). Traditional MMPI-2 validity indicators and initial presentation in custody evaluations. *American Journal of Forensic Psychology, 14*(3), 55–63.

Shaffer, M. (2010). Shared parenting: A cautionary note. Spring/Summer 2006 issue of *Nexus.* Retrieved May 20, 2010 from http://www.law.utoronto.ca/visitors_content.asp?itemPath=5/13/0/0/0&contentid=1448

Shuy, R. W. (1998). *The language of confession, interrogation, and deception.* Thousand Oaks, CA: Sage.

Silverstein, B. (1989). Enemy images: The psychology of U.S. attitudes and cognition regarding the Soviet Union. *American Psychologist, 44*(6), 903–913.

Simmons, C. W. (March, 2000). Children of incarcerated parents. California State Library. California Research Bureau. Sacramento: CRB Note, 7(2), 1–11.

Slovic, P. (1987). Perception of risk. *Science, 236*(4799), 280–285.

Smith v. Quigg. (2006-Ohio-1494).

Soslo, R. L., Maclin, O. H., & Maclin, M. R. (2008). *Cognitive psychology* (8th ed.). Boston: Allyn and Bacon.

Sporer, S. L., & Schwandt, B. (2007). Moderators of nonverbal indicators of deception: A meta-analytic synthesis. *Psychology, Public Policy, and Law, 13*(1), 1–34.

State v. Boston. 46 Ohio St. 3d 108, 545 N.E. 2d 1220 (1989).

State v. Burrell. 20056 Ohio 34 (2011-Ohio-2553).

State v. Cornwell. (Feb. 27, 1998). 11th Dist. No. 95-T-5379.

State v. Johnson. 677 N.E. 2d 1281 83 Ohio Misc. 2d 26 (Ohio Com. Pl. 1996).

Stolle, D. P., Wexler, D. B., & Winick, B. J. (2000). *Practicing therapeutic jurisprudence: Law as a helping profession.* Durham, NC: Carolina Academic Press.

Substance Abuse and Mental Health Services Administration (SAMHSA). (2009). National Survey on Drug Use and Health. http://oas.samhsa.gov/NSDUH/2k9NSDUH/2k9ResultsP.pdf

Summit, R. (1983). The child sexual abuse accommodation syndrome. *Child Abuse and Neglect, 7,* 177–193.

Summit, R. (1992). Abuse of the child sexual abuse accommodation syndrome. *Journal of Child Sexual Abuse, 1*(4), 153–164.

Supreme Court of Ohio. (2009). *Parenting coordination: Working with high conflict families.* Columbus, OH: Author.

Tarasoff v. Regents of University of California. 551 P 2d 334 (1976).

Thelen, M. H., Rodriguez, M. D., & Sprengelmeyer, P. (1994). Psychologists' beliefs concerning confidentiality with suicide, homicide, and child abuse. *American Journal of Psychotherapy, 48*(3), 363–379.

Traylor, A., Price, J. H., Telljohann, S. K., King, K., & Thompson, A. (2010). Clinical psychologists' firearm risk management perceptions. *Journal of Community Health, 35*(1), 60–67.

Tsuchiya, N., & Adolphs, B. (2007). Emotion and consciousness. *Trends in Cognitive Science, 11*(4), 158–167.

Undeutsch, V. (1982). Statement reality analysis. In A. Trankell (Ed.), *Reconstructing psychologists in criminal trials* (pp. 27–56). Deventer, The Netherlands: Kluwer.

Ungerleider, J. T., & Wellisch, D. K. (1979). Coercive persuasion (brainwashing), religious cults, and deprogramming. *American Journal of Psychiatry, 136,* 279–282.

U.S. Department of Health and Human Services (1999). Blending perspectives and building commmon ground: A report to Congress on substance abuse and child protection. Author.

U.S. Department of Labor. (2010a). Retrieved Apr. 24, 2010 from http://www.bls.gov/news.release/empsit.nr0.htm

U.S. Department of Labor. (2010b). Retrieved Apr. 24, 2010 from http://www.divrocerate.org/

Vandenbos, G. R. (2007). Unconscious process. In *APA Dictionary of Psychology.* Washington, DC: American Psychological Association.

Vanneman, R. (1999). Sociology 441: Stratification. Retrieved Oct. 27, 2009 from http://www.bsos.umd.edu/socy/vanneman/socy441/trends/divorce.html.

Virginia Department of Professional and Occupational Regulation. (November 7, 2003). *Study of the utility and validity of voice stress analyzers.* Retrieved Dec. 14, 2010 from http://www.dpor.virginia.gov/dporweb/bpo_Final%20Voice%Stress%20Report%20BPOR.pdf.

Vlosky, D. A., & Monroe, P. A. (2002). The effective dates of no-fault divorce laws in the 50 states. *Family Relations, 51*(4), 317–324.

Vrij, A. (2005). Criteria based content analysis: A qualitative review of the first 37 studies. *Psychology, Public Policy, and Law, 11*(1), 3–41.

Vrij, A. (2010). Statement validity assessment, Chapter 8. Retrieved Dec. 21, 2010 from www.docstoc.com/docs/5255888/Statement-Validity-Assessment.

Vrij, A., Granhag, P. A., & Porter, S. (2010). Pitfalls and opportunities in nonverbal and verbal lie detection. *Psychological Science in the Public Interest, 11*(3), 89–121.

Vrij, A., & Mann, S. (2006). Criteria based content analysis: An empirical test of its underlying processes. *Psychology, Crime and Law, 12*(4), 337–349.

Wagner, K. D., Pollard, R., & Wagner, R. F. (1993). Malpractice litigation against child and adolescent residence programs. *Journal of the American Academy of Child and Adolescent Psychiatry, 32*(2), 462–465.

Waldrop, M. M. (1992). *Complexity: The emerging science at the edge of order and chaos.* New York: Simon and Schuster.

Walker, A. G. (1999). *Handbook on questioning children* (2nd ed.). Washington, DC: ABA Center on Children and the Law.

Wallerstein, J. S. (1991). The long-term effects of divorce on children: A review. *Journal of the American Academy of Child and Adolescent Psychiatry, 30*(3), 349–360.

Wallerstein, J. S., & Lewis, J. (1998). The long-term impact of divorce on children: A first report from a 25 year study. *Family and Conciliation Courts Review, 36,* 368–383.

Ward, J. (2006). *The student's guide to neuroscience.* New York: Psychology Press.

Weiner, R. L. & Haney, C. (Eds.). (2004). Capital punishment in the United States. Special Issue of *Psychology, Public Policy and Law, 10*(4). Entire volume.

Weinfield, N. S., Sroufe, L. A., & Egeland, B. (2000). Attachment from infancy to young adulthood in a high risk sample: Continuity, discontinuity and their correlates. *Child Development, 7*(3), 695–702.

Weiser, B. (January 28, 2011). Court rejects judge's assertion of a child pornography gene. *New York Times.* Retrieved Jan. 4, 2011 from http://www.nytimes.com/2011/01/29/nyregion/29ruling.html.

Wellman, F. L. (1932). *The art of cross-examination.* New York: Macmillan.

Wernicke, C. (1874). *Der aphasische Symptomenkomplex.* Breslau: Cohn & Weigert.

Whitehead, P. D., & Popenoe, D. (2000). Changes in teen attitudes toward marriage, cohabitation and children. The National Marriage Project. Retrieved May 15, 2010 from www.Virginia.edu/marriageproject/pdfs/print_teenattitudes.pdf.

Williams, C. R., & Arrigo, B. A. (2002). *Law, psychology, and justice: Chaos theory and the new (dis)order.* Albany: State University of New York Press.

Wojcikiewicz, J. (2009). *Forensics and justice: Judicature on scientific evidence 1993–2008.* Poland: Dom.

Wolf, J. (January, 25, 2007). Shared parenting bill scheduled for public hearing in Washington State. *Jennifer's Single Parents Blog.*

Woody, M. H. (1997). *Legally safe mental health practice.* Madison, CT: International Universities Press.

Woolard, J. L., Reppucci, N. D., & Redding, R. E. (1996). Theoretical and methodological issues in studying children's capacities in legal contexts. *Law and Human Behavior, 20*(3), 219–228.

Wright, D. C. (2002). The crisis of child custody: A history of the birth of family law in England. *Columbia Journal of Gender and Law, 11,* 175–270.

Wright, L. (2002). Comment: Interviewing children in child custody cases. *Journal of the American Academy of Matrimonial Lawyers, 18*, 295–309.

Wrightsman, L. S., & Kassin, S. M. (1993). *Confessions in the courtroom.* Thousand Oaks, CA: Sage.

Yazdani-Isfehani v. Yazdani-Isfehani. 170 Ohio App. 3d 1 (2006).

Young, G., O'Brien, J., Gutterman, E., & Cohen, P. (1987). Research on the clinical interview. *Journal of the American Academy of Child and Adolescent Psychiatry, 26*, 613–620.

Index

730 Evaluation, 135

A

Abel Assessment for Sexual Interest (AASI), 64–65
Abuse allegations. *See also* Conducting forensic evaluations
case studies of investigations, 72–76
child sexual abuse accommodation syndrome and, 29
conducting the interview, 220–224
contested custody cases and, 32–34
ex parte motions in initial filing phase and, 142–143
forensic evaluations of, 69
general guidelines for interviews concerning, 219–220
implications of constructive memory on, 58
interim pretrial phase, 144
investigative interviewing in equivocal cases, 67–69
judicial perspectives on, 48
parental alienation syndrome and, 163
reportage concerning, 205
semi-structured interview guides, 235–236
timing of with relation to hearing and judgment phases, 144–145
Abuses, judicial decision making and, 25
Adjustment Disorder diagnoses, 83
Affective disorders
bipolar disorder, 182–184
major depressive disorder, 185–187
Affidavit example, 227–233
Age of children
dependence of capacity and performance on, 51
therapy and, 152, 154

Alcohol
effect of parental use on children, 194
patterns of use and abuse, 188
Alienation, 27–28
Alternative dispute resolution (ADR)
parent coordination, 159–161
parental alienation and, 163–164
recommendations for in forensic evaluations, 206–207
Ambiguous speech, 211–212
American Prosecutors Research Institute (APRI), investigative interviewing recommendations, 68
Assessment tools
child custody evaluation and, 130
use of with BPD individuals, 175–176
Attorneys. *See also* Lawyers
actions taken against evaluators by, 104–105
conducting investigative interviews in the presence of, 67
over-identification of evaluators with, 71
pretrial contact of custody evaluators with, 202
Attractors, 3
Audiotaping, interviews concerning allegations of sexual abuse, 135

B

Back-dooring of assumptions, 83
Battered Mothers Custody Conference, 115, 124
Berry v. State, 88
Best interest statutes, content analysis of, 19–24
Best interests
definition of in Michigan statute, 19–20
doctrine, 11

operational definition of, 25
shared parenting legislation and
    standards of, 18–26
Bias, 4–5
    allegations against custody evaluators,
        112
    problems of in forensic evaluations and
        investigations, 129–130
Bifurcation, 2
Biological assessment options for substance
    abuse, 191
Bipolar disorder, 182–184
Blind justice, 4–5
Borderline personality disorder (BPD)
    case management for, 175–178
    categories and characteristics of, 165–166
    causation of, 168–169
    child abuse and, 170–175
    comorbid conditions, 167
    intimate relationships and individuals
        with, 170
    invalidating environments and, 169–170
    recommendations for interaction with
        clients with, 175
    standards for defining, 168
    tendency toward distortion, 166–167
Brain function, current theory and research
    on, 56–60
Brown v. State, 87–88
    implications of, 88–89
    scientific evidence and, 89

C

California Protective Parents Association,
    115
Capacity, definition of, 51
Case examples
    abuse allegation investigations, 72–76
    ambiguity in presentation of custody
        issues, 213–216
    bipolar disorder, 183–184
    borderline personality disorder, 177–178
    civil suit action files against custody
        evaluator, 115–116
    contested custody case with positive
        outcome, 34–37
    critique of a child interview, 247–262
    depression, 187
    equivocal communication, 212
    experience of a forensic psychologist,
        125–127

forensic practitioners and financial
    issues, 133–134
importance of interview taping, 135–136
malpractice actions against forensic
    practitioners, 113
Case management, individuals with
    borderline personality disorder,
    175–178
Change of circumstances, 145
Chaos theory, 1
    principles of, 2–3
Charleston County D.S.S. v. Father,
    Stepmother, and Mother, 92
Child abuse
    borderline personality disorder and,
        170–175
    relationship of with illicit drug use, 189
Child custody evaluators. See also
    Conducting forensic evaluations
    perspectives on of investigative
        interviewing, 69–70
    psychological assessment procedures,
        96–98, 130
    recommended procedures for, 134–138
Child pornography, complexity involved in
    sentencing in cases of, 217–218
Child sexual abuse, history of in individuals
    with BPD, 170
Child sexual abuse accommodation
    syndrome (CSAAS), 28–29
Child therapy, establishing security
    through, 152
Children
    capacity and performance of, 51
    conducting investigative interviews of,
        66–69 (See also Conducting forensic
        evaluations)
    developmental differences and parenting
        schedules, 45
    diagnosis of PTSD in, 83
    evaluation of in contested custody cases,
        197–198
    impact on of dysfunctional family
        situations, 7–8
    in camera interviews of, 5–6, 48–51
    instructions for enhanced security of,
        245–246
    mental health treatment of in custody
        situations, 10
    parental alienation syndrome and, 27–28
    rates of visitation with father's post
        divorce, 16

recommendations for psychotherapy of, 206
right of election of, 48–49
Civil suit actions
    forensic practitioners and, 113–116
    risks of for forensic mental health practitioners, 106
Client information form, 240
Clinician experts. *See also* Therapists; Treating professionals
    areas for cross-examination of, 82
Cognitive behavioral therapy, 82
Cognitive interviews, 66
Communication, equivocal, 211–212
Companionship time, scheduling of, 25–26
Complexity theory, 1, 216–217. *See also* Chaos theory
    application of to human affairs, 7
Comprehensive Assessment of Psychopathic Personality (CAPP), 179
Conducting forensic evaluations
    ancillary contacts, 201–202
    guidelines for interviewing children, 219–225
    obtaining information from independent sources, 199–200
    pretrial attorney contacts, 202
    primary contacts, 197–201
    recommendations, 205–207
    reportage, 202–205
    semi-structured interview guides, 235–236
Confirmatory bias, 112
Confirmatory distortion, 112
Conflict of interest, 128
Consciousness, 59
"Consistent with" statements, 89–90
Constructive memory, 58
Consultations
    example: critique of a child interview, 247–262
    forensic practitioners and, 132
Content Based Criterion Analysis (CBCA), 89
Contested custody cases. *See also* Conducting forensic evaluations; Custody; Domestic relations cases
    abuse allegations in, 32–34
    bipolar disorder in parent, 182–184
    borderline personality disorder and mothers in, 170–178

depression in parents involved in, 185–187
diagnosis of post-traumatic stress disorder in, 83
experts and, 33, 47
narcissistic personality disorder and fathers in, 180–182
parenting schedules in, 32
risks to others in, 117–119
role of evaluators in, 39
substance abuse and, 189–190
use of psychological evaluations in, 32–34
Coparenting, 11
    team, 70
Countertransference bias, 112
Court orders, 137–138
Court system, self-organizing complex systems of, 4
Court-appointed witnesses, 79–81
Court-ordered therapy, 69–70
Coverture, 12
Credibility, expert opinions on, 86–91
Criminal defendants, evaluation of in contested custody cases, 198–199
Criteria Based Content Analysis, 62
CSAAS. *See* Child sexual abuse accommodation syndrome
Custody
    children's right of election, 48–49
    evaluations (*See* Conducting forensic evaluations)
    gay marriage and, 213
    in camera interviews of children in disputes of, 5–6
    legal history of, 12–14
    types of, 10–11
    visitation evaluators, 79
Custody evaluation
    civil suit and malpractice actions related to, 112–116
    licensure board complaints related to, 106–112
    personal risks to forensic practitioners related to, 116–117
    risks involved in, 104
Cyberstalking, 123

D

"Dangerous parenting disorder," 180. *See also* Narcissistic personality disorder
Dangerousness predictions, 117–118

Data
   assigning meaning to, 136–137
   Daubert criteria and the collection of,
      95–98
   fortuitous collection of, 75–76
Daubert decision
   analysis of credibility based on, 62, 84
   implications of for domestic relations
      court cases, 94–98
   psychological assessments and, 129–130
   Rule 702 and, 84
Decision making
   best interests doctrine for, 11
   effect of on children, 7–8
   judicial patterns of, 25
   self-organizing complex systems and,
      4–5
Defensive practice
   checklist for, 138–139
   ethical perspectives, 127–129
   evaluation and investigation, 129–130
   recommendations for, 130–138
Depositions, 52–53
Depression, 185–187
Detection of deception, scientific evidence
   and, 89
Developmental guideposts in relation to
   personal safety, 154
Developmentally appropriate questioning,
   68
Distortions, 55–56, 82
   tendency of BPD individuals for, 166–167
Divorce
   application of parent alienation
      syndrome in legal cases, 28
   guardian *ad litem* involvement in
      proceedings, 46
   initial filing phase, 142–144
   judges, 48–51
   lawyers, 47
   legal history of, 12–14
   litigants in proceedings, 46
   role of experts in proceedings, 47
   sociolegal trends in, 14–18
   substance abuse and, 189–190
Divorce Act of 1968 (Canada), 16
Documentation, necessity of for forensic
   practitioners, 131
Domestic relations cases
   civil suit and malpractice actions related
      to, 112–116
   complexity in, 213–218

effects of change on, 213–216
hearing and judgment phase, 144–145
initial filing phase, 142–144
interim pretrial phase, 144
licensure board complaints related to,
      106–112
personal risks to forensic practitioners
      in, 116–117
sequence of events in, 141–142
Domestic relations court. *See also* Family
      court
   admissibility of hearsay in, 91–94
   course of contested divorce cases in,
      31–34
   court-related evaluations in, 33
   depositions for, 52–53
   evaluators as witnesses, 79
   goal of investigations in cases, 55
   guardians *ad litem* as witnesses in,
      79–81
   interactions of factors in, 7–8
   legal standard issues in, 70–72
   length of divorce proceedings in, 53–54
   pre-trial motions in, 51–52
   problem of expert opinions on
      credibility, 87–91
   psychological assessment procedures
      applicable to, 97–98
   Rules of Superintendence (Ohio), 37
   treating professionals as witnesses in,
      81–83
   types of witnesses in, 78
Domestic Rules of Relations Procedure
      (Massachusetts), 43–44
Domestic violence, parenting coordination
      and, 160
Doyne, Stephen, 114–115
Dual roles, avoidance of, 127–128
Dysfunctional family situations, impact of
      on children, 7–8

E

Ecclesiastical divorce, 12
Echo, 180
Emergency motions, 51–52
Emotional arousal, memory and, 58–59
Emotional memories, 58
Emotionally vulnerable children, borderline
      personality disorder and, 169–170
Encoding, emotional arousal and, 59
English Common Law, 12

Enhanced security, instructions for, 245–246
Equivocal abuse cases
    ambiguous communication and, 212
    case studies of investigations of, 72–76
    dangers to child witnesses in, 148–151
    Federal Rules of Evidence, 84–85
    investigative interviewing for, 67–69
    mediation in, 156–158
Equivocal communication, 211–212
Ethical standards, 127–129
Evaluation of Competency to Stand Trial—
    Revised, 99
Evaluations. *See* Conducting forensic
    evaluations
Evaluators. *See also* Conducting forensic
    evaluations
    court-appointed, 47
    ethical considerations for, 127–129
    negative contributions of, 72
    over-identification of with specific
        attorneys, 71
    practicing defensively, 129–130
    recommended procedures for, 134–138
    risks to in child custody cases, 104–106
    role of in contested custody cases, 39
Ex parte motions, 13
Ex parte orders, 142–143
Excited utterance, 92
Expert evidence
    preparation of, 99–100
    presentation of, 99
Expert witnesses
    Canadian rules of evidence for, 85–86
    Federal Rules of Evidence concerning,
        83–84
    role of in domestic abuse court cases,
        78–83
Experts
    contested custody cases and, 33, 47
    incompetent, 77
    opinions of on credibility, 86–91
Explicit memories, 58
Eyewitness memory, 89

F

Fact witnesses, 78
False allegations
    determination of custody in Arizona
        and, 20
    incidence of and parent alienation
        syndrome, 28

False memories, creation of by investigators,
    151
Families, changing definitions of, 39, 44–45
Family court. *See also* Domestic relations
    court
    application of parental alienation
        concept in, 28
    evidentiary variables in, 5
    models of, 8–10
Family Court Division of the Philadelphia
    Court, 8
Family Court of Clark County, Nevada,
    8–9
Family law, therapeutic jurisprudence-
    based approach to, 6
Fathers, narcissistic and antisocial
    personality problems in, 178–182
Fathers for Equal Justice, 124
Fathers for Equal Rights, 124
Federal Rules of Evidence (FRE), 83–85
    expert witness opinion on credibility,
        87–91
    hearsay, 91–93
Final appealable order, 54
Financial issues relevant to forensic
    evaluators, 132–134, 237–238
Forensic assessment
    abuse allegations and, 69
    affidavit example, 227–233
    billing policy and financial
        responsibility, 237–238, 242
    complex system dynamics and, 3
    conducting (*See* Conducting forensic
        evaluations)
    forms related to, 239–244
    specialized instruments for, 99
Forensic mental health practitioners
    civil suit and malpractice actions
        against, 112–116
    emergence of the Internet and increased
        risk, 123–125
    ethical perspectives, 127–129
    evaluation and investigation by, 129–130
    financial issues related to, 132–134
    licensure board complaints related to,
        106–112
    necessity of documentation for, 131
    perceptions of risk of, 119–122
    personal risks to, 116–117
    risk management, 130–131
    risk vulnerabilities of, 105–106
    risks to others, 117–119

seeking consultations, 132
use of informed consent by, 131
Fractals, 3

G

Gay marriage, custody decisions following
    dissolution of, 213
Grisso Understanding and Appreciation of
    Miranda Rights, 99
Guardians *ad litem*, 46
    appointment of in custody cases, 32, 141
    as sources for custody evaluation
        information, 201–202
    attendance of at depositions, 52
    communications with, 137, 202
    presence of at *in camera* interviews, 50
    role of as witnesses in domestic relations
        court cases, 79–81
Guidelines for Forensic Practice, 130–131

H

Hague Convention, 142–143
Healthcare Integrity Protection Data Bank
    (HIPDB), 110
Hearing and judgment phase, abuse
    allegations during, 144–145
Hearsay
    admissibility of in domestic relations
        cases, 91–93
    Ohio case law illustrations regarding,
        93–94

I

Identification of potential perpetrators,
    Abel testing for, 64–65
Illegitimate drug use, effect of parental
    behavior on children, 194
Illicit drug use, patterns of abuse, 188–189
Implicit memories, 58
In camera interviews of children, 5–6,
    48–51
Individuals, self-organizing complex
    systems of, 3–4
Informed consent, use of by forensic
    practitioners, 131
Initial conditions, sensitive dependence
    on, 2
Initial filing phase, 142–144
Intellectual assessment, 96

Interim pretrial phase, abuse allegations
    during, 144
International abductions, *ex parte* orders
    and, 142–143
Internet, emergence of and risk to forensic
    practitioners, 123–125
Internet stalking, 123–124
Intervenors, provision of psychological
    reports to, 177
Intervention options, 145–146
    parental substance abuse, 195
Interviews
    appropriate procedures for *in camera*
        interviews, 49–50
    conducting in abuse allegation cases,
        220–224
    critique of example, 247–262
    evaluation of, 224–225
    general guidelines for interviewing
        children, 219–220
    in camera, 5–6
    investigator procedures for, 66–69
    recording of in evaluations, 198
    semi-structured guides for, 235–236
Invalidating environments, effect of on
    vulnerable children, 169–170
Investigations
    case studies of in equivocal abuse cases,
        72–76
    legal standard issues in, 70–72
    standardized procedures for, 55
Investigative interviews
    perspectives of child custody evaluators
        on, 69–70
    perspectives on of investigators, 65–69
    procedures for, 50
Iteration, 2

J

Joint custody, 10–11
Judicial perspectives, 48
Jury nullification, 217

L

Larrison v. United States, 88
Lawyers, 47. *See also* Attorneys
    conducting investigative interviews in
        the presence of, 67
Leading questions, minimization of, 68
Legal concepts, 8–11

Legal history, 12–14
Legal risks to forensic practitioners
    civil suit and malpractice actions, 112–116
    licensure board complaints, 106–112
Legal standards, 11
    issues of in investigations, 70–72
Legal system, therapeutic jurisprudence in, 4–5
Liberalization of divorce laws, 16–18
License actions, risks of for forensic mental health practitioners, 106–112
Linear thinking, domestic relations cases and, 216–217
Linguistic analyses of transcripts, 61–62
Litigants, 46
Lying
    linguistic analyses of transcripts, 61–62
    nonverbal interview behavior and, 64
    polygraph, 62
    problem of, 60–61
    use of neuroscience to determine, 63–64
    Voice Stress Analysis, 63

M

Major depressive disorder, 185–187
Malpractice
    actions taken against forensic practitioners, 112–113
    insurance concerns for forensic psychologists, 110
    psychological-psychiatric-therapeutic practices and, 105
Mandatory reporting, 69
Marijuana, use patterns, 188
Marriage, rates of, 39
Massachusetts, Domestic Rules of Relations Procedure, 43–44
Matrimonial law, 8
    liberalization of, 10
    Michigan statute defining best interests, 19–20
Mediation, 156–158
Mediators, practice hazards for, 158
Mental illness
    bipolar disorder, 182–184
    borderline personality disorder, 165–178
    major depressive disorder, 185–187
    narcissistic and related personality patterns, 178–182
    substance abuse, 187–195

Mothers with borderline personality disorder, parenting issues of, 170–175
Motions, pre-trial, 51–52
Motivated forgetting, 59–60

N

Narcissistic personality disorder, 180–182
Narcissus, 180
Neglect, relationship of with illicit drug use, 189
Neuroscience, use of to determine truth-telling, 63–64
Neurotic borderline personality disorder, characteristics of, 165–166
New York City Family Court, 8
Nicotine
    effect of parental use on children, 193–194
    use patterns, 188
No-fault divorce, 16–17
Nonconfidentiality statement, 241
Nonlegitimate bias, 4–5
Nonverbal interview behavior, 64
Norton, Caroline, 13
Nuisance suits, risks of for forensic psychologists, 120–121

O

Ohio
    case law illustrations regarding hearsay, 93–94
    parenting time rule, 39–43
    review of county court rules, 38–39
    Rules of Superintendence, 37, 43
One-sided appointments, 134
Open-ended questions, 66
    use of by child custody evaluators, 69–70
    use of in investigative interviewing, 66, 68
Opie v. State, 88

P

Parallel distributed processing, 57
Paranoid ideation, tendency of individuals with BPD for, 174–175
Parent coordination, 159–161
    parental alienation and, 163–164
Parental alienation disorder (PAD), 29

Parental alienation syndrome (PAS), 27–28,
    161–164
Parental conflict, shared parenting and,
    26–27
Parental depression, 185–187
Parental preferences of children, *in camera*
    interviews and, 48–51
Parenting, individuals with BPD and,
    170–175
Parenting coordinators, 159–160
    knowledge of BPD, 177
    vulnerabilities of, 160
Parenting schedules
    contested custody cases and, 32
    county court rules for (Ohio), 38
    research findings regarding, 45
    state rules for, 43–44
Parenting time
    guidelines for, 39–41
    suggested plan for, 41–43
Parents, evaluation of in contested custody
    cases, 197–199
Patterns, chaos theory and, 2–3
Peacemaker Test, 37–38
Perception, theories of, 57–58
Perceptions of risk, forensic practitioners
    and, 119–122
Perceptual processing, 57
Performance, definition of, 51
Personal bias, 112
Personal risks to forensic practitioners,
    116–117
Personal safety
    developmental guideposts in relation
        to, 154
    risks to for forensic mental health
        practitioners, 106
Personality testing, 96
Police officers, investigative interviewing
    procedures of, 66–69
Polygraph, 62
Possession parent tape instruction, 246
Post-decree phase, intervention options in,
    145–148
Post-traumatic stress disorder (PTSD),
    diagnosis of in contested custody
    cases, 83
Practice hazards for mediators, 158
Pretrial peregrinations, 51–53, 141–142
Primary contacts, conducting forensic
    evaluations, 197–201

Professional supervision services, 147–148
Projection, tendency of individuals with
    BPD toward, 174–175
Psychological assessments
    analysis of applicability for domestic
        relations cases, 97–98
    scientific and legal requirements for,
        129–130
    use of for substance abuse, 192–193
Psychological evaluations
    case management of BPD individuals
        and, 175–176
    use of in contested custody cases, 32–34
Psychopathology
    child custody cases and, 103–104
    equivocal abuse allegations and, 165
Psychopathy, construct of, 178–179
Psychopathy Checklist–Revised (PCL–R),
    179
Psychosocial concepts and research, shared
    parenting, 26–27
Psychotic borderline personality disorder,
    characteristics of, 165–166
Pure version technique interview, 66

Q

Quasi-judicial immunity, 114–115
    parent coordinators, 160

R

R. v. Mohan (Canada), 85–86
Recantation, 29, 92–93
Recommendations in forensic evaluations,
    205–207
Reflexive theory, 57
Relative supervised visitation, 148
Release of information, 239
    authorization, 243–244
Reportage
    child custody evaluations and, 202–204
    discussion section for forensic
        evaluations, 204–205
    forensic evaluation referral question and
        procedure, 204
    forensic evaluation results, 204
    potentially dangerous patients and,
        117–118
Repression, 59–60

Reunification therapy, 154–156
    parental alienation and, 163–164
    recommendations for in forensic
        evaluations, 206–207
Rhode Island Family Court, 8
Risk management, 130–131
Risks to others in contested custody cases,
    117–119
Rooms to Grow (Ashtabula County, Ohio),
    32–33
Roving Reporter instruction, 152, 206, 245
Rule 702, 83–85
Rule 703, 84
Rule 704, 84
Rule 705, 84–85
Rules
    parenting time, 39–43
    review of from Ohio county courts, 38–39
    state, 43–45
    use of Peacemaker Test to evaluation,
        37–38
Rules of Evidence
    Canadian, 85–86
    U.S. tradition, 83–85
Rules of Superintendence (Ohio), 37

S

Scientific Content Analysis (SCAN), use of
    to determine truth, 73–74
Scientific evidence
    detection of deception and, 89
    evaluations and investigations and,
        129–130
    implications of *Daubert* decision on
        presentation of, 95
Secrets instruction, 152, 245
Self-organizing complex systems, 3–4
Sensitive dependence on initial conditions,
    2
Settlement conference, 53
Sexual abuse
    child sexual abuse accommodation
        syndrome, 29
    history of in individuals with BPD, 170
Shared parenting, 11, 25–26
    best interests standards and legislation
        of, 18–26
    mediation and, 156–158
    psychosocial concepts and research,
        26–27

Skepticism, 82
Social behavior
    impact of divorce legislation on, 14–18
    impact of shared parenting legislation
        on, 18–20, 25–26
Social services investigators, information
    from for custody evaluations, 199–200
Social workers, investigative interviewing
    procedures of, 66–69
Sociolegal trends in divorce, 14–18
Sole custody, 10
Special interest Internet sites, 124
Stalking, 123–124
State v. Boston, 90–91, 93–94
State v. Burrell, 94
State v. Cornwell, 94
State v. Johnson, 148–150
Statement Validity Assessment (SVA), 62
Statistical analysis of divorce rates, 14–18
Strange attractors, 3
Substance abuse, 187–188
    biological assessment options for, 191
    current patterns of abuse, 188–190
    equivocal allegations of, 190–191
    individuals with BPD and, 170–171
    intervention options for, 195
    psychological testing for assessment of,
        192–193
Suicidal ideation, 186–187
Superior Court of DC—Family Court
    Operations, 9
Superior Court of Nevada County,
    California, 9
Supervised visitation, 146–147
    paid professional supervision services,
        147–148
    recommendations for in forensic
        evaluations, 206
    relative, 148

T

Tarasoff case, 117–119
Teenagers
    parenting schedules and, 38
    right of election of, 48–49
Tender years doctrine, 13–14
    replacement of with best interests
        standard, 19
Testimony. *See also* Expert witnesses
    "consistent with" statements and, 89–90

The Ikarian Reefer case (U.K.), 86
Therapeutic jurisprudence
    basic argument for, 7
    Peacemaker Test, 37–38
    principles of, 4–7
Therapists
    areas for cross-examination of, 82
    as sources for custody evaluation
        information, 200–201
    do's and don'ts for, 153
    experience of and BPD individuals, 167,
        176–177
    risks of in child custody cases, 105–106
    role of as witnesses, 81–83
    role of in investigative interviews, 67
Time line creation, 72–73
Tobacco
    effect of parental use on children,
        193–194
    use patterns, 188
Treating professionals
    areas for cross-examination of, 82
    role of as witnesses, 81–83
Truth/lie distinction, 60–61
    determination of by expert witnesses,
        87–91

U

Ultimate issue, 84
Unconscious processing, 59

Unemployment, rates of divorce and, 14–16
Unilateral filings, *ex parte* motions and,
    142–143

V

Videotaping
    interviews concerning allegations of
        sexual abuse, 135
    use of for investigative interviewing of
        children, 66–69
Violence
    capacity predictions, 117–118
    use of Psychopathy Checklist–Revised as
        predictor of, 179
Visitation. *See also* Parenting schedules
    contested custody cases and, 32–34
    supervised, 146–148, 206
Voice Stress Analysis (VSA), 63
Vulnerabilities for forensic mental health
    practitioners, 106

W

Wet mind theory, 56–57
Witnesses
    evaluators, 79
    guardians *ad litem,* 79–81
    treating professionals, 81–83
    types of in domestic relations court
        cases, 78

For Product Safety Concerns and Information please contact our EU representative GPSR@taylorandfrancis.com Taylor & Francis Verlag GmbH, Kaufingerstraße 24, 80331 München, Germany

Printed and bound by CPI Group (UK) Ltd, Croydon, CR0 4YY
01/05/2025
01858542-0001